In Performance

T0364128

**EDITED BY
CAROL MARTIN**

In Performance is a book series devoted to national and global
theater of the twenty-first century. Scholarly essays providing
the theatrical, cultural, and political contexts for the plays and
performance texts introduce each volume. The texts are written
both by established and emerging writers, translated by
accomplished translators and aimed at people who want to put
new works on stage, read diverse dramatic and performance
literature and study diverse theater practices, contexts, and histories
in light of globalization.

In Performance has been supported by
translation and editing grants from the following organizations:

The Book Institute, Krakow
TEDA Project, Istanbul
The Memorial Fund for Jewish Culture, New York
Polish Cultural Institute, New York
Zbigniew Raszewski Theatrical Institute, Warsaw

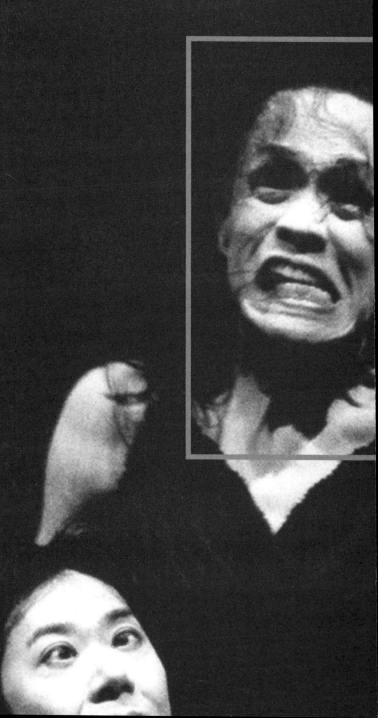

NIPPON WARS

AND OTHER PLAYS

TAKESHI KAWAMURA

Edited and introduced by
Peter Eckersall

Translated by
Shoichiro Kawai
Leon Ingulsrud
Sara Jansen
Aya Ogawa
and **Peter Eckersall**

LONDON NEW YORK CALCUTTA

Seagull Books 2011

Original text © Takeshi Kawamura
Translation © for *Nippon Wars*, Shoichiro Kawai and Leon Ingulsrud
    for *The Lost Babylon*, Sara Jansen
    for *Aoi* and *Komachi*, Aya Ogawa,
    for *Hamletclone* and *The White House in the Hills of Argos*,
     Peter Eckersall
Photographs © Individual photographers

Note: Under international law, the rights for all plays are reserved and
permission must be obtained from the writer. Inquires should addressed
to Takeshi Kawamura and T Factory (www.tfactory.jp)

ISBN-13 978 0 8574 2 002 2

British Library Cataloging-in-Publication Data
A catalog record for this book is available from the British Library

Designed by Bishan Samaddar, Seagull Books, Calcutta, India
Printed and bound by Hyam Enterprises, Calcutta, India

CONTENTS

My deep gratitude is extended to Takeshi Kawamura for sharing his theatrical vision and generosity of spirit. He is a true person of the theater. Thank you also to Kawamura and Yoshiko Hirai for their friendship and work on this project. Thank you to Professor Carol Martin for her scholarship and keen editorship of the In Performance book series and to the team at Seagull Books. Finally, thank you to Naomi Ota and Dr. Philip Flavin for research assistance at the University of Melbourne. The Australian Research Council supported some of the work on this project.

Shoichiro Kawai and Leon Ingulsrud's translation of *Nippon Wars* was first published in the Japan Playwrights Association series *Half a Century of Japanese Theater*: *1980s* (VOL. 2) (Tokyo: Kinokuniya, 2002, 68–110). Act II of *The Lost Babylon* was published in *The Drama Review* 44(1) (2000). Sara Jansen has revised her translation and the complete work is published for the first time. Kawamura's *Hamuretto Kūron* (*Hamletclone*, 2000) was first published in Japanese in Tokyo by Ronsōsha in 2000 and was subsequently updated by Kawamura in 2002. My translation of *Hamletclone* was first published in my book *Theorizing the Angura Space*: *Avant-garde Performance and Politics in Japan*, *1960–2000* (Leiden: Brill, 2006). Acknowledgments and thanks to Koninklijke BRILL NV for permission to republish *Hamletclone*. Kawamura's *Aoi* and *Komachi* were translated for a New York performance season by Aya Ogawa and are available here in English for the first time. *The White House in the Hills of Argos* is also published here for the first time.

This publication is supported by a grant from the Research and Research Training Committee, Faculty of Arts, the University of Melbourne.

Japanese names are written given name first, as is Kawamura's preference.

Peter Eckersall
August 2010

TAKESHI KAWAMURA: MEMORY, SOCIETY, THEATER-MEDIA

Peter Eckersall

> If the characteristics of capitalism are speed, rationality and brevity, the theater is clearly anti-capitalist (Kawamura 2002: 267).

Takeshi Kawamura (b. 1959) is among the most important playwrights of his generation with plays spanning nearly three decades of contemporary theater production in Japan. Kawamura's plays are now performed by notable Shingeki (modern repertory) companies and high-profile theaters, including the New National Theater (Shin Kokuritsu Gekijō) and the Setagaya Public Theater (Setagaya Paburiiku Shiataa), both in Tokyo. Kawamura began working in the theater in 1980 when he founded the Daisan Erotica Company while studying at Meiji University in Tokyo. For 20 years, he produced, directed, and sometimes acted in his plays, progressively refining the distinctive frenetic style of performance and 'cyberpunk' edge of his theater company, famous among theater audiences and critics. Kawamura ended the company in 2001 with the belief that he needed more flexibility than what the running of an ensemble company allowed (see Eckersall 2006). In the same year, Kawamura founded T Factory with producer Yoshiko Hirai. Sometimes Kawamura still brings together former members of Daisan Erotica for smaller-scale experimental productions; and he is Professor of Performing Arts at the Kyoto University of Arts and Design, teaching the next generation of theater-makers.

The plays collected in this anthology explore traumatic postwar history and its consequences. An inability to address the past in meaningful ways contributes to the current sense of malaise that many critics see as a new Japanese crisis. The controversy, for example, over how the Japanese occupation of parts of China (1931–45)[1] and Korea (1910–45) is represented in middle-school textbooks continues to have detrimental effects on Japan's foreign policy.[2] Moreover, the occupation of post-war Japan by the US-led allied forces (1945–52) set the scene for a national polity based on multinational capitalism and the enduring influence of the US. The plays explore how the relatively stable era of post-war development (especially in the 1970s–80s) ended in what Tomiko Yoda and Harry Harootunian call the *fin de siècle* "long post-war" (2006: 1): "If the recognition of the end of the postwar hit a Japanese society already reeling from the millennial malaise of the 1990s, the events of 9/11 on the other side of the globe would convince them that the new century announced even worse things to come" (ibid.: 2). Rapid changes in society—linked to globalization, terrorist insurgencies, and Japan's declining economic capacity—have created unprecedented social division and anxiety in Japanese society. Japan's famed consensus and homogeneity, if ever truly underpinning its apparent success in the post-war era, was now visibly failing.

With a dramaturgy of citations, manifestos, and cinematic references to the recent dystopian past, Kawamura dramatizes and denaturalizes the spectre of unease in contemporary life in Japan. Scenes from his plays sometimes quote directly from political commentary and films; at other times, the citational connection is more lateral and reflective. For Kawamura, theater is a source of social and cultural memory and a way of reviving the past in order to consider its attributes:

> The essential idea that I wish to convey is the awareness
> that theater directors are both thinkers (*shisōka*) and

---

1 Dating Japan's occupation of China is complicated by the fractured nature of Japan's imperialist drive into China and sources of resistance to Japanese forces. Japan occupied Manchuria in 1931 and the second Sino-Japanese War was declared in 1937. Japan surrendered in 1945.

2 While historians continue to debate Japan's wartime experience, textbooks have often glossed over the violence of war and sometimes avoid discussing Japan's aggressive militarism. For further information, see Yoshiko Nozaki (2008).

critics (*hyōronka*), as are, of course, playwrights. [. . .]
The director is a critic of contemporary society, a thinker
who derives ideas in the act of critiquing, and the play an
intellectual apparatus that ponders over society. This is
my fundamental stance towards plays (Kawamura 2002:
267; my translation).

In other words, Kawamura explores the ways in which things are
both remembered and forgotten socially, politically, and culturally.
Like the cascading litany of past existence of the fallen in his play
Hamuretto Kūron (*Hamletclone*, 2000)—where actors recite "I was
Yukio Mishima", "I was Pol Pot", "I was sarin gas" as they are shot
and reanimated—or the cyborg warrior's memory implants in *Nippon*
Wuōzu (*Nippon Wars*, 1984), memory in Kawamura's plays becomes
both an accurate and inaccurate means of fixing patterns in society
and of showing how history is constructed as an expression of power.

JAPAN'S CHANGING CULTURAL ENVIRONMENT

The plays in this anthology span a paradigmatic shift in Japan's
theater landscape in which theater artists have moved away from
making works in ensemble Angura (fringe) systems of production
to making art as part of the cultural industry (see Eckersall 2006:
41–51).[3] The drying-up of corporate support for the arts during
Japan's 1990s' recession, together with changing social attitudes
toward working in old-style theater collectives, has made working
in ensembles both less appealing and less feasible economically.[4]
This makeover of the production system is a consequence of the
widespread influence of globalization in Japan and changes in the

3 The culture industry refers in critical Marxist terms to culture's reification and
ideological patterning in capitalist society (see Adorno 2001). Since the 1980s,
the term has been popularized by advocates of neoliberalism who link the arts
with societal, community, and economic development (see Florida 2002).

4 Interestingly, recent research in the US points to the exact opposite situation,
and the rise of many young theaters working as ensembles [see *The Drama
Review* 54(3) (2010)]. In Australia as well, a new generation of performance
groups, including Black Lung and My Darling Patricia, are ensembles.

Japanese economy. More than 80 percent of Japan's GDP is now found in the service sector and culture industries, a marked contrast to the 1960s, when Japan's post-war recovery rested on industrial production and manufacturing. While the arts are, in some sense, privileged with a supra-economic high cultural status, they are increasingly seen as commodities intersecting with media and other forms of value-enhancing cultural production. As the sociologist Yoshio Sugimoto writes:

> In place of industrial capitalism, which relies on mass-produced and cost-effective industrial goods for mass consumption, the Japanese economy is increasingly *dependent upon the production and sales of cultural goods*, which now form its lifeline both domestically and internationally (2009: 14; emphasis added).

Evidence of this dependence is the rise of prefectural and national sponsorship for the arts[5] and a market-place approach. Formally ad hoc production processes are gradually incorporated into the cultural milieu of prefectural theater programming, arts markets, and the like, with the result that theater in Japan has become more homogenized yet also more professional.

Taken together, the plays in this volume show how Kawamura's playwriting and dramaturgy have become more complex and poetic. *Nippon Wars*, from 1984, is an energetic even belligerent text that was successfully restaged in 2001–02 as a commentary on the postmodern spectacle of 9/11 and its aftermath (see Eckersall 2006).[6] By contrast, *Aoi* and *Komachi*, dating from 2003, show Kawamura as a

---

5 See Ikuya Sato (1999) for a sociological mapping of the changes to contemporary theater in relation to the late 1990s' cultural economy.

6 In closing his restaging of *Nippon Wars* with the overused image of the collapse of the Twin Towers followed by a projection of the words: *Eiga?*, *Sensō?*, *Engeki?* ([is this] film, war, theater?), Kawamura risked being too obvious. But given the context of a play that is in many ways about the cultural 'logic' of warfare, the commentary is valid. *Nippon Wars* explores the context of radicalism and how this can be both programmed and compensated for in society. Kawamura's commentary on 9/11 points to the postmodern spectacle of the

mature playwright—poetic, visionary, angry—but able to explore his vision in a subtle rewriting of the canonical form of Noh. Kawamura's plays have grown in scale and technical ability in part due to the rise of this new cultural economy. T Factory plays have featured accomplished professional actors drawn from diverse genres including Noh, Takarazuka, modern theater, and Butoh. They are made in partnership with gifted designers in well-equipped theaters where a sophisticated artistic vision can be realized. Observing Kawamura direct his plays over many years, I have seen how his creative vision has expanded to include more imaginative possibilities for staging his works and his interactions with his team necessarily become multilayered and collaborative. One way of reading the plays in this anthology is to look at the shift from the idiosyncratic, rough-edged style of Daisan Erotica in *Nippon Wars* and *Rosuto Babiron* (*The Lost Babylon*, 1999) to a 'producer system'[7] at work in making *Aoi* (2003) and *Komachi* (2003) and *Argos Zaka no Shiroi Ie* (*The White House in the Hills of Argos*, 2006, the only play in the anthology that Kawamura didn't direct). *Hamletclone* is perhaps a turning point in the sense that it was the last large-scale Daisan Erotica production. As a play about the effects of globalization on Japan that enjoyed international critical success, *Hamletclone* anticipated a new phase of international theater reception and production working its way into the Japanese theater scene.[8]

---

attacks and to the ways that 9/11 was used by George W. Bush and the so-called coalition of the willing, including Japan and Australia, as a staging platform for the invasion of Iraq.

7 The producer system has been popularized by funding bodies such as the British Council for the Arts and encourages artists from the "small to medium sector" (the fringe or "*angura* space") to partner with funding organizations and venues who produce their work. Producing theater is a specialist role and releases artists from many more mundane producing tasks to focus on creating works. At the same time, questions such as what, where, and who makes work become more complicated and mediated by producers. The arts also become more corporatized and driven by the market.

8 This point is accurate for Japanese literature more broadly. Toshiko Ellis shows how, for writers since 1980s, "the author–nation relationship no longer marks the essential starting point of writing activity" (2009: 212).

Kawamura carefully analyzes the conditions of making theater in Japan in his essay "Yasashii gendai engeki" ("Contemporary Theater Made Easy"), where he states:

> [D]espite the theater being fundamentally anti-capitalist, it exists within the capitalist industry of entertainment and seeks success. And while there are theater people who choose to ignore or deny the entertainment industry as they conceive of theatrical works, I do not. In placing myself within this capitalist system of the entertainment industry, I find the anti-capitalist aspects of the theater of interest, but also a burden (2002: 267; my translation).

What kind of burden is Kawamura talking about? Modern theater is arguably no longer a popular medium. It cannot be collected as an artifact, and even commercial theater forms like musicals are financially risky. Even so, theater remains influential in other ways: as a form of cultural capital, for example, it is often highly valued. Theater scholar Baz Kershaw argues that repertory-style theater in the UK encourages a neoliberal agenda and promotes "normative social values in the behaviour of its participants" (1999: 31–2). For Kershaw, plays offer only muted social criticism, an effect that is contained by the bourgeois apparatus of the theater's institutional and architectural framework. On the other hand, Jacques Rancière has recently argued for the need to break the binary of the stage separating the audience; to create instead a non-hierarchical and possibly anti-capitalist relationship by giving the spectator a central role as a participant in art (2009: 13). Arguably, all good theater engages audiences in conversations about the world but, as these perspectives show, debates continue about how effective theater is as medium of political activism. Moreover, examples of theater with influences dating back to the early twentieth century continue to offer resistant and/or anti-capitalist perspectives. Moving between this historical avant-garde paradigm and the cultural–economic–political tangles of contemporary theater production constitutes the burden that Kawamura mentions above.

To create theater that resists normative ideas while also commenting on the ways in which theater is shaped by its institutional contexts is Kawamura's aim. This is particularly evident in his recent works, especially *Hamletclone* and the plays that follow in this volume, all of which address metatheatrical questions of form and genre through narratives about history, capitalism, and theater.[9] A self-conscious authorial voice disrupts the internal dramaturgy in these texts. For example, the character of the Old Gay Prince in *Hamletclone* (played by Kawamura himself in the Tokyo production) sitting at the back of the theater with a microphone. Dressed in faux Shakespearian ruffles and breeches, he comments sardonically on the action below. He lives to see both the failure of his revolution—staged in the play—and the failure of his dream for theater to realize an alternative world. In the final scene, he lies dying, shot by the character of the thief doubling as a nationalist politician. Parodying the closing moments of *Hamlet*, he laments: "Again, the happy ending is suspended at the end of the twenty-first century," and the play ends on an uneasy note of intransigence. After all the chaotic energy of the work, the play suggests that nothing can be done to interrupt Japan's failing vision of a society unable to find new energy or sense of purpose.

THEATER AS HISTORY; THEATER AND THE SOCIAL CONDITION

Many of the transformations taking place in Japan are reflected in this volume. Kawamura began making theater in the 'bubble economy' era of the 1980s, a time of unprecedented economic growth and speculative capitalism. Japanese art often drew on

---

9 A metatheatrical reference is usually self-referential, sometimes including comments or quotations about theater's existence as a medium or construction as an artifact. The sense of knowing this about theater and its imbrication in historical and contemporary referents is shared with an audience.

science fiction, creating striking postmodern images of apocalypse, perhaps as a way of representing the superficial euphoria of the time (Uchino 2000, Eckersall 2006). The animated film *Akira* (Katsuhiro Ōtomo, 1988) typifies this trend. Symbolized by the postmodern architectural monuments of the bubble decade, Tokyo is suddenly, momentarily, destroyed by an atomic bomb in the film's opening sequence. But the city appears reborn in the next scene as if to simply erase the trauma of the bomb and the subsequent memories of what is presumably the task of reconstructing the city from memory. *Akira* is a film riddled with a sense of historical crisis and millennial anxiety. Moreover, the bubble era and the following 'lost decade' of the 1990s show Japan at extremes—of economic excess and in a state of crisis, of an alluring capitalist spectacle, and subsequent human emptiness and hardship.

It is argued that the remaking of Japan from the 1960s to the 80s—from an emergent post-war new order in step with America to the era of turbo-capitalism—erased the complexity of Japan's history from the popular imagination (see Yoda and Harootunian 2006). Such a perspective is explored in Kawamura's first successful play, *Nippon Wars*. Loosely based on the iconic science fiction film *Blade Runner* (Ridely Scott, 1982), *Nippon Wars*—which won Kawamura the respected Kishida Drama Prize in 1994—is set in a futuristic apocalyptic landscape where cyborg soldiers are programmed to fight in wars under the command of the overlord figure of the General. In the first part of the play, the cyborgs seem to have their latent humanity awakened when they develop self-awareness and rebel against their standing orders. It becomes apparent, however, that their rebellion is part of their programming and they remain dependent machines; their new-found freedom is, in reality, expected, sanctioned, and fully normative in terms of the existing status quo. This scenario is akin to the human-replicant figures in *Blade Runner* who frantically treasure photographs of moments documenting memories from their past that suggest human subjectivity. As the film shows, the photos, in fact, belong to family members of the scientists who design the androids. The images capturing family memories are reused as "implants" to allow the androids to feel empathy and improve their interactions with humans. The android memories are therefore quotidian moments exploring the relationship between history and subjectivity that, in turn, question ideas of freedom and identity. History becomes stage-managed and is presented as a form of agency sanctioned and remade as a means of power.

Like *Nippon Wars*, *The Lost Babylon* is inspired by a popular science fiction film, *Westworld* (Michael Crichton, 1973) and they both utilize subculture-cyberpunk themes. *The Lost Babylon*[10] is set in a theme park where people hunt other humans. *Furōsha*, unemployed homeless people, are given low-paid jobs as hunter's prey and are trained to perform real-looking cinematic deaths when they are shot by the gamers. As in *Westworld*, where players face off against robots in fantasy battle scenarios, things begin to go wrong and people begin to actually die. A cowboy robot, memorably played by Yul Brynner, begins to hunt humans in *Westworld*; and in *The Lost Babylon* the "heart stop" bullets, designed to momentarily give the impression of death, are replaced with "blood bullets" or live ammunition. At first it is unclear if the subsequent deaths are another part of the game, more realistic and more thrilling; but gradually, the machinery of violence takes over and the border between what is real and what is part of the game is no longer discernable. Kawamura uses these film citations as a means of underscoring confusion about reality and virtuality in postmodern culture. As Sara Jansen argues, the play "presents a confusing but not unfamiliar world in which the esthetic and grotesque violence of comics, action films, and video games spills over into everyday

---

10 *The Lost Babylon* has also been performed in English in an artistic exchange project by the Adelaide-based Shifting Point Company and Daisan Erotica. Russell Fewster directed the production featuring two Daisan Erotica members alongside local actors at the Adelaide Fringe Festival in February 2006.

life" (Kawamura and Jansen 2000: 114). Moreover, some 25 years after *Westworld*, virtual-reality violence is so fully patterned in computer games that the play shows wealthy gamers rejecting the virtual and returning to the "thrill" of a live hunt. *Nippon Wars* and *The Lost Babylon* heighten the sense of apocalypse connected to the breakdown of the 1980s' capitalism and the subsequent loss of historical memory in the 1990s by portraying the ways in which we can no longer distinguish what is real and what is simulated.[11]

With its radical theatrical style and subject matter, *Hamletclone* is a pivotal work for Kawamura, introducing debates about theater and life in Japan in the new century. In one sense a rejoinder to Heiner Müller's *Die Hamletmaschine* (*Hamletmachine*, 1977), a play about the history of post-war Europe and the failure of communism, the sprawling structure of *Hamletclone* rejects the formal cohesion of conventional theater. It is intentionally fragmented and difficult to understand, and aims at inciting multiple responses and interpretations. As noted elsewhere, *Hamletclone* shares with Shakespeare's *Hamlet* the subject of a ruling family in crisis; it is a social and political satire that targets contemporary Japanese society and its place in the world (Eckersall 2006, Moriyama 2004). In Kawamura's version, Hamlet's split personality and hopelessly dysfunctional family embody recent social, economic, and political troubles suggestive of Japan's post-war history. The play begins with the audience standing on the stage, trapped behind barbed wire and looking into the auditorium. In the Prologue, a thief wandering among the audience describes in jumbled unconnected sentences the chaos of civil war and the desire to play Hamlet. Allusions to Japanese radicalism become intermingled with images of refugees and the flotsam of globaliza-

---

11 Much of the discussion on Kawamura's work in the 1980s and 90s is featured in essays by Peter Eckersall (2000) and Tadashi Uchino (2000). Further commentary is seen in Sara Jansen's translation of Kawamura's *The Lost Babylon* (2000) and an interview with Kawamura by Carol Martin (2000). All of this was edited by Carol Martin for a special issue of the *Drama Review* 44(1) (2000). See also Naoto Moriyama (2004).

tion. As Giorgio Agamben argues, the image of the "camp," the creation of a space of bare life entailing a state of exception (1998: 174), stands for the moral condition of contemporary society. In Kawamura's barbed-wire prison, the camp is transposed in the opening scene as a "colony" where the Japanese national anthem ("Kimigayo") is played, and the Japanese flag of the rising red sun (Hinomaru) blows in the breeze. The audience come to realize that the wire is electrified and the colony is a prison and a concentration camp. The flag, represented as a video projection in Kawamura's production, mutates into lurid colours: a waving hallucination of the national symbol. Historical figures are paraded before us only to be shot by soldiers patrolling the auditorium. Troubling events and crimes taken from the daily newspapers are mentioned. Rapes and murder, attacks on homeless people, suicide, and the Aum cult's attempt to stage a coup by gassing the Tokyo subway are linked as interconnected consequences of the Japanese condition at the turn of the millennium. The Old Gay Prince, using words taken from an anarchist propaganda text, offers a systematic analysis of the steps needed to stage a military coup. Rival neonationalist and schoolgirl gangs vie for power. In the closing scenes, the uprising is staged and then quashed. Coalitions of rival forces form the new government, but as always, the politics remain forever the same. The play ends on a note of despair. The Prince is shot and his dream of transmutation into a hybrid figure of possibilities and transcendence is denied.

While *Nippon Wars* shows human subjectivity as programmed feelings merely awaiting the right time to be switched on, *Hamletclone* shows only fragmentation and a surplus of images. Kawamura notes in an extended interview during this time:

> In 1989, the emperor died and it was the end of the Shōwa era.[12] The Berlin Wall also came down. In other

---

12 The Shōwa era (1925–89) or the reign of Emperor Hirohito (called Emperor Shōwa after his death), covers the period of the Second World War, the bombings of Hiroshima and Nagasaki, and the post-war occupation and reconstruction under the aegis of the US alliance. Needless to say, the Shōwa Emperor remains a controversial figure in Japan.

words, there seemed to be many important historical events unfolding during that time. As a result, my work began to reflect a need to face these big moments in history. Until that era, as a theater artist, I was known as a member of the little theater movement (*angura*), as someone working in that tradition. In other words, I was writing my stories and directing them with my own company. However, I was becoming tired of making theater in this way, theater based solely on one story. Given what was happening in the world around us and the magnitude of historical events that we saw, it seemed to me that this kind of theater-making based on story was no longer able to address the questions that were being asked. Another kind of theater-making was becoming necessary (2004).

In shifting to a more interpretative and poetic dramaturgy, Kawamura was connecting his esthetic interests to the work of other artists, especially Müller but also UK playwrights Martin Crimp and Sarah Kane. Kawamura directed Kane's *4:48 Psychosis* (translated by Takehiko Tanioka) in 2003, the first Japanese production of Kane's work. Along with Crimp, Kane created bleak and stilted visions of society that were the legacy of Thatcher-era Britain. *Hamletclone* shares this textual intensity and acerbic social vision; its "jumbled, poetic clusters standing for text" (Sierz 2000: 33) are the sign of a writer keen to explore the limits of text and theatricality in the new century.

THE CANON 'CORRUPTED BY MEMORY'

Aoi and *Komachi* are two modern Noh plays by Kawamura that are, in equal parts, dramatic poem, performance art, and contemporary dance. They are contemporary adaptations of the canonical plays *Aoi no Ue* (Lady Aoi, attributed to Zeami, *c*.1363–1443) and *Sotoba Komachi* ("Komachi at the Stupa", written by Kan'ami, *c*.1333–84).

Adapting premodern theater for modern and avant-garde contexts, while occasionally attempted before the Second World War, developed from the late 1950s and especially in the 60s. Yukio Mishima's *Kindai Nō Gakushu* (1956) [*Modern Noh Plays* (1981)] took five well-known plays from the traditional Noh repertoire and re-imagined them in modern style. The story of each is recognizably from the Noh, but the dramaturgy and dialogue are modern. Japan's premodern cultural history was revived in the Shō-gekijō (small theater movement) of the 1960s. It energetically adapted acting styles and esthetics from traditional performance, synthesizing folk tales and community rituals from the past with contemporary themes and issues drawn from leftist politics. As David Goodman attests:

> Post-shingeki [Goodman's term for Shō-gekijō] has two main characteristics. First, it is characterized by the identification of a character or characters with an archetypal, transhistorical figure (a god) into whom they metamorphose; and second, by concern with the interrelated questions of personal redemption (salvation of the individual) and social revolution (salvation of the world) (1988: 10).

Kawamura's modern Noh plays draw on the narrative and cultural–esthetic aspects of Noh. Moreover, his plays use transhistorical themes to try and understand how Japanese society remains connected to the past.

Prefacing modern Noh also is the fact that Noh plays traditionally follow a set pattern. Memories of the past are recalled and then restaged in order to better contemplate the nature of life and gain redemption for past transgressions and disappointments. As the Noh scholar Komparu Kunio says, Noh reanimates "an experience from the past in the form of a reversal of self" (1983: 61). Thus, a karmic sense of resolution is achieved in Noh when moments from life are made other-worldly and replayed as a kind of ripple effect (or reversal) of an original action or moment of crisis. While the principal aim of Noh is to reveal insights into Buddha-nature, it is exceptionally well suited to exploring personal narratives as a form of national history. This is because the re-enactment of life-changing experiences in Noh evokes personal memories that are at the same time taken from Japan's literary–cultural tradition and are historically based. Stories of suffering, love, battles, grief, and madness in Noh constitute key moments in Japan's cultural history and its elements are foremost in Japan's esthetic traditions. Noh drama also reanimates the past by connecting this world with a phantasmic world of ghosts waiting to return to tell their stories, often intense experiences of grief and mourning. This sense of moving between history as social memory and history as a personal traumatic past is paradigmatic of Noh. Kawamura explores the complexity of meaning in comments about Mishima's Noh plays:

> In the *Modern Noh Plays*, I think you can see this kind of political and cultural ambivalence that Mishima showed. These problems are addressed in the *Modern Noh Plays*: the fact that he was looking at the Noh, as a type of performance that is recognised as being ancient and traditionally Japanese, and at the same time that he was trying to fit that into a very western idea of theater. When you look at [his] work—both the strangeness of the old theater and the incongruity of the western theater seem to come together. What he was trying to incorporate seems to be very important even in Japanese society today. It is a question of distance [and perspective] between Japan and the west (quoted in Eckersall 2006: 48).

Like most Noh plays, *Aoi no Ue* and *Sotoba Komachi* stress Buddhist themes and are staged as offerings of prayers to the souls of the departed. Both are popular plays from the Noh canon and their stories are widely known in Japan. Kawamura uses these stories not so much to revive the past but to make visible the strangeness of present-day Japan. In *Aoi no Ue*, Lady Aoi, wife of the famed Prince Genji, is possessed by a phantom and becomes ill. Her presence is represented on stage by a folded-over kimono or *kosode*. A priestess is called to exorcise the phantom, but instead, the vengeful spirit of Lady Rokujō, an older rival for Genji's affections, appears in a jealous rage. Buddhist prayers finally subdue her demon-like presence. No longer overcome by hatred, Rokujō is able to attain nirvana.

Sotoba Komachi is also a play of emotional extremes. A ruined old woman who covets her long-faded beauty appears on the stage as a mad dishevelled beggar. At the site of a stupa, a Buddhist monument near the Katsura River, she is possessed by the ghost of Fukakusa no Shōshō, a suitor from her youth. Fukakusa was to court her for a hundred nights, returning to her hut each evening to profess his love. Tragically, he dies on the ninety-ninth night and their relationship is left unconsummated, just as Komachi intended. Akin to an act of purgatory, she is possessed by Fukakusa and replays his suffering until prayers calm the vengeful spirit.

As with Mishima's *Modern Noh Plays* (which Kawamura directed in the late 1990s), Kawamura's plays place the themes of these two plays in modern settings. Kawamura's *Aoi* is set in a hair salon owned by Hikaru, the husband of Aoi, who has a mysterious illness. Hikaru has a strange obsession with hair, which his young assistant Tōru thinks is a factor in Aoi's illness. In fact, Aoi is convinced that the hair of Rokujō—Hikaru's former lover who helped him establish the salon—is mixed with her hair. Images of black tangled hair are prominent design features in Kawamura's production, adding to the overall feeling of unease. Later, Rokujō appears trying to seduce Hikaru, reminding him of how they killed her former husband together. Hikaru resists her advances and remains connected to Aoi saying that they are suffering from the sexual abuse they experienced as children. In the final scene, Aoi returns revealing a newly shaved head. She asks Hikaru to cut her hair. He begins to make invisible cutting motions, all the while declaring his love for her hair. The play ends enigmatically; "Your hair, it's so beautiful," he says, as the script calls for a "gentle breeze blow[ing] apart the mountains of hair." Soft billowing strands of hair that soon become tangled are projected on the stage, symbolizing the threat of violence and intense memories merging with the present. When Hikaru mimes cutting Aoi's hair, a ghostly possession takes place. The final image of cascading entangling hair connotes the transmutation and merging of bodies, an essential part of the cyberpunk *anime* that Kawamura loves. It is an impossibly transgressive DNA-like fusion of Rokujō, Aoi, and Hikaru.

Komachi begins in a derelict movie theater in the time of war. An unemployed film director discovers a wartime propaganda film called *Graceful Nation*, starring the legendary screen beauty Komachi, now long retired. An old man (Komachi's servant) questions the man and asks him to leave. As the man leaves, he senses Komachi sitting in the auditorium and becomes entranced by her scent. Later, the man visits a noodle shop and gets drunk on sake. Komachi appears and dances in memory of old-time film actresses. Later still, the man is abducted and given some old filmscripts written by Major General Fukasawa. These were specially written for Komachi but never filmed, as Fukasawa, after visiting Komachi for 99 days, died in the war. The man is told that he resembles Fukasawa and the servant insists that he must direct Fukasawa's screenplay. Komachi appears, not as an old hag but as a beautiful young woman. Her role is wordlessly performed by Butoh performer Kasai Akira. His dance is an interpretation of poetic images and descriptions of human sensations written by Kawamura in the script.[13] Possessed by the spirit of Fukasawa, the director begins to rave about wartime atrocities and seeks

---

13 Interestingly, here Kawamura writes a part to be danced, and the performer and director must interpret the textual references through movement in their rehearsal. This is also like Noh, where the main actor (*shite*) dances most of their role and their text is sung by a chorus.

redemption. Komachi strangles him in tangles of film. At the end of the play, the old woman is reborn, "blossoming like a flower."

Canonical works such as Noh are defined by their reiteration and reinscription across time and place. In Marvin Carlson's words, plays from a canon are "corrupted by myth or memory as a grounding for restoration and reinvention" (1996: 51). In other words, the gaps between the memory of the canon and its reprise open new possibilities for a performance of a canonical work. Noh plays, because they have such a long history, give us a wide field of interpretation and reinvention. Writing his own modern Noh plays, Kawamura's work is ineluctably entangled with the past—the plays' reanimation and adaptation embody a transhistorical vision. Audiences are meant not only to experience the moment of the performance and its immediate allusions to contemporary events, but its view of the plays is also informed by intergenerational, non-linear, and phantasmic sensibilities. We are encouraged to see the works as fractured and sensory, their consideration of history and of culture as underscored by ambiguity.

This is also the case for the final play in this collection, *The White House in the Hills of Argos*, loosely based on the Greek tragedy *Electra*. A number of Kawamura's earlier themes work in concert here; for example, the family as political entity seen in *Hamletclone* reappears in the guise of a tragedian family dynasty. Japan's subaltern status to America, a theme explored in *Hamletclone* and *The Lost Babylon*, returns in this play, acting as a critical response to the US invasion of Iraq and Japan's non-combatant military support. Figures from Greek myth mix with regular everyday Japanese characters: Kawamura inserts a humorous debate between the playwright Euripides, who is now retired and enjoys drinking sake, and Shimaoka, who has come to visit Euripides, seeking some handy writing tips. As in *Komachi*, a film is being made in *Argos*. The space of live action and the more constructed semiotic gaze of cinema are intersecting currents in the storyline.

In versions of the play written by Sophocles and Euripides, the character of Electra plots with her brother Orestes to kill their mother Clytemnestra and her lover Aegisthus, who together murdered their father Agamemnon, King of Argos. *The White House in the Hills of Argos* takes place in their family home. Other modern playwrights, including Jean Giraudoux, Jean-Paul Sartre, Heiner Müller, and Eugene O'Neill, have used the Electra story as the basis for plays with modern perspectives on violent family struggles. Müller's *Hamletmachine* gives a privileged space to Electra to articulate a feminist revolutionary tract ("This is Electra speaking / From the heart of darkness / To the capitals of the world.") and it is this revolutionary Electra that comes to Kawamura's play although only as a parody of this ideal. Kawamura transforms Electra into the embittered daughter of a movie actress and a failing copy of Müller's revolutionary trope. In the final scene, we learn that Electra has been unable to enact her revenge and instead, as recounted by Shimaoka,

> [S]he leaves the house and writes novels. As the daughter of a famous actress, her private life becomes a stream of steamy scandals. Adultery, attempted suicide, abortion, causing traffic accidents, violence, court cases, gaol. All the time, the city lives on with the fear of terrorism. In a corner of the city, in an out of the way place, a sister and brother meet once again.

This is a bittersweet comment on the stalling of Japanese society and lack of gender equality amidst the complications of global capitalism. It is a fitting end for a daughter of the Japanese bourgeoisie, one who writes cool postmodern novels about the emptiness of the world. From outsider transgressor-feminist, she blends back into the city space and becomes invisible.

Kawamura's plays are concerned with memory and disputed history, evident in the many textual and cinematic citations from historical sources. His abiding interest in society and his fundamental belief in theater as a source of social debate are coupled with a vision of Japan being eaten by capitalism, on the perpetual edge of collapse. This pessimism, however, is countered by a sense of nostalgia, ribald humour, and humanity. All of Kawamura's plays are adaptations that can be read as conversations between art and social trends, trends that are not only bleak but sometimes absurd. The plays are also about human relationships. As Kawamura asserts, "In contemporary society [. . .] there is an urgency to explore the structure of other people's relationships; theater becomes a privileged intellectual apparatus [in this task]" (2002: 267). In adapting the canon, Kawamura is struggling with a form that is ideologically and esthetically rooted in countless moments in history *and* in the prosaic everydayness of the contemporary human condition.

There is also the question of how we might read and perform these plays beyond the Japanese context. Do they warrant becoming global texts that might be seen in new productions or are they so closely connected to local ideas and events that their wider appreciation is not possible? As my analysis of these plays has shown, Kawamura's vision is both local and international. With commentaries on aspects of life as diverse as ecology, capitalism, and social relations, his plays are transhistorical. They offer insights into myths, genres, and ideas that circulate in media, culture, and art. Like much of what defines good art, Kawamura's is a singular vision reflecting on issues and themes in the world that are of larger concern; the specific cultural space intersects with a global flow of ideas.

To close, we might think about the image used on the cover of the Japanese publication of the script of *Hamletclone*, also used as one version of the poster for the production.

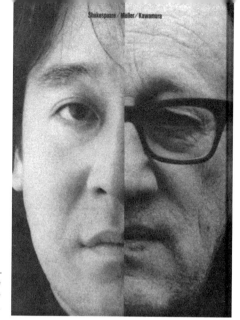

IMAGE 1. The cover of the book *Hamletclone* (Tokyo: Ronsōsha, 2000).

The joining of the half-faces of Müller and Kawamura symbolizes the artist's thinking about the importance of Müller's text to theater culture; how *Hamletmachine* was a moment of change challenging all artists who come to theater after Müller. Müller–Kawamura is also an image of the Japanese artist growing through an accumulation of ideas. In the transhistorical figure of Müller–Kawamura, the 'writer' takes on the Japanese theater's implicit and emergent globality and makes it an aspect of the wider esthetic–cultural condition of Japan. Rather than making clear distinctions between past and present-day Japan, Kawamura's plays work toward a blurring of all things. Like the ghosts in Noh plays, Kawamura's characters live phantasmically in several times and places at once. Kawamura's worldview is humanistic yet divided. His writing is a matrix of interwoven moments of history and culture. As the thief says in the prologue to *Hamletclone*: "I am the prince who lives in the age of late capitalism. To be in this age or not to be [. . .] that is the question." In the final analysis, Kawamura's plays are questions for living.

ADORNO, Theodor W. 2001. *The Culture Industry: Selected Essays on Mass Culture* (J. M. Bernstein ed. and trans.). London and New York: Routledge.

AGAMBEN, Giorgio 2001. *Homo Sacer: Sovereign Power and Bare Life* (D. Heller-Roazen trans.). Stanford: Stanford University Press, 1998.

ALLISON, Anne. 2006. *Millennial Monsters: Japanese Toys and the Global Imagination*. Berkeley: University of California Press.

BAUDRILLARD, Jean. 1994. *Simulacra and Simulation*. Sheila Faria Glaser trans. Ann Arbor: University of Michigan Press.

CARLSON, Marvin. 1996. *Performance: A Critical Introduction*. London and New York: Routledge.

ECKERSALL, Peter. 2000. "Japan as Dystopia: Kawamura Takeshi's Daisan Erotica." *The Drama Review* 44(1): 97–108.

———. 2006. "After Angura? Recent works by Kawamura Takeshi" in Edward Scheer and Peter Eckersall (eds), *The Ends of the 60s: Performance, Media and Contemporary Culture*. Sydney: University of New South Wales and Performance Paradigm, pp. 41–51.

ELLIS, Toshiko. 2009. "Literary Culture" in Yoshio Sugimoto (ed.), *The Cambridge Companion to Modern Japanese Culture*. Melbourne: Cambridge University Press, pp. 199–215.

FLORIDA, Richard. 2002. *The Rise of the Creative Class: And How it's Transforming Work, Leisure, Community and Everyday Life*. New York: Basic Books.

GOODMAN, David. 1988. *Japanese Drama and Culture in the 1960s: The Return of the Gods*. New York: M. E. Sharpe.

KAWAMURA, Takeshi. 2002. "Yasashi Gendai Engeki" (Contemporary Theater Made Easy) in *Butai Geijutsu*

(Performing Arts). Tokyo: Tokyo zōkei geijutsu daigaku butai geijutsu kenkyû senta, pp. 264–70.

———. 2004. Interviewed by Peter Eckersall.

———, and Sara Jansen. 2000. "*The Lost Babylon* by Kawamura Takeshi, Translated with an Introduction by Sara Jansen." *The Drama Review* 44(1): 114–35.

———, and Carol Martin. 2000. 'Kawamura Takeshi: New Ideas in/for Japanese Theatre; An interview with Carol Martin.' *The Drama Review* 44(1): 109–13.

KERSHAW, Baz. 1999. *The Radical in Performance*: *Between Brecht and Baudrillard*. London and New York: Routledge.

KOMPARU, Kunio. 1983. *The Noh Theatre*: *Principles and Perspectives*. Tokyo: Weatherhill and Tankosha.

MARTIN, Carol. 2000. "Japanese Theatre, 1960s–Present." *The Drama Review* 44(1): 83–5.

MORIYAMA, Naoto. 2004. "A Phantom of Suburbia: Kawamura Takeshi's 'Hamletclone'" in Peter Eckersall, Tadashi Uchino and Naoto Moriyama (eds), *Alternatives*: *Debating Theatre Culture in an Age of Confusion*. Brussels: Peter Lang, pp. 95–107.

NOZAKI, Yoshiko. 2008. *War Memory, Nationalism and Education in Post-War Japan, 1945–2007*: *The Japanese History Textbook Controversy and Ienaga Saburo's Court Challenges*. London and New York: Routledge.

RANCIÈRE, Jacques. 2009. *The Emancipated Spectator*. Gregory Elliott trans. London and New York: Verso.

SATO, Ikuya. 1999. *Gendai Engeki No Firudowaku*: *Geijutsu Seisan No Bunka Shakaigaku* (Contemporary Theatre Fieldwork: A Cultural Sociology of Artistic Production). Tokyo: Tokyo Daigaku Shuppankai.

SCHECHNER, Richard. 2002. *Performance Studies*: *An Introduction*. London and New York: Routledge.

SIERZ, Aleks. 2000. *In-yer-face Theatre*: *British Drama Today*. London: Faber & Faber.

SUGIMOTO, Yoshio. 2009. "'Japanese Culture': An Overview" in Yoshio Sugimoto (ed.), *The Cambridge Companion to Modern Japanese Culture*. Melbourne: Cambridge University Press, pp. 1–20.

UCHINO, Tadashi. 2000. "Images of Armageddon: Japan's 1980s' Theatre Culture." *The Drama Review* 44(1): 85–96.

YODA, Tomiko, and Harry Harootunian (eds). 2006. *Japan after Japan*: *Social and Cultural Life from the Recessionary 1990s to the Present*. Durham: Duke University Press.

CHARACTERS

MIDDLE-AGED MAN

YOUNG MAN

GIRL

CROWD

WOMAN

I (female)

MAN/Ó (male)

O (male)

R (male)

J (male)

B (male)

P (female)

M (female)

F (female)

K (female)

RIGHT

LEFT

GENERAL Q

SUE ELLEN

NIPPON WARS

TRANSLATED BY SHOICHIRO KAWAI AND LEON INGULSRUD

Text projection: Calm down. The world is just moving. That's all. But don't misunderstand. The world is, if nothing else, against you.

Music. Light comes up slowly. People are seeing off Young Man in military uniform as he leaves for the front. A variety of banners. Middle-aged Man is among them. A voice is heard from deep below the stage.

VOICE. Lesson 25. Program designated "Departure for the Front." Begin.

MIDDLE-AGED MAN. Ladies and Gentlemen, our country and her people are in a state of war. Our country shall be victorious. Our men shall win many battles through the strength and courage of Mr. (*actor's name*), whom I present here. He is holding, as it were, our country in his hands. Mr. (*actor's name*), you are the first student to be drafted. You are the pride of our town. Mr. (*actor's name*), a word, if you please.

YOUNG MAN. Thank you, I am still young, but I will fight for the United Capitalist Republic of Nippon.

MIDDLE-AGED MAN. Three cheers for the United Capitalist Republic of Nippon.

The crowd cheers three times.

YOUNG MAN. I am going now. Thank you, everybody. (*Bows several times.*)

The crowd cheers. A girl rushes to him. Girl calls out the name of the actor playing Young Man. He responds by also addressing her by her real name.

GIRL. Take this with you. (*Hands him an amulet.*)

YOUNG MAN. Thank you. Goodbye for now.

GIRL. Please fight bravely for our country. I'll keep the home fires burning.

Young Man calls her by her real name and takes her by the hand.

GIRL. And I will . . . wait . . . until you come back.

YOUNG MAN. I'm sorry (*actor's name*), I don't know what happened . . .

GIRL. Never mind. I hear it happens to lots of guys.

YOUNG MAN. I'm really sorry. I was tired and upset that night. But, (*actor's name*), I'm not always like that. Look, I have a hard-on now.

GIRL. It's all right. I know.

YOUNG MAN. If you feel too lonely, use this. (*Hands her a vibrator.*)

GIRL. What? What's this?

YOUNG MAN. I bought it in Kabuki-chō. You know what it is. Don't play innocent.

GIRL. I don't know. I don't know what you're talking about.

YOUNG MAN. If you don't know, read *Hustler*. If you turn this, it moves, see?

GIRL (*looking at it*). You're going to the front, (*actor's name*).

YOUNG MAN. Yes. This is a real war. I'll fight for the UCRN,[1] the United Capitalist Republic of Nippon.

GIRL. For the UCRN . . . But what is the UCRN?

Young Man and Girl gaze forward. Again, the crowd gives three cheers. The piercing shrieks of sirens. Cries—"Alert!" "Raid!"— are heard. The people scatter for cover. Screams. Overlapping the clamour, the tune of "Le Internationale" begins to sound solemnly. A gunshot. Man, with a gun, appears from the back of the house and stands on an elevated platform.

MAN. The UCRN is the country of my birth, my home country.

The clamour of the air-raid becomes the clamour for a deserter. The crowd notices Man and cries "Deserter! Deserter!" It surrounds Man. He fires into the air. The crowd disperses quickly.

---

1 In the original Japanese, the abbreviation "Nichiren" is used instead of the initials UCRN. This makes it a homonym for the Nichiren (Lotus Sutra) sect of Buddhism.

MAN. History is my friend.

CROWD. Shut up.

MAN. You assholes. There's no hope for you. Get lost.

The crowd disappears at once.

MAN. I've come a long way, carried by the memory of an unknown history. I know nothing. Yet, I know everything. I am nothing but an arrogant neurotic.

He fires. A screen comes down with the legend: THE TWELFTH YEAR OF EMPEROR SEIKI'S REIGN. THE UNITED CAPITALIST REPUBLIC OF NIPPON WAGES WAR AGAINST CALGARIA.

MAN. I joined the Rebel Canary a year ago. I needed a war for myself.

He fires. Another screen comes down: THE THIRTEENTH YEAR OF EMPEROR SEIKI'S REIGN. ALL-OUT WAR IN CALGARIA. THE UCRN FORMS AN ALLIANCE WITH THE REPUBLIC OF AMERIGO.

MAN. But I ran. Here I am, a man who escaped from the secret underground base of the Rebel Canary. A man who has lost his own war is now standing here in the night.

He fires. Another screen comes down: THE SIXTEENTH YEAR OF EMPEROR SEIKI'S REIGN. WORLD WAR. TOTAL WAR. THE UCRN INSTITUTE. A POLICY OF TOTAL CIVILIAN WAR EFFORT.

MAN. Oh, my semicircular canals are sloshing . . . Nausea like carsickness. I could puke my guts out. History is making me sick. (*He is about to vomit.*)

Another shot. Another screen: THE SEVENTEENTH EMPEROR SEIKI'S REIGN. THE UCRN ESTABLISHES CONSCRIPTION. THE ANTI-GOVERNMENT ARMY REBEL CANARY MOVEMENT MAKES A STATEMENT.

This is followed by another screen: THE TWENTIETH YEAR OF EMPEROR SEIKI'S REIGN. STUDENTS GO TO THE FRONT.

MAN. Fuck. Bullshit. I was born and raised here. (*Fires into the air.*) What do I have to shoot at? The bullet that I shoot in the air—won't it come down? I've come so far, so far . . .

Silver sheets of paper flutter down from the sky. Man picks one up and reads.

MAN. "A REAL WAR. NOT A GAME, NOT CHILD'S PLAY. ARE YOU BORED? HOW ABOUT FIRING A REAL GUN? ARE YOU WITH IT, THE BATTLEFIELD IS WAITING FOR YOU."[2] What the hell . . .

A voice—"There he is!"—is heard. Unidentified people appear and shoot at Man.

MAN. The bullet. The fucking bullet that I shot into the air has come down . . . (*Falls.*)

Matsuda Seiko's "Sweet Memories"[3] is heard. Woman appears and sings before Man, who is carried away by the people.

WOMAN. Somebody, solve this equation of history and memories. Removable logic. False set-up. Trick backdrop. Isn't there anyone who can solve it? This equation? . . . The fear that you might die if you close your eyes, trying to sleep. You! Do you wanna feel this fear?

"Sweet Memories" grows louder.

WOMAN. Please. Don't kiss me, because, because, I . . .

Murmurs, which gradually become louder. Lights up. A room. Young men and women are sitting in a circle, playing games in a strange language. They keep playing for a while. A voice is heard from the back of the room.

VOICE. Lesson 100. Program: "Conversation." The scheduled number is complete. Change your thought, and get a reward. The leader is going to give you a smile.

---

2 The silver papers are an updating of the *aka-gami* (red papers), which are traditional Japanese conscription notices. The writing style gives the notices a somewhat informal, almost comic, feel.

3 Mastsuda Seiko was a major pop star of the 1980s and early 1990s. "Sweet Memories" was one of her biggest hits and is extremely familiar to a Japanese audience. The lyrics are full of a sentimental longing for the past.

Everyone stops playing. They look relieved. The leader J appears holding Man in a coma and throws him down.

J. How are you doing today?

A YOUNG MAN. So-so.

ANOTHER YOUNG MAN. You're the one who made the mistake.

A YOUNG MAN. Are you kidding? It was you.

J. Forget it. We have lots of time. Your term's two and a half years.

A YOUNG MAN. Is he a new one, J?

J. Conscript number 72502. He must be good if he was sent here.

A YOUNG MAN. Bullshit. He doesn't look so tough.

J. Hey, R. I'll cut your marks for that.

R. Who gives a shit. If you wanna cut 'em, cut 'em.

J. Just watch it. (*Looks at the new man.*) He's still under anaesthesia. We'd better wake him up. You all, give him a warm welcome, all right? (*Sprays something over Man's face.*)

Man wakes up and looks around.

J. Welcome to the Blue Whale Room!

ALL. Welcome to the Blue Whale Room!

MAN. Blue Whale Room . . . Who . . . who am I?!

J. A slight loss of memory is to be expected when you've been shot by the Algin Z[4] anaesthetic gun. He'll eventually recover his memory.

MAN. I am . . . I am . . .

J. What is your name?

MAN. I am . . .

J. Tell me your name, son.

MAN. I am . . .

J. The memories you had of your former name have been removed by Algin Z. Everyone here in this room went through the same thing. Names are nothing. Their only function is

---

4 The name of a popular energy drink, like Red Bull.

IMAGE 1.1 'Welcome to the Blue Whale Room!'
Nippon Wars. Open-Air Theater, Toga International Festival, 1986.
Photograph by Hisako Kagami.

expediency. You no longer have your old name, son. From now on, your name is "Ó."[5]

A YOUNG MAN. J, what the hell . . .

J. I know how you feel, O. But this comes directly from the General. I know you're already called O. But I'm sure the General has something in mind. This young man is Ó from now on. You understand, don't you, O?

O. Yes sir.

J. Be his friend. You're the smartest one in this room.

5 Pronounced "O dash." The meaning implied is that Ó is a variant or alternative version of O.

R. Shit.

MAN. Ó . . .

J. Yes, you are Ó from now on.

O. Hi, Ó. I'm O. We might as well get to know each other.

O takes the hand of Ó, who still looks blank.

R. Look at him. Dreamy-eyed, like he's just jerked off.

B giggles.

M. He's kinda cute.

K. It's good to have another boy.

O. Stop it, girls.

J. Quiet. See. He's looking around. You were all just like him when you first came here. It's slowly sinking in that he's Ó.

Ó. Where am I? . . .

All laugh.

F. That's what we all say at first.

J. You are in the Blue Whale Room.

The sound of waves.

Ó. The Blue Whale Room . . .

J. We are in the stomach of a blue whale, which mutated to this size because of the radiation from the seventh battle of San Sebastian. We are drifting in the black sea, off the UCRN.

Ó. Why am I here?

Everyone laughs.

R. We're fighting a war, you asshole. Didn't you know that?

Ó. War?

M. You got one of those Silver Slips, didn't you? Man, this is a real war.

Ó takes out the silver paper from his pocket.

J. You were drafted.

Ó. Drafted?

J. That Silver Slip is a draft notice, what they used to call Pink Slips.

Ó. Pink Slip!? (*Drops to the floor.*)

J. What's up?

Ó. My legs went weak.

J. You know conscription has been re-initiated, don't you?

Ó. But . . .

J. It's war. It's not child's play, not a game. The UCRN is in the middle of a war, a war in which people really die. You've heard in the news how we're losing in Calgaria.

Ó. But I . . .

J. You are so accustomed to peace. I know it's a sudden change. Hard to get used to. We were all like that. Right? (*Gabble.*) Our country is in a state of emergency. Your country, the United Capitalist Republic of Nippon.

Ó. But the country . . . It's . . .

J. Who do you owe your life to?

Ó. Nobody.

J. What?

Ó. My life's my own. I take it in my own hands.

R. Hey, he's got balls.

Ó. I die for myself, not for anyone else.

R. Yippie-Kai-Yae!

O. Cut it out, R.

J. R, you just lost three marks.

M. Serves you right, jerk.

R. Shut yer fucking cunt.

M. What! Motherfucker!

J. M, that's two marks for you.

Ó. Why am I here?

J. Oh, yes, I almost forgot. (*Takes out a file.*) "Ó from West Tonkie."

O. West Tonkie. That's where I'm from.

J. "A member of the anti-government partisan Rebel Canary for the past year, before escaping." (*Murmurs.*) So you're a deserter from the Rebel Canary, eh? Pretty mysterious background. Mysterious and dangerous. But that's probably why you were chosen for this room. Danger is very attractive. People love danger even if they're scared of it.

P. Yeah!

J (*drops the act*). Yeah! How was that? Did I look cool?

O. J . . .

J (*recovering himself*). P loses two marks.

P. What the hell? Hey, how come?

Ó. This is a violation of my civil rights.

J. A civil rights violation! Did you hear that? Civil rights violation, huh! Somebody, bring me the Xerox. (*F brings it.*) You apparently don't read newspapers. Look Ó, this is a copy of the *Daily News*, the seventeenth year of Emperor Seiki's reign, September the first. Here are the details of how conscription was passed by the House. You were engaged in anti-government activities and didn't know about this?

ALL. Stupid asshole!

Ó. What, you! . . .

J. In short, it's these! (*Numerous silver papers fall through the air.*) Isn't it beautiful? You must have seen something like this before. Twinkling silver papers falling down through the gaps in the blue sky. Did you see any sort of flying vehicle?

Ó. Flying vehicle?

J. I'm asking you if you saw a flying vehicle scattering these papers?

Ó. No . . . Well, maybe.

J. No, you didn't. No one let them fall. They come pouring out of this blue sky, just like a mountain spring.

Ó (*reading a silver paper*) "A REAL WAR. NOT A GAME, NOT CHILD'S PLAY. ARE YOU BORED? HOW ABOUT FIRING A REAL GUN?"

J. The moment you took that paper in your hands is recognized as the moment you accepted the call. Only the bored ones pick them up.

Ó. This is bullshit.

J. Well, weren't you bored? (*Ó can't say anything.*) Were your days so filled with bliss that you didn't have time to get bored? Why'd you run away from the Rebel Canary then?

Ó. That's because . . .

J. The sky knows everything. That big blue sky knows everything in your mind.

Ó. I hate the blue sky!

ALL. You stupid asshole!

J. All right. He'll get it eventually. I was just like him at first. I felt constricted. That's what everyone feels in the beginning. But that's what's called a persecution complex. You'll come to understand. This is relatively free space.

Ó. Free . . . I haven't heard that word for a long time.

J. Oh, by the way, let me introduce myself. I'm J, sub-leader of this Blue Whale Room. I keep things organized. Nice to meet you. (*Offers his hand.*)

Ó. Free space . . .

J. Free space means space that is not completely restricted. (*Forcibly shakes Ó's hand.*) You can think whatever you want. You're to complete the two-and-a-half-year military drill while you're here on probation, and then you go to the real front. This isn't the old kind of militarism. Let me be clear: here you're free to do whatever you want. That's why boys and girls are together here. You may fall in love, make love, or jerk off!

B. How about tonight?

P. No.

B. Come on. You'll have a good time.

P. No.

B (*snickering*). Huh, I know you want it.

Ó. We might be killed.

J. Sure. But at least you won't be bored.

O. Boredom or death.

R. I choose death. Bang, boom.

> *R and B start to play "war."*

M. Humanism's old-fashioned, bro.

O. Let's fight together, Ó.

J. That's right. You're the elite here.

Ó. Elite?

ALL (*proudly*). Yes, we're the elite.

J. They've been chosen because they have special aptitudes for battle. You who are wild, strong, quick, and have various special abilities. You are the war elite.

ALL. Yes, the war elite.

Ó. That's a weird kind of elite.

ALL. Yes, a weird elite. (*Realize what they have said and become angry.*) What did you say?

J. Don't belittle their powers, Ó.

R. Yeah, don't fuck with us, asshole.

Ó. Go fuck yourself, dick-wad.

R (*knocked down*). Oooh.

J. Take R, for instance.

> *R makes very quick movements.*

R (*blahs meaninglessly*). Chonwa. Chonwa. Chonwa. Chonwa.

Ó. What's so special about that?

J. R, open your hands.

> *Something crumbles from R's hands.*

J. He caught forty Seiki Flies, flying at Mach speed, too fast for us to see.

ALL. Wow.

J. Seiki Flies. These are also mutants created by radioactivity. Next, B.

B brings a huge bar and breaks it.

ALL. Wow.

B giggles.

J. You know what that was that he just broke? Marble.

Ó. Marble?

J. You ain't seen nothing yet. F and K.

F and K start playing cat's cradle, yelling encouragement at each other.

Ó. So what?

J. Cat's cradle with wire.

ALL. Wow.

Ó. Is that all?

J. You ain't seen nothing yet.

Ó. You're right, I ain't.

J. P, do it.

P flaps his fan and imitates a hen. After several big motions, he makes a popping sound with his cheek.

Ó. What now?

P (*taking out an egg*). I laid an egg.

ALL. Wow.

J. You ain't seen nothing yet.

Ó. I've seen enough.

J. Go on, M.

M opens her eyes and mouth wide and breathes in and out. Sound of the wind is heard. All cry out, "What is it?" M breathes violently and causes a vortex. All spin around.

J. Enough. Stop it, M. Stop.

The vortex ceases.

J. She could cause a typhoon.

ALL (*panting*). Wow.

Ó. Now, this is something.

J. You ain't seen nothing yet. O, start.

O. Yes.

J. O is the brightest one in the room. Look into his eyes.

> *Ó and O stand face to face.*

O. Think of something. Place a thought in your brain. I'll read it.

J. You see. He's a telepath. He reads people's thoughts.

Ó. Thought . . .

O. Yes, any thought you like.

J. You ain't see . . .

O. Quiet.

J. Sorry.

> *A metallic sound.*

O. Your name.

Ó. Ó.

O. Your former name.

Ó. I forgot.

O. This is West Tonkie.

Ó. Yes, do you know it?

O. You're thinking of your hometown. I can see it. I'm looking at it. The railroad is stretching out forever. The Western Line running through the wheat field. It's like the wheat field Van Gogh painted just before he died. The station is called "Satisfaction." You get off the train. The same beautiful scenery. I see. The dime store in front of the station. You bought your first wristwatch there. The pub "JR" on the corner. You used to fight there, drinking beer. The cheap motel along Route 31. Yes, that's where I made love to her for the first time. The radio was playing the Doors. You pass the bus stop for Tonkie Park and you'll soon be home. (*Ó starts whistling lightly.*) The same old house. The white swing. You open the dark brown door. Yes, you're starving. You go straight to the kitchen. The same smell. Corn soup made from the corn that grows in the backyard. Roast turkey. You always had three eggs scrambled. You want beer. Yes, you like beer before anything else. Mom, where's the beer? Cold beer. Your mother brings a can of beer. The same face . . . (*Something happens to O. He cries out suddenly and can't breathe.*)

J. What's the matter, O? (*O continues gasping.*)Take him away. Take him to bed.

> *O is carried out.*

Ó (*recovering himself*). What happened?

J. I don't know. He was doing all right. Maybe it's because he hasn't done this for a while. Don't worry. What did you think?

Ó. He was describing the exact scene I was imagining.

J. Yes. Are you impressed?

Ó. Yes, I see what you mean.

J. But you too must have some kind of power if you were sent to this room.

Ó. Me?

J. Yes. You must have. You haven't realized it.

Ó. Me?

J. You have two and a half years to find out.

Ó. Two and a half years . . .

J. I'll teach you.

Ó. Two and a half years . . .

J. Yes, after two and a half years, you'll be one of us, the elite.

Ó. . . . No! (*Produces a gun.*)

J. Battle stations.

> *In an instant all surround Ó with guns in their hands.*

J. You fool, do you think you can win a fight against professionals?

Ó. I don't like this. (*Tries to shoot.*)

J. Shoot.

All shoot.

Ó. They got me . . . (*Falls.*)

J. Stubborn fool.

F. What do we do with him?

J. Leave him. A few dozen shots of Algin Z . . . He'll be out for at least two days.

All leave. Music is heard from afar. Woman emerges on the stage. Ó wakes up.

WOMAN. Do you want me to sing?

Ó. What? . . . No.

WOMAN. If you want me to, say so. That's all I can do now.

Ó. What?

WOMAN. Sing . . . That's all I can do now.

Ó. You're alive.

WOMAN. What?

Ó. You're alive. I'm glad.

WOMAN. Silly. Do you have a smoke?

Ó. I'm sorry. I'm out.

WOMAN. It's all right. There's one left.

Ó. You still have trouble?

WOMAN. What?

Ó. You still have trouble sleeping at night?

WOMAN. Yes.

Ó. The sleeping pills I gave you . . .

WOMAN. I don't take pills. It's too easy to become addicted. I read the book you lent me, though. It was so good I couldn't sleep.

Ó. That detective story . . . it's good, isn't it?

WOMAN. Did you figure out who done it?

Ó. No. It's impossible.

WOMAN. Me neither. I never got it.

Ó. No one done it.

WOMAN. That's right, I forgot. No one done it. All the suspects proved their alibis.

ó. Not a bad idea for a detective story.

WOMAN. No. But why were so many people killed, when there was no one who done it?

ó. I don't know. But . . .

WOMAN. But what?

ó. Do you remember what the private detective said after he solved the case? "The night . . . it was all because of the night."

WOMAN. "It was all because of the night . . ."

ó. Do you remember how the story started?

WOMAN. "You're a cold person. My ex-wife used to say."

ó. And the last line was . . .

WOMAN. "It's probably because you think too much during the night. Man is but a ragbag full of memories."

ó. You have a good memory.

WOMAN. But I can't remember the title.

ó. You think too much during the night.

WOMAN. I'm . . . tired.

A voice is heard.

VOICE. Kill the woman, Hiroyuki.

ó. What?

VOICE. She's a spy for the government.

Woman smiles.

ó. You are . . . !?

WOMAN. Now I remember the title of the novel.

VOICE. Kill her, Hiroyuki.

ó. I'm sorry. (*Points the gun at her.*)

WOMAN. The title of the novel was . . . (*As she speaks, she raises her own gun slowly and points it at her temple.*)

VOICE. Kill her, Hiroyuki.

Both guns are fired simultaneously. At that instant, it becomes brighter: R, B, P, M, F, K, and J are seated at that table in a row, facing the audience. Six of them have their hands clasped in front of their faces and have their eyes closed.

M. Our dear homeland, the UCRN, we thank you tonight for this good supper. Amen.

ALL. A-men. B-men. C-men.

M. We thank you, O Unseen One, for letting us live another day. Amen.

ALL. A-men. B-men. C-men.

M. UCRN stands for UNITED CAPITALIST REPUBLIC OF NIPPON.

ALL. A-men. B-men. C-men. This is getting old!

J. Now, let's eat.

All talk.

R. Hey, B, give back my kangaroo meat.

B. I didn't take it.

R. Then where is it?

J. Relax. You can have mine.

R. Yeah!

Ó looks blank and is in the same posture as he was before.

Ó. Wh—Where am I?

M. Look, he's coming to at last.

K. He wants to know where he is.

R. Hey, bro. We already had that where-am-I stuff in the last scene. Lay off that hero shit. What are we, actors?

P. That's right. And I'm going to play the heroine.

B. Me too.

R. You can't.

B. The hell I can't! (*Snaps his fork in half.*)

J. Settle down and eat quietly.

R. Oh come on, let's play heroes.

ALL. Yeah!

Ó. Now I remember. This is the Blue Whale Room.

P. Did you see that acting? Sends shivers down my spine.

M. Doesn't it?

K. Doesn't it?

Ó (*suddenly serious*). Hungry, hungry, I'm hungry. Hungry, hungry,
I'm hungry.
All the hungry young men and all the angry young men
Couldn't put hungry together again.
(*As soon as he finishes singing, he starts to eat like a horse.*)

R. Look at him.

F. Let him eat. He hasn't eaten for two days.

J. But . . . but I can't figure him out.

P. Don't give up, J.

J. Yeah. I'm the leader, aren't I?

O appears.

O. Hi. Sorry about freaking out like that.

F. Are you all right?

O. Yeah, I'm OK. I had some kind of fit. I'm more delicate than you
think. (*Coughs.*)

R. Don't make me laugh.

O coughs.

B. I don't buy that for a second.

R. All right. Now eat.

Everyone is taken aback by the way Ó and O eat. Then, J speaks.

J. OK, everybody, let's eat. (*Starts to eat.*)

R. You know what I think?

M. What?

R. I think the war's gonna get tougher and tougher.

F. I heard four Nazi warships were sighted in the Iowa Sea.

ᴋ. Nazi?

ᴍ. Yes, Nazi. Who'da thunk it?

ꜰ. J, is it true that the Nazis have more nuclear missiles than anyone?

ᴊ. Well, I'm not sure.

ᴘ. They bring in nuclear weapons, it's game over for the UCRN, eh?

ʙ. Amerigo will help us.

ʀ. Dream on. That sort of thinking is so infantile.

ʙ. Are you saying I'm infantile?

ʀ. You're too independent.

ᴍ. You mean "dependent."

ʀ. Yeah. You're fucking dependent.

ʙ. Well, why don't you tell us what to do if you're so smart? (*Breaks his spoon.*)

ʀ. We'll win it ourselves. That's why we're here, right, J?

ᴊ. Well, I'm not sure.

ʙ. Hey, P, let's fuck tonight.

ᴘ. Fuck yourself.

ʙ (*laughs*). I know you want it.

ᴘ. Yeah, but not with you.

ʙ. Come on, it's not like it'll hurt you.

P pours water over B.

ʙ. Ugghh!

ʀ. OK. Calm down. Now calm down.

ʙ. It won't hurt you, will it?

ᴘ. It will.

ʙ. What?

ꜰ. Now, now, now.

ᴋ. Does it really hurt, d'you think?

ᴊ. Well, I'm not sure.

F. But it's kind of strange.

K. What?

F. Sitting all together like this, I wonder if we're ever really going to the front.

All pause in their eating except Ó and O.

R. Hey J, what's combat like?

J. Well, I'm not sure.

R. Can't you say anything else? (*Makes the motion of strangling J.*) You're the only one who's actually been in a real war.

J. Ugghh. All right, I'll tell you. It's like hell. Hell.

P. Hell.

R. Come on, stop fucking with us. You've seen *All Quiet on the Western Front*. You've seen *Apocalypse Now*. You've seen *Rambo VII, Platoon*.

M. I haven't seen *Rambo VII*.

F. You don't have to.

J. It's hell over there. (*Stands up.*) I, Private J, was Marlon Brando on Rarotonga Island.

R. What the hell are you talking about?

J. I was a god to the natives on Rarotonga Island, just like Marlon Brando in *Apocalypse Now*!

B. Bullshit.

J. It's true. I got tired of the war.

R. What d'you mean tired, you motherfucker?

J. I'm not trying to piss you off. But I'm fed up with killing. Do you know who I was before I came to the Blue Whale Room?

M. No.

J. You're lucky that you didn't meet me then. Good evening, ladies and gentlemen, may I present Jack the Ripper.

Music.

O. What, you're Jack the Ripper?

J. Not a rip-off or a jack-off, not Rip Van Winkle but Jack the Ripper.

O. Bullshit.

J. You think I'm dead. But I'm not. Yes. Thanks to some delicate maneuvring by the government, I have survived. Why? Because my inherent sense of cruelty and violence was a perfect match for the profile for this room.

R. This room?!

J. Yes. The Blue Whale Room. According to research conducted by the UCRN Criminology Association, my qualities exactly match the qualities of the war elite. We're going to bring the memory of Jack the Ripper into the battlefield. But of course, murder in daily life and murder in the context of a war are not the same. In battle, you get tired of it after only killing ten people.

R. Ten?

J. If you kill ten, no one's left. And so I became Marlon Brando. (*O reads a poem by T. S. Eliot.*) Just like this, alone in a cave.

M. What did you do then?

J. I reached a conclusion. Murder is for yourself. . . .Who do you murder for in battle?

O. For our friends, our countrymen.

J. Be more specific.

R. For the UCRN.

J. That's right. But can you really die for the UCRN?

O. Are you allowed to say that, J?

J. Shut up and recruit. Let us confirm the situation. I am your leader, J, commissioned by General Q. There are other troops besides us, the Emperor Penguin Room, the Bottle-nosed Dolphin Room, the Sperm Whale Room. I know that in those rooms nationalistic discipline is strictly adhered to. Which is to say . . .

ALL (*except Ó*). Which is to say . . .

J. Your bodies belong to the UCRN.

ALL. Our bodies belong to the UCRN!

J. Save the UCRN.

ALL. Save the UCRN!

J. But you are the elite. General Q intends to turn an entire battle-field over to you. You are not necessarily going to die for the UCRN.

O. What does that mean?

J. You'll know when your term is completed. You're free, that's what General Q said. Ugh! (*Shows intense suffering*.) Shit! The memory of Jack the Ripper . . .

P. You live too much in the past.

J. Ugh, ugh. This is a bad one. (*Falls down and rolls over*.) Ugh, ugh.

F. J, are you all right?

All run toward J, who suddenly stands up.

J (*drooling*). You saw me rip.

M. What the fuck.

J. I'm Jack the Ripper. I want women. I want young women. (*Chases the women, his mouth watering*.) I wanna fuck. Give me fuck.

Ó slams the table. All look at him.

Ó. Are you really ready to fight a war?

J. I'm ready. I'm ready to fuck.

Ó. Get lost.

J. You saw me rip . . . (*Goes out, chasing the women*.)

R, O, Ó and B are left.

Ó. I hate this stinking place.

R. Still worried? You just ate a meal here.

Ó. But . . .

R. It's not so bad once you get used to it.

Ó. But where's the dessert?

All collapse.

B. Well, aren't you momma's boy.

R. If you want to take off, it's easy. There's a small submarine called the *Devilfish* at the back of the room. The keys are in it. I'd go but the Rebel Canary is after me. Besides . . .

O. Cut the theatrics. Even if you got back to Tokyo, the streets are full of unemployed workers. It's the worst depression of the Emperor Seiki era. They call it "super-stagflation." We're the lucky ones. The Silver Slips took care of us. At least we don't have to worry about food. Stay here with us.

Ó. But I was a member of Rebel Canary.

O. Don't be a fool. Get rid of your ideology. Throw it to the plankton. Get real, Ó from West Tonkie. I was so happy to see it all again. I mean the pictures of West Tonkie in your thoughts. That wheat field. The view along the highway. Did you go to Guatemala Elementary School?

Ó. Yeah.

O. Me too.

Ó. You went to Guatemala Elementary School?

O. I went to Guatemala Junior and Senior High School too.

Ó. Me too!

R. Hey, this isn't an alumni meeting, you hicks.

Ó. Where are you from?

R. Me? I'm from Sakhalin.

Ó. Sakhalin! Fuck, you're the real hick, aren't you?

O. Yeah. The Sakhalin mountain ape.

R. Shut the fuck up. He's from Andalusia.

Ó. Wow, Andalusia, where they still use paper to wipe their asses.

B. What's wrong with wiping your ass with paper?

R. Hayseed.

B. Don't be ignorant. It's the farmers of Andalusia who support the economy of the UCRN.

R. Get lost, hick.

B. The hick's getting mad.

O. Oh, shit. B's mad now.

B. B-B-B-B-B! (*Rages about, attacks R.*)

R. Back off, country boy.

B. I'll kill you, city boy.

J holds down M.

J. You saw me . . .

M. Get him off me.

Ó. Still at it?

J holds down M.

J. I'm Jack the Ripper.

M. Ahh . . . !

O. Quiet! The General's coming.

All freeze.

O. I can feel General Q's body heat.

Noises are heard.

J. O, are you sure?

O. I can feel it. I can feel General Q's heat.

The sounds become louder.

J. He's right. It's a surprise inspection by General Q!

Q appears on the elevated passageway smoking a cigar. Sawada Kenji's[6] song "Miscast" is heard. Q comes on stage singing, followed by Right and Left, spokesmodels of the battlefield. J and the others salute. Ó follows suit reluctantly. Q, still singing, inspects their salutes, their clothes, and their belongings.

Q. Oh, you wonderful people! Human existence is a colossal miscasting. It's worse than if Jane Russell had played Scarlett O'Hara. Don't you think?

---

6 Sawada Kenji (also known as "Julie") was a major pop star of the 1970s and 80s, known for his flamboyantly androgynous persona.

RIGHT. Yes, yes, I agree.

Q. Oh man, people are so unhappy, aren't they?

LEFT. Oh, I'm burning.

Q. Yes, we are all burning with the pain of human intelligence.

LEFT. My pussy is burning.

Q. Yes, the pussy is the great spark of intelligence.

LEFT. Do me quick, General.

Q. To do it quick means to come too soon.

RIGHT. Do me quick, General.

Q. For the sake of all those who suffer, I can't do it with you. (*Left and Right hit General Q in the groin.*) Uggh! (*Doubles over.*) I've got no cum. (*Jumps up.*) My penis was burnt by napalm in the battle of San Sebastian. You knew that, didn't you, J?

J. Yes sir, but you've still got your balls, sir.

Q. Yes indeed, and balls of fire they are. A dirty joke. By chance, my balls escaped being burned. But since then, I have not experienced the ecstasy of ejaculation. Do you understand my pain, J?

J. Yes sir, General.

Q. Don't lie to me. (*Kicks J's groin. J doubles over. Q kicks everyone in the groin one at a time.*) Good. You are all doing fine. Let me introduce you to the new spokesmodels of the battlefield: Miss Right and Miss Left.

RIGHT and LEFT. Pleased to meet you.

All start to drool.

Q. You are not to love.

ALL. No, sir.

Q. Good. Love retards thinking. The new man should not be involved with love affairs. I'll show you the simplest form of our new love.

Right and Left open their legs wide. All gather around them.

Q. Now line up. Behave yourselves. (*They line up.*) Good. This is indeed a new democracy.

Ó. Hey, why are *you* in line?

M. I'm lesbian.

Ó. I see.

> *They start fucking Right and Left, but J and M, who started first, take too much time.*

Q. How about that? The great miscasting of our existence as human beings. When the world collapses, you'll be something more than human.

O. Hurry up. We're waiting!

R. I'm a bit too ready!

B. I'm about to come.

R. J takes too fucking long.

> *All gather and bitch about it.*

Q. Behave yourselves. Where's your sense of democracy?

B. Hey, there's another woman over there!

> *Woman struggles.*

Ó. You, you're . . . !

> *The sound of the sea.*

Q. Welcome back, I.

O. Welcome, I!

LEFT. Who is that woman?!

> *Q hushes Left.*

Q. It's Miss I, the first spokesmodel of the battlefield.

RIGHT and LEFT. Oh, pardon our ignorance, please.

I. Q, you are miscast. You are the only miscast one here.

Q. I knew you'd come back. Everyone does. They always come back here, knowing everything.

I. I'll tell you something, Q.

Q. Don't say a word.

O. What happened, I?

Q. You'll find out eventually, O. Don't push it.

O. What?

Q. I, come to my quarters tonight after midnight. I'll give you a real good one. I'll make you come all night with a super-deluxe electronic vibrator.

I spits at Q.

Q. J, programs!

J. Yes, sir. Salute!

All come forth, line up, and salute.

Q. J, which one is the newcomer in this room?

J. Ó, step forward.

Ó steps forward in front of Q.

Q (*touching Ó's body*). Wonderful . . . This is a perfect human being. You still don't understand any of this. I know how you feel. But you'll gradually understand. You have plenty of time. J, I want a sit-rep of the war.

J. Yes, sir.

A TV is brought in. The situation of the war is projected on the screen.

J. After forming an alliance with Assist, Cal raided Nanjing with their secret special forces unit.

Q. Nanjing too, at last.

J. There is a temporary lull in the battle of Calgaria, but guerrilla warfare is expected to break out at any moment. Given this situation, it is probable that Cal is going to be involved in the World War semi-permanently.

Q. You all understand this? Any questions?

ALL. No sir.

Q. Then we'll move on to the programs. Since you're a newcomer, Ó, stay there and watch. The troops have to master two hundred lessons in two and a half years. They have various names. This is a new type of military drill created by Sue Ellen.

Ó. Sue Ellen?

Q. She is the sum total of our thoughts, our total brain. You'll come to know her. Now, everyone, show me the results of your work.

J holds a microphone. The sound of a siren.

J. All of you in the belly of the Blue Whale, we are going to start our lesson. Places. (*All take up their positions.*) Breathe in. Breathe out. Breathe in. Breathe out. You're stuffed. (*All move their mouths according to the instructions.*) Woodpecker. Fellatio. Vampire. Neuralgia. Concentrate. Lesson 7: Burst of laughter. (*All burst into laughter.*) Lesson 10: Joy. (*All smile.*) Lesson 5: A shy smile. Lesson 34: A wry smile. Lesson 35: Orgasm. Lesson 39: Grief. Lesson 40: Wailing. Lesson 43: Crying with joy. Lesson 45: Surprise. Moving on to lesson 50: Anger. Lesson 51: Shouting. Lesson 52: Controlled anger. Lesson 55: Violence. Lesson 57: Giving up. Lesson 58: Mastur-bation. Lesson 59: Insignificance. Lesson 60: Self-confidence. Lesson 61: Obedience. We are skipping up a level. Lesson 70: Death. (*All collapse. J checks whether they are really dead.*) If you can do this, you've completed the elementary level. R, you are not completely dead. Lesson 71: Returning to life. (*All get up at once.*) Now, we move on to physical training. Lesson 80: Karate. (*All shout as they take up postures for karate.*) Lesson 81: Tricks. Lesson 82: Playing games.

All walk around on can-stilts and play soccer.

Q. What do you think of this kind of drill? It gives you practical skills.

6. I don't understand.

Q. It's very different from the Rebel Canary, eh? What did you learn there? The same old stuff . . . how to use your gun, how to use explosives, how to fight a guerrilla war, how to find spies . . . That's all useless bullshit. The enemy we face is far greater.

6. What do you mean "greater?"

Q. I'll show you our final trump card. J, get them ready for lesson 100: Conversation.

J. Lesson 100: Conversation.

All sit in a circle.

Q. This is communication. You exchange your own ideas. But you cannot use any existing language. You let your ideals whirl around the circle. On top of the circle sits Sue Ellen, our total brain, observing us. Let's begin.

J. Begin.

All talk to one another in a strange language. They speak faster and louder as they grow more excited, more agitated. Still speaking their strange language, they face the audience. The emergency siren is heard, and the sound of the sea becomes louder, like a storm. Something has happened. Vibration. All are trembling. The sound of an explosion. All fall to the floor. Screams.

Q. What happened? What's going on?

J. The enemy submarine *Sea Bat*, searching for us, exploded near the tail of our Whale. There are no survivors.

Q. Did we attack?

J. No, we didn't do anything at all.

R. What happened, then?

P. I feel like something exploded in my head.

Q. You did it, troops.

O. What do you mean, General?

Q. You blew up the *Sea Bat*.

ALL. What?

Q. Your "power id" materialized for the first time. Our research shows that the concentration of your thoughts can create explosive power. It's Neuro-Kinetic Energy.

O. Neuro-Kinetic Energy?

Q. Neuro-Kinetic Energy has only been a theory, until now. We've been waiting all century for this moment. J, bring us champagne for a celebration.

J. Yes, sir.

Q. Everyone, you will soon depart for the front. (*Takes a glass of champagne and hands one to I.*) You saw it, I, didn't you?

I. But there's no telling what will happen.

Q (*ignoring her*). You have just joined the war. We drink to your war!

Ó. Our war?

A voice is heard.

VOICE. Well done, everybody. Here is your reward—the sound of the battlefield.

O. I know that voice!

Q. Thanks, Sue Ellen.

Loud music. Slowly, lights down. Several gunshots are heard in the darkness. Ó wakes up suddenly. P is lying beside him.

Ó. I was dreaming.

P. What's up?

Ó. What are you doing here?

P. What the hell are you talking about? You let me in.

Ó *(looking at the empty bottles around them).* We drank too much.

P. I'm hammered. You're hammered.

Ó. Oh, my head aches.

P. I should have known.

Ó. What?

P. As soon as you hit the bed, you started snoring.

Ó. What do you mean?

P. Don't get caught up with a battlefield spokesmodel. There are lots of nice girls like me.

Ó. What are you talking about?

P. Chill out. You don't have to marry me right away.

Ó. I had a dream. I was blindfolded and my hands were tied behind my back. I was shot and killed.

P. That means you're frustrated. Don't make love to the spokesmodels. They're a disgrace to women. Do you know the rate of marriage between people in the same room? In Sunfish Room where I used to be, it was ninety percent. Oh, shit. I shouldn't have mentioned marriage. Hold me.

Ó. I can still feel bullets in my body.

P. Come on, hold me.

IMAGE 1.2 **The androids get drunk.**
Nippon Wars, Kinokuniya Hall, Shinjuku, 1986.
Photograph by Hisako Kagami.

6. In the dream, I was alive after I was shot. I pretended to be dead but I was alive. Someone saw me and shouted something, looking at me.

P. Hold me!

A voice—"Hold her."—is heard. I lights her cigarette in the dark.

6. You . . .

I. Hey, sweetie, you're too uptight.

P. Get lost. You're disgusting. You battlefield spokesmodels are complete sluts.

I. I didn't choose this.

P. Get away. Filthy bitch.

I. I know . . .

P. What?

I. A year ago, there was a spokesmodel named P in the Sunfish Room.

P. That's a lie.

I. You know a man named Alpha.

P. You mean Alpha. Alpha. (*Starts to cry.*)

I. You don't have to hide it.

P. Alpha. My Alpha.

I. They tricked you.

P. No. He just went to the front.

I. He's dead. General Q said he died an honorable death in Calgaria.

P. You lie. You're a goddam liar.

I. Why should I lie to you about your lover?

P. Liar. (*Cries.*)

I. Miserable little dope. You should have known this would happen if you have an affair with someone in the same room. Women in the rooms avoid affairs. You know why? Because they don't want to suffer.

P. Alpha is alive. He has to be alive.

ı. When all is said and done, war is just a game for men.

    P runs away.

ó. You.

ı. What do you want?

ó. You were in the Rebel Canary, weren't you?

ı. Why do you ask that?

ó. I shot a girl who looked just like you.

ı. How can I be here if I'm dead.

ó. I know . . . Have you been here long?

ı. Yes, I've been here longer than anyone else. If I were a soldier, I would have gone to the front a long time ago. I've watched many of them go.

ó. How are they now?

ı. Some are dead, some are still fighting. It depends. I heard you're from West Tonkie.

ó. Yes.

ı. I'm from East Tonkie.

ó. Well, what a coincidence.

ı. Not now.

ó. What do you mean?

ı. I used the submarine *Devilfish* and escaped to East Tonkie. I went to the orphanage where I grew up.

ó. You were in an orphanage?

ı. Doesn't matter now. I lost what I was.

ó. Was it destroyed in an air-raid or something?

ı. Yeah, sort of. I have memories of living in the orphanage until I was four. A painting by Lautrec on the wall. The linden tree you could see outside the window. (*Produces a photo.*) Look. This is me, when I was three. It's in front of the gate of the orphanage. But now . . . (*She is in a daze for a second.*) Do you have a photo?

Ó searches his pockets and takes one out.

6. My mother.

I. Oh, she's beautiful.

6. This is my house.

I. It's a beautiful house. The wheat field, sparkling. There's quite a difference between West and East Tonkie.

6. Why do people here want to talk about their memories all the time?

I. Living here, it seems like your memories are all that count. You'll soon understand.

R, O, B, M come in, roaring drunk, followed by Right and Left.

R. Hi there! How're you fucking?

M. I need more booze.

O. Oh, am I drunk.

LEFT. Come on, pass the booze.

O. No. No more. Hey, you two. What are you doing there?

B. Don't be fucking around behind our backs, new guy.

R. Right. If you fuck us up, I'll tie a rope around your cock.

M. I need more booze, fucker.

R. Drink this, bitch.

M. I said I need more, asshole.

They shout at each other.

RIGHT. Miss I, have a drink with us.

LEFT. Miss I, tell us about your experiences. We want to learn from you.

I. Never fall in love. That's all.

LEFT. That sounds cool! But we'll never fall in love with these jerks anyway.

B. What did you say, bitch?

R. You cunt.

M. Forget them. Let's go.

M, Right, and Left go out.

O. Oh, I'm done. (*Vomits.*)

R. Shit. What a mess! This is why I hate these bright boys. What a fucking waste!

I. Are you all right, O?

Ó. I want to ask you something.

B. Ask J.

Ó. I want to ask you.

R. Pay up. If you want to ask us something, give us money.

Ó hands R some money. R tears it into pieces.

Ó. Why'd you do that?

R. There's no use having money in this room. What do you want to know?

Ó. First. About Neuro-Kinetic Energy.

R. What about it?

Ó. What the hell is it?

B. How should we know?

Ó. But you created it.

O. We don't know how we did it. We just did it.

R. Do you want us to do it again?

B. Yeah, let's show him.

R and B strain themselves. Sound of a fart.

R. Oh man, that stinks. Fuck you.

B. You did it.

Ó. The other thing is about Sue Ellen. What is a total brain?

O. Sorry, we don't know about her either. We just know that she's somewhere in the depths of this room.

Ó. You don't know anything.

R. I don't give a fuck. We have all the booze we need. What else do you want?

I. Shall I tell you about Sue Ellen?

O. Do you know something about her, I?

I. Where's J?

B. He's sleeping, dead drunk.

I. Look around and make sure nobody's around.

Ó. We're alone.

I. Promise that you won't tell this to anyone.

R. What the hell. I'm getting sober.

I. I'll show you Sue Ellen.

O. Are you serious?

I. Yes. We're friends.

R. So she's a cunt just like you.

I. Shut up. Keep quiet. Close your eyes.

    R, O, Ó, and B close their eyes.

I. Do you care if you die with your eyes closed? We're at the bottom of the sea. Hear that? The sound of running water. It's like waking up in your coffin after being buried. Just like this. No sound. Nothing to do but wait for a slow death. You scream. You scratch till your nails come off. But nothing happens. It's hopeless. You can't do anything in the dark. Take three steps forward. (*The four obey.*) You understand for the first time where you're from and where you're going.

O. We're from far far away and we're going far far away.

Ó. No. It's just a matter of perspective.

I. Quiet. Take two steps back. Answer the questions. Do you have the memory of being loved?

O. No.

B. Maybe.

Ó. I don't know.

I. Do you have the memory of having loved? (*All are quiet.*)

I. Answer the question. Do you have the memory of having loved?

Ó. I don't know.

I. Did you hear that, Sue Ellen?

The atmosphere of the room suddenly changes. There is an open space in the middle, where a brain is floating in the air in the darkness. Several women surround it with candles in their hands.

R. What the hell is that?

I. That's Sue Ellen. She is breathing only in idea and thought. Do you read me, Sue Ellen?

SUE ELLEN. I read you, I. It's been a long time.

R. Blah blah blah . . .

I. She is the total brain that supports the intelligence in this room.

B. I'm gonna try poking it.

B is thrown back by an invisible barrier.

I. That's the barrier of thought.

O. The barrier of thought?

I. Although she has no body, she can exert an invisible force by thinking.

Ó. By thinking?

O. She can exert force just by thinking. That's fantastic. That's the ultimate power to intelligence.

I. You could say that. Her intelligence is the sum total of all human intelligence. Isn't that so, Sue Ellen?

SUE ELLEN. Don't flatter me, I.

O. Her intelligence runs everything here, eh?

I. Yes.

SUE ELLEN. But I'm not an authority figure. I'm just a sad, lonely woman.

R. Yeah, but you're the bitch in charge, aren't you?

SUE ELLEN. Hey, here's one with guts. What's you name?

I. He's R, Sue Ellen.

SUE ELLEN. Nice to meet you, R.

R. When are you gonna let us fight?

SUE ELLEN. Are you eager to fight?

R. Sure thing. Any time.

o. How did she get to be this way? She was an ordinary woman before, wasn't she?

I. Yes. She was once a brave soldier. She was a war hero from the Emperor Penguin room. But she was blown up in the war before last.

o. And her brain was all that was left, eh?

I. She was transformed into a new entity that can only think. She hasn't made a single mistake since.

SUE ELLEN. No. I'm not so powerful. I'm just an unhappy woman who can no longer love.

B. I'll hold you, baby.

B is blown back again.

I. Don't you ever learn?

B. She must have been a fox.

o. Don't you have a photo or something?

SUE ELLEN. This is an old picture of me.

A photograph of Sue Ellen when she was alive is seen in the darkness. It is a photo of Ingrid Bergman.

R. Wow, she's beautiful!

SUE ELLEN. This was me, when I could still believe in things.

o. What about now?

SUE ELLEN. I can't believe in anything.

I. Stop it, Sue Ellen.

SUE ELLEN. I've thought too much.

I. Stop it, Sue!

SUE ELLEN. I'm sorry, I. I didn't mean to upset you.

ó. Tell me where the Whale is swimming right now.

SUE ELLEN. The Whale is about two thousand metres above the "Crying Sea." The bottom of the sea here is covered with skeletons of dead soldiers.

ó. Where are we going?

SUE ELLEN. To the coast of Calgaria.

R. Calgaria?

O. That's the front line.

Ó. Are we going to fight?

SUE ELLEN. I don't know.

Ó. What about Neuro-Kinetic Energy?

SUE ELLEN. It's your own power. If you use it, the UCRN cannot be beaten.

Ó. Are we going to get killed?

SUE ELLEN. I don't know.

O. Where are we from?

I. O, don't.

SUE ELLEN. O, you're like I. You think too much at night.

O. Where are we from? What are we, floating in the sea, awakened by the sound of the Whale's breathing at midnight? Tell me, Sue Ellen.

O rushes toward her, but is blown back by the barrier.

O. What is that dream that we always dream? The dream in which we're thrown out into cosmic space, floating among the planets, not knowing if we're alive or dead?

I. Stop it, O.

Ó. Miss I, what is this?

I runs away.

R. What's up, O? You freaking out again?

O. Please, Sue Ellen!

SUE ELLEN. If you insist . . .

Gunshots. O is shot. R, B, and Ó are shot, one by one. They fall. Sue Ellen disappears. I comes out with a gun from the back of the room, followed by Q and J.

Q. Well done, I. That was close.

I. I was . . . I scared myself.

Q. J, erase the memories of these four.

J. Yes, sir.

> *J approaches the four. It slowly gets dark. A voice is heard in the middle of the darkness.*

VOICE. Emergency. Emergency. Cal Laser Tank Troops have captured Harna, the capital of Nanjing. The President of Nanjing, Ri Eipeni, has committed suicide in his palace. Calgaria district is again in a state of tension and the troops on both sides are prepared for all-out war. And now for the domestic news There will be snowfall in the early morning. A small hand-made bomb was thrown into the carriage of Governor-General Suzuki Takenobu. Four men including the Governor-General were killed in the explosion. Hours later, martial law was declared in the capital of Tokyo. I repeat. Tokyo the capital of the UCRN is now under martial law.

> *Ó rises.*

Ó. A dream again. Am I dreaming again? Something's been wrong ever since I came here. If I am dreaming, why does it feel so real? If the dream world is real, am I supposed to live in that world too? You have to tell me, Sue Ellen.

O. Quiet, Ó. In the dream world there is dream version of you. This is neither dream nor reality. This is the third world.

Ó. What's that?

O. I already told you. We're in the belly of the Whale.

Ó. I . . .

O. You are your third self. Look. You have friends in the third world.

> *R, B, P, M, F, and K can be seen in the dark.*

ALL. You understand, Ó?

> *Each speaks, stating their blood type and zodiac sign.*

F. I'm F. (*Inserts own star sign and blood type.*) I'm still a kid at heart. I'm bright and cheerful but a little sentimental. I sometimes write poems, influenced by my brother, who is two years older than me.

M. I'm M. (*Inserts own star-sign and blood type*). When I was seven, my father ran away with a lover. I was brought up by my mother after that. I became a criminal at fifteen, and went straight again at twenty when I met my boyfriend. I might look tough, but sometimes I cry at night. My boyfriend is working at a confectionery factory in South Sakhalin. I write to him once a week.

B. I'm B. (*Inserts own star sign and blood type*). I'm from Andalusia. I'm a farmer.

R. Good, hayseed.

B. Shut up. If I have a stern character, it's because of the cold climate in Andalusia. Cold has a great influence on the character. But I think I'm cheerful at heart.

K. I'm K. (*Inserts own star sign and blood type*). I was born in a regular household in Ikursk. My father is a junior high math teacher. My mother teaches elementary school. I was an only child raised without want or worry. I've never known poverty. I've never known true hunger. If I had to have a serious problem, it's that I've never had a serious problem. But right now, I have lots of friends and I am enjoying every day.

R. I'm R. (*Inserts own star sign and blood type*). I was born near the sea of Sakhalin. It was a nice place. Seagulls flying around. I was brought up near the sea. My character? I'm very cheerful. I'm what you would call an open-hearted guy. Everyone thinks I'm wild, but if you spend some time with me you'll see what I'm really like. I'm actually gentle and warm-hearted.

P. My name is P. (*Inserts own star sign and blood type*). I'll soon be too old to get married. I really want to get married. Is anyone interested? Let me tell you about myself. My hobbies are knitting and listening to music. I like pop music. I went to a bridal finishing school for one year after junior college. I can handle flower arranging and tea ceremony without trouble. I have a bright personality and can become friendly with just about anybody. My ideal man is kind and tolerant. I'm not picky about looks.

o. I'm O. (*Inserts own star sign and blood type*). I'm from West Tonkie. I graduated from Guatemala High School. Do you remember the high school dance?

ó. Yes. You mean the one on Christmas Eve?

o. The girls couldn't take their eyes off you.

ó. Bullshit.

o. The band made a "boom" and the party poppers were popping all over the place. We drank punch without alcohol. Teenage boys and girls smelling of milk.

ó. Were you at that dance too?

o. You danced with a girl named Chiko for the first time when you were a sophomore.

ó. How do you know that?

o. Do you have any photos?

ó. Photos?

o. Any old photos?

ó. I have some of my home and mother.

o. Show them to me.

ó. Sure.

> *O receives photographs from Ó. His hands are trembling. After looking at them, he hands them back, slowly.*

o. Thank you.

ó. What's wrong, O?

o. First your pyorrhoea flares up. Then your semicircular canals begin to swirl.

ó. What?

o (*bending over in pain*). Then your eyesight goes, your hearing, and you feel a deep anxiety. You lose hold of your emotions and your existence itself . . . Oh, oh! (*Runs off.*)

ó. O, what happened? O!

> *The sound of party poppers, music, dance. Everyone is dancing an easy and slow dance. The atmosphere is bright and happy.*

Ó. What is this? Where am I?

R (*dancing*). You're finally awake.

Ó. Where am I?

M (*dancing*). Is that all you ever say?

K (*dancing*). You forget where you are whenever you dream.

Ó. Dream? Was that a dream?

F. You were asleep for three whole days.

R. I bet you're hungry again, eh?

> *All laugh.*

P. Come on. Join in. It's the room's annual dance.

Ó. Dance?

B. A generous move on their part—they let us off the drills for a day. Come on, let's dance. Find a partner.

R. Even B has a partner.

B. Shut up, you asshole.

Ó. Where's O?

R. No idea. He's probably drunk and barfing again somewhere. Come on. Dance.

Ó. I don't feel like dancing.

P. What a loser.

> *Ó sits alone away from the others. I comes up to him.*

I. Why, don't you dance?

Ó. I had another strange dream.

I. Come on, dance. This is your last chance to dance.

Ó. What do you mean?

I. Don't yell at me. I'm only telling you this: when the war is going badly, dances are more frequent.

Ó. You mean . . .

I. The trainees in this room will leave soon for the front.

Ó. I see.

1. It's a good plan. Q, I mean, Sue Ellen was really thinking. They're going to send us to the front satisfied and happy. We're free here. We can do anything—drink, gamble, make love.

6. I don't think so.

1. Well, do you think the world outside is so full of freedom?

6. No.

1. You have to admit we have more freedom here than what they have outside.

6. I know what you mean, but . . .

1. Let's talk about something else. I don't like arguing. Especially between men. (*Looks toward the dancing people.*) I remember the dances we had in high school.

6. You too!

1. What's wrong? You look pale.

6. I don't seem to be able to distinguish between dreams and reality. We used to have dances like this at my high school too.

1. Yes? Doesn't this take you back?

6. It does. Aren't you going to dance?

1. I didn't dance even in high school.

6. How come?

1. I was too proud. I wanted to dance, but I just sat smoking in the corner, looking down my nose at everybody.

6. Like you do now.

1 (*laughs*). Yeah, like now. I was just dying to dance. Teenagers are strange. When a boy you like comes up to you, you get even more proud and cool.

6. I was like that too.

1. You?

6. I'm like that now.

1. You haven't grown up.

6. No.

1. . . . Soon they'll be in battle.

Ó. Is there really a war going on?

I. What?

Ó. Nothing. You wanna dance?

I. Sure.

> *Both rise. O runs in, his face pale.*

Ó. O!

O. Ó, look at me!(*Produces a knife and points it toward his wrist.*)

> *Scream. The dance circle is broken up. B tries to stop O. A crashing sound. The room sways. The emergency siren sounds.*

J. Our Whale is under attack by two enemy warships. Battle stations.

R. Hey, something's wrong with O.

J. Forget about him. Battle stations!

> *All scatter. O is standing rigid.*

Ó. Hey, O. What's the matter, O?

J. Hey, I told you to take up battle stations.

Ó. But O is . . .

J. Are you disobeying me?

> *A voice—"That's all right, J."—is heard. Q comes in, accompanied by Right and Left clad in operating gowns, pushing an operating table.*

J. But General . . .

Q. He might as well know. Ladies and gentlemen, stand by.

> *J sprays something over O. O becomes rigid. Right and Left strip him down to his shorts and lay him out on the operating table.*

Q. It seems like the sewing machine and the umbrella have finally met on the operating table, eh?

LEFT. We're ready, sir.

J (*puts on a mask*). Shall we begin?

Q. Just a second. (*To Ó*) Don't be shocked. It's a simple process. You're beginning to figure it out, aren't you?

Ó. I dream more often than I used to.

Q. They aren't dreams.

Ó. What?

Q. In this room is a third world, which is neither dream nor reality. O has told you that much, hasn't he? All our science and intelligence have yet to find out what this world is. We call the phenomena in this room "a third world."

Ó. What is it?

Q. I told you, we don't know.

Ó. What does that have to do with this?

Q. Observe carefully. Start the operation, please.

J. Yes, Dr. Spock.

Q. What's that.

J. General Hospital.

Q. Cut it out.

J. I'm sorry. Scalpel, please.

> *Right hands him a scalpel. J places it against the chest of O.*

J. Wow! (*Throws down the scalpel.*) I'm sorry. Scalpel, please. (*Right hands it to him. He places it against the chest.*) Wow! (*Throws it down. Repeats it several times.*)

Q. What the hell are you doing?

J. I'm sorry, sir. I'm afraid of blood.

Q. Move over. Scalpel. (*Cuts O's chest open.*) Ladle. (*Puts the ladle into the chest, ladles out the blood and tastes it.*) How is it?

J (*drinks*). It's just right.

Q. Good. Ear pick. (*Scrabbles in the chest with the ear pick.*)

J. Ahh. It tickles.

Q. Oooh . . . here it is, a big ball of earwax. (*Blows into the chest.*)

J. Ahh, it tickles.

Q. The chest seems OK. Let's cut open the skull. Gaff tape. (*Tapes the chest.*) Scalpel. (*Opens the head.*) Good God! Look!

> *Right, Left, and J look into the head.*

J. It's here, just as I expected.

LEFT. The right-hand tank is empty.

J. There's clearly been too much use of emotion.

Q. Hey kid, come and have a look.

Ó peeks in, scared.

Ó. What the . . .

Q. Isn't it wonderful?

Ó. I can't believe . . .

Q. This is not a dream. Not a dream, boy.

Ó. I refuse to believe this.

J. Don't be an idiot.

Ó. I won't believe this! *Ever!*

Q. Don't run away. (*Ó crouches, his hands covering his head.*) Since the beginning of the reign of Emperor Seiki, the UCRN has promoted the development of microbe bombs and androids. That's how we prepared for war. The computers concluded that there would be a war, based on all the data in the world. We could not avoid a war. As early as in the tenth year of Emperor Seiki's reign, the UCRN completed the first android: Type R3VZ. They don't age, of course. The problem was that they had emotions. Even the engineers who made them didn't think that androids could have emotions, like O here, or J, Right, and Left.

Ó. What?!

Q. The first emotional skill they acquired was laughter. Then crying, and anger. In three years, they learned to master complex feelings. That is, bashfulness, humor, coyness, loneliness, regret . . . Type R3VZ was gradually becoming human. But there was one emotional skill they hadn't acquired. Can you guess which one? (*Ó thinks.*) Love. Affection was the most difficult. Can a machine love? It turns out that it is possible. A Type R3VZ fell in love with my late wife.

J. Let's not talk about that now, General.

Q. J, bring it here.

J. But, sir!

Q. Quick. (*J brings in a kind of board.*) One spring night in the four-teenth year of the era, a Type R3VZ committed adultery with my wife. At last, we had made a complete human being. The moment his steel penis entered my wife's vagina was a great historical moment for humankind!

6. Where's that R3VZ android now?

Q. After I reported it to the authorities and received permission, I destroyed him. (*J fires.*) An android can't be killed with an ordinary gun. (*Takes the gun from J.*) I shot him with this spe-cial gun for androids. In the midst of their fourth session, I shot him in the back.

6. Him . . .

Q. He wasn't a machine anymore. He was a man. I held him before he died, and did my duty. I reconfirmed his affection. I asked him "Do you have the memory of being loved?"

J. "No."

Q. "Do you have the memory of having loved?" (*J moves his mouth slightly.*) He seemed to say something but I couldn't hear it. It is written here. (*Takes off the cloth covering the board J has brought. It is a monument that reads: "Do you have the memory of being loved? NO. Do you have the memory of having loved? . . . [Indecipherable] TYPE R3VZ.*") We made this in secret to commemorate the birth of the perfect human being. The first android in history. A year later, my wife killed herself. The UCRN's skill in manufacturing androids has improved greatly. For example—

RIGHT. I'm the male libido-releasing sexatroid Type A.

LEFT. I'm sexatroid Type V1.

J. Officer-obeying Type B20.

Q. We had a lot of trouble getting this far. The Type R3VZ was not a perfect human being. He lacked the most important feature of a human being. He lacked memory.

ó. Memory . . .

Q. Yes. A man's memory is what he cherishes most. Androids don't have memories of their infancy and teens. So we started programming them with memories at an early stage, just when they start to have emotions. We extract an individual's memory—which is stored in the capital—at random and implant it without knowing whose memory it is. The government has access to everyone's memory.

ó. Then O's memory is . . .

Q. Yes, coincidentally, it was your memory up through high school.

Ó kicks the monument.

ó. I'm dreaming.

Q. No you're not. Look at O's brain. A work of science. Almost a work of art. Give me some gaff tape. (*Seals O's head with tape.*)

ó. Then in this room . . .

Q. Yes, as it turns out you were sent to a room where you and I are the only ones who aren't andro—

O suddenly wakes up and starts to strangle Q.

Q. Help. Hel—

J. Stop, O. Why do you want to kill the General?

O. He is the one. He is the . . .

J. What are you talking about? In a sense, the General is your father!

The strength goes out of O.

O. My father . . .

J. Your parents are not in West Tonkie, the General gave you life.

O releases Q, exhausted.

Q. Phew. Calm down, O. Look, the war is not going well. In a few days you will be the first to leave for the front, all right? (*He leaves, followed by J.*)

O. My parents are your parents. (*Produces a photograph.*) This picture is a lie . . . I feel as if I've been thrown into outer space. I am neither alive nor dead . . . I'm NOT HUMAN!

Ó. Calm down. Calm down, O.

O. I can handle it. I know the truth now. But what about the others? They don't know anything yet I can't listen to them talking about the past anymore.

Ó. I feel the same way.

A voice—"We were listening."—is heard. It is R's voice. R, I, B, P, M, F, and K come out from all directions.

R. I heard it all, O.

M. I had a feeling something was wrong. We were always kind of different.

P (*taking out his photograph*). They do a good job. I'll say that for them. (*Tears it up.*)

Each of them tears their photograph. Piercing sounds of a siren. J rushes in.

J. The alert is cancelled. We're outside the range of the enemy warship's radar. Everybody, prepare for drills!

They do not move.

J. What are you waiting for? Get ready for drills! (*R, O, I, B, P, M, F, K, Right, and Left take up positions.*) Don't relax too much even after you've accomplished something. Don't cheer till you're sure you're out of the woods. We'll jump right into the program. Breathe in and out. Breathe in and out. We'll skip the warm-up. Concentrate. Now, let's begin. Lesson 1: Laughter. (*All do as J says.*) Lesson 2: Sorrow. Lesson 3: Anger. Lesson 7: Burst of laughter. Lesson 34: A wry smile. Lesson 35: Orgasm. Lesson 40: Wailing. Lesson 45: Surprise. Lesson 51: Shouting. Lesson 57: Giving up. (*All look drained of emotions.*) Good. Very good. Perfect. Perfect human emotions. Make no mistake. You're human. More than human. That's all for today. Get ready for dinner. (*Leaves.*)

All prepare for dinner without a word. Silence. All sit down when the preparations are completed. They close their eyes and clasp their hands.

ɪ. Dear God, the world is now in perpetual twilight. Amen.

ᴀʟʟ. Amen.

ʀ. Dear God, all men are living as the dead. Amen.

ᴀʟʟ. Amen.

ᴍ. Dear God, we no longer look to a bright morning, a dripping rain is hitting the pavement. Amen.

ᴀʟʟ. Amen.

ᴘ. Dear God, we are all . . .

ᴀʟʟ. Amen.

ᴘ. Dear God, we cannot even kill ourselves. Amen.

ᴀʟʟ. Amen.

ꜰ. But Dear God, we do not say, "Save us." Amen.

ᴋ. But Dear God, we do not say, "Save us." Amen.

ᴀʟʟ. Amen.

ᴏ. Dear God, all the brains are now heading out into the universe like an injured white horse. Amen.

ɪ. Dear God, Your horizon is different from ours. Amen.

ó. Dear God, this war, our war, sees the universe at the end of the retina, and starts again toward another darkness. Because . . .

ᴀʟʟ. Because.

ʀ. Because this war is not our war. Amen.

ᴀʟʟ. This is not our war. Amen! (*All slowly turn over the table in front of them and rise.*) This is Nippon's war. But it's not ours!

ɪ. Weapons . . .

Steel rods are handed to All.

ʀ. What are we going to do?

ᴏ. We point the Whale toward the horizon.

ᴍ. What's the password.

ɪ. More than human.

ó. Destroy. Destroy everything.

All start destroying the room with their rods. A storm of metallic sound. They keep on hitting. The sound of the sea becomes louder. The room sways.

R. The Whale, the Whale is freaking out!

J rushes in.

J. What the hell are you fuckers doing?!

Ó. Destroy. Destroy everything.

All start hitting again.

J. Watch out. The Whale's going to breach.

The Whale breaches and all tumble down.

J (*quickly stands up and takes out the gun for androids*). We do not allow rebellion.

Ó. Tie him up.

R and B tie up J.

I. It doesn't work. The Whale's too tough.

M. What do we do?

R. Shoot it.

O. No way.

I. Sue Ellen.

O. What?

I. Sue Ellen's brain is controlling the Whale. If we destroy her, we might make it.

P. But it's impossible to fight her.

Ó. Let's try, win or lose. Miss I, show us Sue Ellen again.

I. Look out into the universe. Use your imagination and see your own universe . . . Turn around. Say a word.

Each says a word: HOPE, DESPAIR, HAPPINESS, DESIRE, SOLITUDE, DEPRESSION, PLEASURE, SOUND OF THE SEA, CORRUPTION, DESERT, STARDUST.

I. Sue Ellen, we're going to fight you.

In the darkness, Sue Ellen appears with a roaring sound.

SUE ELLEN. What's going on, I?

I. We've come to destroy you, Sue Ellen.

SUE ELLEN. Destroy me? You're insane, I. You know me, don't you?

I. If we destroy you, we'll be free.

SUE ELLEN. Free? Free? (*Laughs.*) You still believe in freedom?

R. Don't laugh.

SUE ELLEN. Freedom is like stardust. It's a flower that doesn't exist. It's a place which is nowhere.

R shoots at Sue Ellen.

SUE ELLEN. Impossible, because I am you.

Ó. Destroy her. Your power is being tested. Call up the power you know you have. (*R, B, M, F, K, and P together rush toward Sue Ellen, but are thrown back.*) Again!

This time, an electric current runs through them and they retreat, paralysed.

SUE ELLEN. Children, you are so full of spirit. My dear children. Relax. Everything will be sorted out. All you hopes and fears . . .

A slow lullaby is heard.

Ó. No. Don't fall asleep. M, do it!

M creates a storm, but Sue Ellen is not affected.

SUE ELLEN. Good night, my dear children.

Ó. O, read her mind.

O concentrates.

O. What the hell is this? What kind of universe do you have in your mind, Sue Ellen? Ah, my pyorrhoea. My semicircular canals are swirling . . . I'm losing my eyesight, my hearing, I feel a deep anxiety. I'm losing control of my emotions . . . Sue Ellen, you're not my mother!

The lullaby stops.

R. No. You are not my mother!

SUE ELLEN. Then where is your mother, R?

R. In Sakhalin . . .

SUE ELLEN. Don't lie to me, R. You know you're not human. You are a combat android Type V3.

R. No.

SUE ELLEN. Tell me then, do you have a vision, R?

R. A vision?

SUE ELLEN. A vision that belongs to the human race?

R. Our vision is to destroy you.

SUE ELLEN. You're wasting your time, R. Do you think there is any vision in this revolt? This war represents the last vision of humankind.

R. This war?

SUE ELLEN. Yes. Humans could only pursue their vision through war. They couldn't think of anything except war. And you were created to serve this vision.

6. Don't let her trick you.

SUE ELLEN. War is necessary for human beings. Now, stop making trouble and go to bed. You're going to war when you wake up.

Again the lullaby is heard. All start to get drowsy.

6. No. don't sleep! Neuro-Kinetic Energy. Use your Neuro-Kinetic Energy. (*All regain alertness.*) Only Neuro-Kinetic Energy can defeat her.

SUE ELLEN. Good night, my dear children.

6. This is our last chance. Gather round.

They form a circle for Neuro-Kinetic Energy. They utter a language which is not a language. They stand up, get together, separate themselves, and take up various postures. The Neuro-Kinetic Energy gradually builds.

SUE ELLEN. Ah, what is this . . . ? (*They direct the power at Sue Ellen.*) No . . .

They get together once again to exert their last strength. Sue Ellen explodes.

R. We did it!

Ó. Bring J here. Did you see that, J?

J. You assholes. What have you done?

Ó. Make the Whale surface.

J. But . . .

Ó. Do it now!

J. All right, I'll do it. I'll do it. Come up!

> *The sound of the waves becomes louder. The Whale comes up. A blue sky is seen on the stage. All look up at the sky.*

IMAGE 1.3 **The submarine surfaces and everyone enjoys the fresh air and sunshine.**
Nippon Wars. Theater Apple, Shinjuku, 1987.
Photograph by Hisako Kagami.

P. The air . . . The outside air . . .

M. The blue sky . . .

B. How long has it been since I've seen the sun?

F. I feel great.

O. We weren't free after all.

R. Look at the seagulls. (*Falls.*)

All look surprised for a moment and then fall, expressionless, one after another, as if they were broken machines. Ó, I, and J are left standing.

Ó. What—what the hell happened? (*J laughs.*) J, what does this mean?

J. We're finished, General.

Q appears.

Q. Lesson 200: Revolt. The scheduled lessons are completed. Tomorrow everyone will fight as a first-rate soldier.

Ó. Q, what the hell . . .

Q. Don't worry. They've been running on sea energy for such a long time that they can't make the switch to solar energy right away. They'll wake up in a few hours.

Ó. You son of a bitch, Q.

J. Calm down. The world is moving. That's all.

Q. The last lesson, Revolt, is the most difficult lesson. We had to wait for the right moment. But it all went very well. It was the most successful one we've had so far, thanks to excellent personnel. Good work, J.

J. Thank you, sir.

Q. What would you like to do now?

J. I'd like to take a bath and wash off the sweat, sir.

Q. OK. Off you go.

J. Yes, sir. (*Leaves.*)

Ó (*stupefied*). It was programmed.

Q. Our soldiers aren't sent to the front until they have drunk the nectar called "revolt." It's just one of the programs, but this was one of the most wonderful revolts we've ever had. Don't you agree, I?

Ó. I? You knew?

Q. Anyhow . . . Solar energy is good, isn't it? Look. We'll have a sunset in a few hours. Sweet night comes and then the sun rises again on the horizon. It'll be a bright, brilliant morning for you soldiers who have lived through all the despair, all the hope, and this revolt. You will be resurrected as brave soldiers for the UCRN!

I. A brilliant morning . . .

Ó. Miss I, you knew . . .

I. I'm sorry, Ó . . . (*There is a knife in I's hand. She rushes toward Q. Q avoids her but the knife catches his arm. A gun is fired. Q has the gun for androids in his hand.*) Ahh . . .
I falls. Ó catches hold of her.

Ó. Miss I!

Q. It's all right. I just reduced her energy. Androids don't die so easily. (*Leaves*)

Ó. I. Don't die, I.

I. I'm sorry, Ó. I knew everything from the beginning . . . I knew that I wasn't human . . .

Ó. That's not true. You are human.

I. Everything was a lie. The stars in the sky. The twilight when I wept. The hot soup in the kitchen in winter. Freshly baked biscuits. The taste of honey spreading in the mouth. The dream that I dreamed in a soft bed. They were all lies.

Ó. But that dance. The dance that we had in the high school gym. That was real, wasn't it?

I (*smiles slightly*). I sat smoking in the corner, not dancing, although I wanted to.

Ó. Right!

I. When a boy I liked came over to me, I pretended to be cool.

Ó. Yes. That Christmas Eve dance.

I. That dance was an illusion.

Ó. It's not an illusion. Let's dance. Dance with me.

I. Ó. My memory is the memory of General Q's dead wife.

Ó. That's not true.

I. See, she's dancing. Not me. She . . . is . . . dancing. I am sexatroid alpha type A . . .

Ó. Do you have the memory of being loved?

I. No.

Ó. Miss I . . . She said something, but I couldn't make it out. Indecipherable. Still I don't believe it. I can't see her face as anything but a dead woman's face. The dance was an illusion, but it must have been real between me and Miss I. For we must have been dancing at least in our minds. Not in our memory but in the shadow which is our thought.

J is seen in the darkness.

J. Lesson 198: Crossed in love, completed. Miss I will be alive again in four hours and twelve minutes. (*Leaves.*)

Ó. I won't . . . I won't believe this . . . But as J said, the dead Miss I revived exactly four hours and twelve minutes later. (*I rises slowly and leaves.*) The sun dazzled me. The Blue Whale came to the surface and went south of the Calgarian Sea. I spent days gazing at the sun without eating or drinking. And I thought: Where did I come from and where was I going? Two days later, it was time for O's departure for the front. (*O steps forward ready for departure. A crowd is behind him to see him off.*) A man with my memory, no I myself are going to the front . . . It was a strict human ritual performed by androids.

J. Three cheers for O!

The crowd cheers three times.

O. Thank you. I'll fight hard for our country.

F goes up to him.

F. Here's the amulet. Please come back alive.

O (*holding her hands*). Yes. I'll come back alive.

F. Take care of yourself.

O. I will.

F. Boil the water before you drink it.

O. Yes.

J. Three cheers for the UNITED CAPITALIST REPUBLIC OF NIPPON!

The crowd cheers three times.

Ó. O! (*O looks.*) What are you going to fight for, O?

O. For my family. (*Salutes.*)

Ó. Is that true?

O. For my country.

Ó. Is that true? O!

O. It's true. For my fatherland. (*Stands to attention.*)

J. The national anthem of the UNITED CAPITALIST REPUB-LIC OF NIPPON.

"Le Internationale" is performed by an orchestra. The scene changes and people are seen playing the tune. The conductor is Q. Ó slowly takes out a knife, rushes at Q, and stabs him in the chest. "Le Internationale" stops. All disappear.

Q. So you've done it.

Ó. Do you have this programmed? Do you have one called "assassination?"

Q. You fool.

Ó. I hate you.

Q. Then, I'll tell you something. The last thing.

Ó. What?

Q. Don't you have doubts about yourself?

Ó. Me?

IMAGE 1.4 **The androids walk slowly toward the audience. The stage is full of light and nothing can be seen. The sound of an explosion.**

Nippon Wars. Kintetsu Shōgekiō, Osaka, 1986.

Photograph by H. H. Steinhauser.

Q. Why are you here in this room? Think about it. (*Ó is speechless.*) I figured you'd realize sooner or later. But you're pretty stupid about yourself. Think back. How did you get into this room?

Ó. I escaped from the Rebel Canary, and . . .

Q. Tanaka Hiroyuki escaped from the Rebel Canary. He was caught east of Mecon and shot. Dead.

Ó. What?!

Q. I'm going to die. (*Leaves.*)

Ó. Me too? No!

I comes out.

I. It's the truth.

Ó. Miss I.

I. What Q said is true.

Ó. But that means I'm . . .

I. Let's find out. (*Takes out a gun.*) Shoot yourself in the head with this. If you're human, you'll die, but if you're an android . . . (*Ó takes the gun with a trembling hand.*) Ó, a gamble. The last gamble.

Ó. But . . .

I. Bet it all on zero, Ó! On zero!

Ó shoots himself in the head and falls. The wall collapses and reveals a row of androids behind him. They all shoot at him.

Ó (*sitting up*). I'm alive. I'm ALIVE!

R. Come with us, Ó.

O. We've taken over the Whale. We'll change course, and sail north.

Ó. Where are we going?

R. To Nippon.

I. Come on. Let's go, to our own war.

Ó stands up. A light is seen at the back of the room.

I. Where are you?

6. Inception date (*Actor's birthday*.) I am the thinking-type android, ZERO.

I smiles. The androids walk slowly toward the audience. The stage is full of light and nothing can be seen. The sound of an explosion.

The End

CHARACTERS

MAN	Film director, known for his action films.
WOMAN	Screenwriter.
SOLDIER	Guard.
BOSS	
ATTACKERS	Hired as "live" targets.
MAN A, MAN B, YOUNG WOMAN	Theme park customers.
GIRL	Ghost of Woman's sister, character in Woman's screenplay
BOY, MIDDLE-AGED WOMAN	Characters in Woman's screenplay

THE LOST BABYLON

THE LOST BABYLON

TRANSLATED BY SARA JANSEN

ACT I

A day in early autumn from the afternoon until midnight.

SCENE 1

The silhouette of Boss appears on a television screen placed into the wall. Three men are sitting on chairs. The stage is dark and their faces are not clearly visible.

BOSS. When did you start living like that?

SILHOUETTE A. On the streets, you mean? Eight months ago.

BOSS. You're a poor shot.

SILHOUETTE A. I'll work very hard. I'm ready to die for it.

BOSS. What use are you to me if you die?

SILHOUETTE A. I'll die as if my life depends on it.

BOSS. Aha. That sounds good.

SILHOUETTE A. Really?

BOSS. Any relatives?

SILHOUETTE A. No, none.

BOSS. You look like you've been through a lot.

SILHOUETTE B. I was downsized.

BOSS. At your age?

SILHOUETTE B. Age doesn't matter.

BOSS. You hit the mark 90 percent of the time. Extraordinary!

SILHOUETTE B. Whenever I was on the road for work I'd go to the arcade. I've finished all the games with guns.

BOSS. You must be single.

SILHOUETTE B. What kind of woman would want to waste time on me?

BOSS. What about you?

SILHOUETTE C (*with a slight accent*). I'm an illegal.

BOSS. Aha. You came to this country with great expectations?

SILHOUETTE C. Yeah.

BOSS. Well, you've been misled!

SILHOUETTE C. I'll do anything.

BOSS. Ever used a gun?

SILHOUETTE C. Back home I was in the army.

BOSS. Do you have a grudge against this country?

SILHOUETTE C. Fudge?

BOSS. I mean hatred.

SILHOUETTE C. Oh. No, not really.

BOSS. What about you guys?

SILHOUETTE A. No.

SILHOUETTE B. No.

BOSS. All right, then. You're all hired.

A shooting scene from an action movie is shown on the TV screen.

SCENE 2

A room with a table and a chair. The back wall has a couple of doors. On the table is a laptop computer which is switched on, a bottle of vodka, and a glass. Woman, who just stepped out of the shower, stands facing the audience. She shakes her wet hair to get rid of the excess water and drinks coffee from a large mug.

WOMAN (*mumbling*). An endless, desolate place in the desert. The chirping of insects. A man and a woman embracing . . . No need to be afraid . . . You're not the one who's afraid . . . As long as you can hold on to someone . . . In a situation like this, you realize you're alone. All alone in this world . . . But at night, after the rain clears up, that fear goes away. (*Resolutely puts the bottle and glass away in the desk drawer, sits at the computer, and starts typing vigorously.*) No rain today.

One of the doors opens. Man, blindfolded and carrying a travel bag, is pushed into the room and is followed by Soldier.

MAN. We must be inside now. I heard gunshots on our way over. Are we near a border?

SOLDIER. I'm not very good at geography.

MAN. You made a border, didn't you? It's easy. People fight each other and change the borders of their countries. Nothing to it. (*He lifts his foot as if about to take a step.*) Nothing serious will happen if I take a step, right? You might be bad at geography but you must know something about history, huh?

SOLDIER. You talk too much, pal. Not soldier material.

MAN. A soldier bad at geography isn't too reliable either.

SOLDIER. You don't need geography for local conflicts. (*He starts to take off Man's blindfold.*)

MAN. Thanks, that helps. I was a little carsick. (*Soldier now completely removes the blindfold.*) The light's blinding. It's like I'm seeing the world for the very first time. So this is it, huh? (*Notices Woman.*) It's you . . .

Woman, ignoring him, continues to type.

SOLDIER. I'll check in my pal here.

MAN. This has been bothering me for a while now, but can you stop addressing me so informally?

SOLDIER. Well, what about "master" then?

MAN. Yeah, well, why not? (*Pulls himself together.*) Is this my room?

SOLDIER. Private rooms are at the end of the corridor. This is the common room.

MAN. Will I be served any tea or anything?

SOLDIER. You can make some for yourself. She can tell you where to find everything. (*Exits.*)

MAN. So he says. (*Noticing the coffee mug on the table*) Where did you get the coffee? . . . Ah, I remember. You don't want to be disturbed when you're writing. (*Observes his surroundings.*) The decor and the color of the walls don't matter. What matters is air quality. And smell. (*Sniffs.*) Not bad. Perfect humidity, a scent of hay. I can even hear the sound of waves in the distance. I wonder what all the childish secretiveness is about . . . (*Suddenly sits down.*) I feel sick. I'd better lie down for a while. This place is like the movies. You know, just the other day a young screenwriter asked me if film imitates life or life imitates film. She was my kind of girl . . . (*Pause. Woman is mumbling to herself.*) You still speak your lines out loud. It's all coming back to me now. Three years, or was it four years ago? I hear you're writing a melodrama? Good for you. You always wanted to write melodramas. What was the last script you wrote for me again? That story about that female prisoner escaping from jail? Or was it that yakuza revenge story? You really hated action films. I guess I didn't play a significant part in your success story. But, who knows, maybe it was to your advantage that you started with action movies. It's all about not boring your viewers . . . But isn't it a little strange, a melodrama with this subject matter and in a place like this? Definitely action material.

WOMAN. Like I said, an action melodrama.

MAN. Oh, I see.

WOMAN. Oh, hell. Why do you talk to me when I'm writing? I was just getting into it! (*Takes the vodka bottle out of the drawer, pours herself a drink, and drains the glass in one gulp.*)

MAN. Can I have some? (*Woman throws him the bottle. Man scrutinizes the label on the bottle and drinks.*) Ah.

WOMAN. . . . Damn.

MAN. How long have you been here?

WOMAN. A week.

MAN. Is this your room?

WOMAN. The rooms are in the back.

MAN. Then what are you doing here?

WOMAN. This space is much bigger, more comfortable. Besides, I'm the only one here so far. Why must you talk so much?

MAN. I didn't know you'd already started writing.

WOMAN. I have.

MAN. A bit odd, isn't it?

WOMAN. What?

MAN. Starting on a screenplay without talking to the director first. Is this how popular screenwriters work these days?

WOMAN. If you have something to say, why don't you just come out and say it?

MAN. I don't really care anyway.

WOMAN. I'm just following the producer's orders. He gave me a plot and told me to finish the script as soon as possible.

MAN. Show me the plot.

WOMAN. I don't have it.

MAN. What do you mean you don't have it?

WOMAN. I don't have it on paper.

MAN. Well, then explain it to me.

WOMAN. Too much trouble. You can read the script when I'm done. I'll have to rewrite it anyway.

MAN. I guess you have a point.

WOMAN. You haven't changed a bit.

MAN. I hear that a lot, but lately I don't know whether that's a good thing or a bad thing.

WOMAN. Both.

MAN. Right. How boring.

WOMAN. People often tell me that I have changed. In your case, that's definitely a criticism.

MAN. Jealousy, for sure.

WOMAN. You're all grown-up now.

MAN. You were always jealous. (*Mockingly*) "That woman had connections," "she got the job because she slept with the producer". . . Reminiscing about our time together, aren't you?

WOMAN. Our time together was the worst time of my life.

MAN. I'm honored.

WOMAN. You always turn up at the worst moments.

MAN. This is different, though. You're famous now. There must be a reason we're meeting again to make another flashy action flick.

WOMAN. I just told you it's to be an action melodrama.

MAN. What's the difference? Two people kissing and diving into bed or suddenly shooting at one another, it's all the same to me.

WOMAN. That smells of Samuel Fuller. You're mistaken if you think that it's only men getting hurt.

MAN. Fuller's films are different.

WOMAN. I'm talking about your films!

MAN. I did a pretty good job showing a woman's story in *Cobra, the Female Convict*, didn't I?

WOMAN. Nothing but rape scenes!

MAN. The script was yours, remember?

WOMAN. I didn't have a choice. What was I supposed to do, working for a chauvinistic pig of a producer and a sex-obsessed director?

MAN. Ha ha ha!

Soldier enters.

SOLDIER. What's so funny?

MAN (*laughing*). Huh? Oh.

SOLDIER. One happy man.

WOMAN. He's always been like this.

SOLDIER. So you know each other?

WOMAN. From worse times.

MAN. You've become pretty good at hurting people.

SOLDIER. Are you done laughing? Boss wants to talk to you.

MAN. Finally. I still haven't heard a thing.

Soldier takes the remote control and switches on the television. A silhouette appears.

BOSS. Welcome. How are you feeling?

MAN. It was an interesting trip. A real spy movie.

BOSS. Yes, I remember a film called *Blindfold* . . .

MAN. Is that the kind of film you like?

BOSS. What I want you to create this time is different. I want an action movie.

MAN (*to Woman*). See, didn't I tell you?

BOSS. How is the scenario coming along?

WOMAN. Good. As long as I do it my own way.

BOSS. Of course. I have total confidence in your talent. Develop the story any way you want as long as it suits the theme park.

MAN. Excuse me, but I don't have any information yet about the plot or the budget.

BOSS. You don't need to worry about the budget. You're free to do whatever you want. The plot is this theme park itself. I want you to enjoy being here. Try it out, and develop the film from there. The film will be shown all over the world when the park opens. I don't want a simple commercial trailer for the park. It needs to stand on its own. It has to leave its mark in cinema history! The theme park is still under construction. It's top secret. I'll choose a focus group, a preview audience, from the general public and escort them to the site. The plan is to have them try out the attractions and give me their opinions so that I can further develop this amusement park. You two are also test users. I'm looking forward to your feedback.

MAN. This isn't a dinosaur theme park, is it?

BOSS. Close.

MAN. Wow! Where are the half-naked women?

BOSS. Find that out for yourself, but finish the scenario. I can't repeat this enough: the plans here are top secret. I realize this is a big favor, but until you finish the screenplay I can't allow you to have any contact with the outside world.

SOLDIER. If you have a mobile phone, give it to me now.

MAN (*taking his phone out of his bag*). Wow, this really is like the movies.

BOSS. If you want out, this is the time.

MAN. Yeah, to be met with a mysterious death on my way home . . . (*Gives his mobile phone to Soldier.*)

BOSS. You watch too much TV.

MAN. Well then, according to the rules of the game, this hero, overflowing with excitement, will recklessly embark on a mysterious adventure. I love the movies!

BOSS. That's the spirit, Mr. Director.

MAN. Why did you pick me?

BOSS. We considered a few people. We watched all of their films and counted the number of people getting shot. Your movies had the most.

MAN. So what?

BOSS. That's it.

MAN. I never realized that.

BOSS. Of course not. "Cinema is not theory." Federico Fellini.

MAN. A real film buff, are you?

BOSS. Who do you think is more guilty: John Wayne or Clint Eastwood?

MAN. Huh?

BOSS. Well, who do you think killed more people?

MAN. Unfortunately, I'm a fan of James Cagney.

BOSS. All right, all right. But who's most guilty? You'll find all of their films in your room. Why don't you count?

WOMAN. I'll give you a hand.

MAN. It must be John Wayne.

WOMAN. No, Cagney, for sure.

BOSS. Good luck.

Soldier turns off the TV.

SOLDIER. Are you carrying a gun?

MAN. You must be joking.

SOLDIER. Ever used one?

MAN. Once, in Hawaii. (*Soldier picks up a gun and holds it out to Man.*) What's this about?

SOLDIER. Your passport to this place.

Man turns to Woman.

WOMAN. Why don't you take it? It's a requirement while you're here.

MAN. You too?

WOMAN. Yeah.

Man accepts the gun.

SOLDIER. You like guns?

MAN. I don't hate them.

SOLDIER. An action film director can hardly have an aversion to guns.

WOMAN. I do. But when you're here, you have no choice, really.

MAN. Hold on! What could possibly happen?

WOMAN. Like I said, a bunch of guys come to attack us. We're surrounded.

MAN. Attack? What do you mean? Indians? Martians? The FBI?

WOMAN. Guys who want to get a hold of our secret.

MAN. Wait a minute! Aren't we here to write a script?

WOMAN. It doesn't help to worry like that. The fact that you're here means that you're okay with what goes on here. Behind the construction of this theme park is some big strange secret. I wouldn't be surprised if the government was in on it, or some large-scale international spy network.

MAN. What are we doing in a place like this? They should have called for James Bond or Charlie's Angels instead. (*Soldier giggles.*) You know the secret, don't you?

SOLDIER. No.

MAN. That's a lie. People in positions like yours always have the full story. You don't watch movies at all, do you?

SOLDIER. I love movies. I've watched all of your films.

MAN (*pleased*). Really?

SOLDIER. But here I'm an employee, just like the two of you.

MAN. Yeah, yeah. Soldiers aren't allowed to talk too much. But I bet you have classified information about UFOs too. Aliens are already roaming the earth, right?

A door opens and an Attacker appears with his gun, ready to fire.

WOMAN. They're here! Shoot!!

MAN. What?

WOMAN. You're supposed to shoot!

Man hesitantly levels his gun. Attacker turns to Woman and shoots. Woman drops to the ground, trying to dodge the bullets. Soldier fires. Attacker collapses.

WOMAN. Why didn't you shoot? Do you want to get me killed?

SOLDIER. He's obviously never shot anyone before.

MAN. What the hell . . .

WOMAN. If you don't shoot, you'll get killed!

MAN. So he's dead?

WOMAN. This is no time to simply stand there. We're in the field of an international spy ring! We have a license to kill.

Man approaches the Attacker on the floor. All of a sudden, the Attacker gets up and runs off.

MAN. What's this? He got up! He came back to life!

WOMAN (*trying not to laugh*). This is a zombie factory.

MAN. I've had it. Let's get out of here. What do you think you're doing? This isn't funny! (*Woman bursts out laughing.*) You enjoy being manipulated by a bunch of zombies?

SOLDIER. That's enough for now. (*To Woman*) You're pretty mean, aren't you?

WOMAN. I didn't think he'd fall for it. People usually get suspicious at the mention of an international spy battle, don't they?

MAN. What?

WOMAN. I even threw in the word "zombie" for you. (*Laughing*) Come on now, zombies?

MAN. So this is all just some sick joke? And when exactly did it become a joke? What the hell is all this?

WOMAN. A theme park.

MAN. What's the theme?

WOMAN. You had a park like this in one of your films, remember? What was the title, again? *The Last War*?

MAN. *The Last War* . . . killing people . . . virtual murders. A theme park where you can shoot whoever you want!

WOMAN (*quietly*). Bingo!

MAN. You can actually feel what it's like to aim a gun at a human being, the ultimate amusement park!

WOMAN. Bingo!

MAN. So these guns are fake?

WOMAN. Wrong.

SOLDIER. The guns are real. (*Takes a bullet out of his own gun.*) And, at first sight, these bullets look completely real too, but they're fake. When they hit someone, they burst open and a spurt of blood shoots out. An elaborately crafted substitute. The success or failure of this park depends on how real these bullets look. People who've shot a real gun will still get satisfaction out of this experience. Ever wanted to shoot someone?

MAN. Yes.

SOLDIER. A specific person?

MAN. You mean with the intention to kill? No, but I've always wanted to try using a gun. Is that what you mean?

SOLDIER. That's it.

WOMAN. I don't get it. Why do men think like that?

MAN. A minute ago you were screaming I should shoot if I didn't want to get killed.

WOMAN. I was just repeating the soldier's lines. He's annoyed that I refuse to shoot. I wouldn't do it for anything.

MAN. Why are you here then?

WOMAN. I want to write an action melodrama. That's all. I'm bored with superficial love stories. But I also hate those violent movies in which dumb machos just chase each other. I hereby officially declare I will not use a gun. So the action movie I'm writing will be different from anything you've ever seen. I'm sure it's what Boss wants. So what will it be: Are you in or are you out?

MAN. I'm in. But are you sure you can do it?

WOMAN. How dare you insult me?

MAN. No, no. You have extraordinary talent.

WOMAN (*takes a gun out of the desk drawer*). Here.

SOLDIER. I don't care whether or not you use it, as long as you carry it. That's the rule here.

In an attempt to put the gun away, Woman pulls vigorously at the desk drawer, which falls on the floor. A number of empty vodka and gin bottles roll out.

MAN. It looks like you had a pretty big party.

WOMAN. Got it? Some talent, right? Plot, plot, new plot! Producers keep asking for novel storylines, but when I come up with one, all they can say is: it's too much, it's too dark, not family-oriented enough, not happy couple-oriented enough . . . Whatever! I'm not writing scenarios so married people who can't stand the sound or smell of each other's farts anymore can have their minute of pleasure, or so young couples can feel each other up. What does that make me? The slave of this bunch of idiots? Yes, that's it. I came here to hide!

MAN (*quietly to Soldier*). Is liquor forbidden here?

SOLDIER. No.

MAN. Then there is no problem. (*Takes some vodka.*) The days of wine and roses, huh? (*While he picks up the bottles from the floor*) No need to fret over coming up with a new storyline every time. It's okay to repeat yourself. It's all about how you do it. Say you have this story that resembles an earlier one. People don't remember all of it anyway. Just when they've forgotten how it went, you use that story again. Just dress it up a bit differently. When the make-up and the costumes are new, it's all new. Otherwise, you might as well leave the film business altogether. There's no way that you can be writing only for yourself. Stories are meant for other people, and "slave" sounds too masochistic.

WOMAN. Nice pick-up line! For a fallen female screenwriter anyway. If we were alone I would throw myself at you right now.

SOLDIER. I'll retreat.

WOMAN. I was just kidding. Why so considerate all of a sudden?

A door opens. An Attacker enters with his gun ready to fire.

WOMAN. Again? They're pretty persistent today.

SOLDIER (*to Man*). Your welcome party. Go on, shoot! And this time you'd better do it right!

WOMAN (*in a perfunctory manner*). If you don't shoot, you'll be hit instead.

Man shoots. Attacker collapses.

MAN. My first time.

WOMAN. How does it feel?

MAN. It hurt.

WOMAN. It'll grow more pleasurable once you get used to it.

MAN. A little more foreplay would have been nice.

Attacker gets up and runs off.

MAN. What a relief!

WOMAN. That was close.

MAN. The first time and pregnant straight away . . . that would have been too much. (*To Soldier*) Who are they?

SOLDIER. Part-timers. They're training to become better at being shot.

MAN. On-the-job training, like at McDonalds.

SOLDIER. The attackers appear without warning. You'd better have your gun ready.

MAN. What happens if I don't shoot? Will I be shot instead?

SOLDIER. They'll shoot at you, but they won't aim directly at you. They're trained to just miss the target.

MAN. What happens if someone just refuses to shoot at them?

SOLDIER. People like that won't come here.

MAN (*to Woman*). What are you going to do?

WOMAN. I already have a plan.

MAN. I'd love to hear it.

WOMAN. I'll show them! I'll kill myself! One blow, with my gun — boom! Everyone will be shocked!

SOLDIER. I see. I hadn't thought of that one.

MAN. Hey, are you all right?

SOLDIER. I need to think about the guidelines in case a situation like that occurs.

MAN. Are you okay?

WOMAN. What?

MAN. Call me when you're having a drink. I'll join you.

WOMAN. Why don't you mind your own business? You're not the type to put your life on the line for someone else.

MAN. I'm flattered, but we have to collaborate on this project.

WOMAN. Coming from you, "collaborate" sounds rather scary.

MAN. I'll do whatever you want.

WOMAN. You say that to every woman, don't you?

MAN. I've changed. I believe in true love now.

SOLDIER. I'm off.

MAN. Don't worry about it. Listen in as much as you want. I don't care. Besides, she's the type that's excited when people are watching me fuck someone.

Woman splashes the contents of her glass onto Man's face. Pause. She is wondering what Man's next move will be.

SOLDIER. I think I really should be off now.

MAN (*angrily*). Didn't I just say you can stay!

A number of silhouettes come through the different doors. Man levels his gun but Soldier pulls it back down.

SOLDIER. Wait a minute! Wait a minute!

The three silhouettes are Man A, Man B and Young Woman. They are dressed in street gang-style clothing. They still have their guns ready to fire.

SOLDIER. They aren't enemies. They're fellow testers!

The Men and Young Woman slowly put their guns down.

MAN A. Oh. So it's not just us. You should have warned us. We almost shot him.

MAN B. It's not like anyone will really die or anything.

SOLDIER. But you'll be charged for the cleaning.

YOUNG WOMAN. When did you get here?

MAN. Ah. Just now.

YOUNG WOMAN. How many people did you shoot?

MAN. Well, I just got here, so just one.

YOUNG WOMAN. Just one! What a waste. You have to enjoy yourself more. Look at us! We got here this morning but we've already shot about twenty people, right?

MAN A. Twenty-seven.

YOUNG WOMAN. Our goal is a hundred!

MAN A. Are you a friend of the Boss too?

MAN. Kind of . . .

MAN A. My old man is a friend of the Boss. He sent me here to help him out. She's my girl and he's "my man!" (*Speaks in a kind of gang-rapper slang.*)

SOLDIER. So what do you think?

YOUNG WOMAN. It's the best! Beats any video game.

MAN B. But the guys we shoot get up right away and run off so fast—it spoils the fun. Like it was all just a lie.

MAN A. Same thing when you shoot them. One guy was really over-acting—falling over like this, screaming.

MAN B. Yeah, that was very funny! He was really screaming.

MAN A. You need to improve the training you're giving your part-timers.

SOLDIER. I see. You mean acting classes. I hadn't thought of that. I'll pass it on to the top.

MAN B. Their deaths should be more convincing.

SOLDIER. We already have a remedy for that problem.

MAN B. Can I see your piece? (*Takes Man's gun*.) Wow, a Smith and Wesson semi-automatic! Not bad. But a revolver is the best for that real Western feeling.

MAN. You like Westerns?

MAN B. Yeah. But I don't want to say it too loud or the girls will start calling me grandpa or something.

MAN. Who do you like?

MAN B. Peckinpah.

WOMAN. That mass murderer.

MAN B. I also like Ralph Nelson's *Soldier Blue*.

MAN. You're a real fanatic, aren't you?

MAN B. Did you see *Soldier Blue*?

MAN. Yes. That's the one with Candice Bergen, right?

MAN B. Yeah. (*Looks impressed and grabs Man's hands*.)

WOMAN. The more violent shooting scenes the better?

MAN. Most American directors are mass murderers, you know.

MAN A. Aren't there any automatic rifles here?

SOLDIER. Sure.

MAN A. Really? Then why didn't you give me one from the start? I'm bored with these toy guns.

SOLDIER. I'll get you one. (*Exits*.)

WOMAN. I'm moving to another room.

YOUNG WOMAN. Aren't you going to join us?

WOMAN. No thank you. (*Picks up the laptop*.)

YOUNG WOMAN. Wow! Are you writing something?

WOMAN. Yes.

YOUNG WOMAN. Something about this place?

WOMAN. A screenplay.

YOUNG WOMAN. So you're a screenwriter? What kind do you write?

WOMAN. Boring ones. (*Exits.*)

YOUNG WOMAN. Did I say something wrong?

MAN. Don't worry about it. She's against guns.

YOUNG WOMAN. Then what's she doing here?

MAN. We have some things to take care of together.

MAN A. You dirty old man.

MAN. I was talking about work!

YOUNG WOMAN. You're trying to tell us that we're just a bunch of stupid kids? That's too easy. There are psycho perverts out there. You have no clue how disgusting it feels to have your underwear stolen![1]

MAN A. She's got major stalker trouble.

YOUNG WOMAN. My underwear wasn't only stolen, you know. It was sent back to me covered in semen.

MAN A. I'd like to line up those repulsive masturbating perverts and mow them down with a machine-gun!

MAN. It takes one to know one.

MAN A. You think I'm strange? Am I crazy for wanting to protect myself?

MAN. That's not what I meant.

MAN A. Okay, let's say I am crazy. I'm not harming anyone by play-

---

1 Kawamura hints at a phenomenon that has been widespread in Japan since the early 1990s, namely the theft and sale of women's used underwear. In recent years especially, the sale by high school girls of their used underwear and sailor-type school uniforms accompanied by a photograph of themselves has frequently made the news. The girls are said to sell their underwear as a way to make money to buy clothes, make-up, and mobile phones. This phenomenon, which is referred to as *burusera*, a contraction of the Japanese terms for "bloomers" (*burūmāsu*) and "sailor" (*sērā*), is related to a host of other phenomena, such as "telephone dating services" (*terekura*), "dating clubs" (*dēto kurabu*), and hostess bars (*kyabakura*) which bring men into contact with high

ing this game. I unleash all that's abnormal about me while I'm here and then in the real world, I'm a good boy.

MAN. I see. Crime prevention.

MAN A. That's what the government's hoping for.

MAN. Now you're bringing up the government too. You're not going to trick me!

MAN A. You're a fool. You think this is possible without the government? If the government wasn't involved, this would be some kind of cult.

MAN. Right. I thought it was weird. This must be some cult's military training camp.

MAN A. No, I'm telling you that's not it!

MAN. Can you prove it?

MAN A. My old man is financially supporting this project.

MAN. What proof do you have your dad isn't involved in a cult?

MAN A. My dad's a respectable man! He's very serious about the well-being of this country! What'll we do if war breaks out? What happens if no one knows how to use a gun? My old man thought about that and that's why he's supporting this project! Have a problem with that, old fart?

MAN. Calm down! I hear you. No need to get so excited!

MAN A. This old fart has no idea what goes on in the world!

MAN (*mumbles*). So I'm about to make a propaganda film . . . You must be joking.

MAN A. Joking? You still don't get it, do you? Say someone you love is raped in front of your eyes. Wouldn't you shoot?

---

school girls, who are said to receive money and expensive gifts in exchange for their company. Although probably not as widespread as popularly believed, these phenomena, which received major attention in the Japanese media, do highlight the level to which the eroticization and commercialization of high school girls (*joshi kōsei*) and their specific culture has made its way into Japanese society at large. Related problems that Kawamura also hints at in this play are sexual harassment, and the frequently occurring touching and stalking incidents on crowded trains and in subway and train stations. In the late 1990s, cases in which men approach a woman on a commuter train, for example, and continue to harass the same woman for days or months, often made the news.

MAN. With pleasure!

MAN A. You're evading my questions, aren't you?

MAN. Not really.

MAN A. You don't like to shoot guns?

MAN. Sure I do.

MAN A. You do? Did you just say you like it?

MAN. Yeah.

MAN A. Well, then you're as abnormal as I am. (*Takes Man's hand.*) We'll get through it together.

YOUNG WOMAN. Sorry. When he gets excited, he acts kinda weird.

MAN A. Women should shut up!

YOUNG WOMAN. Are you coming?

MAN. If I'm not in the way.

MAN A. You're not in the way, but don't you dare touch my girl!

MAN B. Look, kid, it's the sheriff!

> *Attackers enter through different doors. Man A, Man B, and Young Woman shoot them one by one as if in a movie. Attackers fall, get back up, and exit.*

MAN (*in blank amazement*). Wow, that's really amazing.

MAN A. Do you finally get it then?

MAN. Hmm . . .

MAN A. So?

MAN. I don't know exactly what it is, kid, but you sure kill people in a beautiful way.

MAN A. What did you just call me?

MAN B. Kid.

MAN A. What's that?

MAN B. Butch Cassidy and the Sundance Kid. Or do you prefer Wyatt Earp and Doc Holiday?

MAN A. I thought of us more as Bonnie and Clyde.

MAN B. What does that make me?

MAN A. You? A stupid little jerk.

MAN B. Stop kidding, will you. All right, you're impotent!

MAN A. Don't get started!

Soldier enters bearing an automatic rifle.

SOLDIER. Here you go. This is what you wanted, right, pal?

MAN A. Yippee!

SOLDIER. Well, have fun with it, boy.

MAN A. Hold on, what did you just call me? Old fool!

SOLDIER. Don't take it out on me. Just focus on killing people.

MAN A. What's with this old fool? (*He points his gun at Soldier.*)

MAN B. Hey, stop that!

An Attacker appears in one of the doors.

MAN A. Good timing! (*Shoots at Attacker. Attacker shakes and moves his body as if he is dancing. He manages to dodge the bullets. All bullets are gone but Attacker hasn't collapsed.*)

ATTACKER A. Will you stop this! This is not part of the deal!

MAN A. Drop dead, you idiot!

ATTACKER A. No one ever mentioned any automatic rifles to me!

SOLDIER. You have been instructed to assume various situations and to act according to the circumstances.

ATTACKER A. I need some time to mentally prepare myself.

MAN A. Fire this, clumsy idiot!

MAN B (*to Attacker A*). Hey, you?

ATTACKER A (*notices Man B*). You?

MAN B. It's you, isn't it?

ATTACKER A. Oh, you are . . .

MAN B. It's me. What are you doing here?

ATTACKER A. I'm being shot. I see, you're on the other side. How did you pull that of?

MAN B. What are you doing on that side? Come on over here.

SOLDIER. Changes in registration are a breach of contract.

ATTACKER A. They told us you're important guests from the privileged classes.

MAN. Ridiculous.

MAN A. I don't care if you know, my man. I'm not gonna let you change sides. You gotta finish the work you signed on for!

ATTACKER A. I wasn't smart enough to get the stupid son of some rich guy on my side, that's all.

MAN A. What? Slap him! I hate guys like you who blame fate or other people for their inadequacies.

MAN. All right. It's just a game. We can all get along. (*Slaps Attacker A lightly on the cheek.*) Ah.

SOLDIER. Direct violence is not allowed. (*Man A slaps him again.*) I'm sorry but I'll have to report this.

ATTACKER A. What could possibly happen if you report this? We're not treated as human beings around here anyway.

MAN. Well, well, well. You've got me interested. Tell me, what's going on.

SOLDIER. Don't go there.

ATTACKER A (*points at Soldier*). It's him. He's the one who first approached me. I had just started living on the streets, in an underpass. He told me he had a good job for me and asked me to follow him. He took me to an office in a big building and immediately ordered me to play violent video games. Next thing I know I was blindfolded and put on a bus. There were a lot of foreigners on the bus too. They spoke many different languages. I didn't feel safe. But I thought I didn't have a future anyway, so I just sat there shaking, trying to avoid throwing up on the bus. When my blindfold was finally taken off I was sat down for an interview. I was asked a bunch of questions. I don't know how but I passed the test. Then I was blindfolded again and put back on that shaking bus, and this time I really threw up. Whatever, I thought, I couldn't care less, so I just let it all out and then I heard one of the foreigners howl.

SOLDIER. Damn. I was the one who had to clean up after you, you know.

ATTACKER A. When we arrived it was the desert, sand everywhere. I was shocked. There were a number of prefab buildings but we were all pushed into one big room. I had puke all over me so I was hoping I could take a shower but I was immediately handed a gun and an instruction manual. No one ever mentioned rifles.

SOLDIER. He's still rambling on about that.

MAN A. See, he's a pain in the ass. Why don't you shove him too?

ATTACKER A (*to Man B*). We were fighting for the same gang. How did we end up on opposite sides?

MAN B. You always blew it at the big moments.

ATTACKER A. I don't understand them, but the foreigners around here are a lot nicer to me than you guys.

MAN A. That means that you're a foreigner yourself. Don't come sneaking into this country as if nothing's wrong! (*About to hit Attacker but Man stops him.*)

MAN A. Why are you doing this?

MAN. Let's be fair here and cut him some slack.

ATTACKER A. I'm going back. It's dinnertime. If I'm even a little late, there won't be anything left to eat.

MAN A. Wait a minute. Do you really think you can go back? (*Slowly puts his gun against Attacker A's temple.*) I'm sick of Westerns. This is war! And you're a captive. (*To Soldier*) We can do this too, right, master?

SOLDIER. The customer is always right.

YOUNG WOMAN. Stop it, please!

MAN A. Shut up! This is war. The only role for women around here is either for one getting raped or one not getting raped . . . it's always rape.

YOUNG WOMAN. I've had it! Let him go!

MAN A. And you're Mother Teresa all of a sudden?

ATTACKER A (*to Young Woman*). It's OK. I won't really die anyway. It's a game.

MAN. A little sick for a game . . . don't you think?

ATTACKER A. Not as bad as your movies.

MAN. So you know who I am?

ATTACKER A. I watched your movies on video when I was still attacking businessmen on the streets at night.[2]

MAN B. I see. No wonder. (*Takes Man by both hands.*)

MAN. Yeah, okay, thanks. (*Holds back.*)

ATTACKER A. Your movies were very helpful, (*to Man B*) weren't they?

MAN B. Yeah, especially the torture scenes.

MAN. Hey, please, let him go! He's probably hungry.

MAN A. No way, man. He's driving me crazy.

SCENE 3

Night. Woman is sitting in the dark meeting room facing the computer and drinking vodka. She's not typing.

WOMAN (*clearly drunk*). Why do you drink . . . I drink because I'm embarrassed that I drink . . . No good, no good, you'll end up like the Little Prince. Why do you depend on vodka so much? . . . I'm trying to make peace with the world, that's all. That's all . . . So then why don't you try firing a gun? . . . What are you saying? I just told you I want to make peace with the

---

2 Kawamura uses the term *oyaji gari* which can be translated as "old men hunting." The term was coined by a group of high school students who were arrested for attacking drunken businessmen at night in Chiba near Tokyo. The students were looking for money to spend on video games and saw the drunken men as easy targets. The incident was particularly shocking as the boys went to a famous private school in Tokyo. Media coverage caused a number of copycat incidents and the term *oyaji gari* became widely known. What stands out for Kawamura about this incident is that the students perceived their behavior as entertainment, as a game. The media explained the crimes as caused by college entry exam stress and the boys' inability to discern reality from the video games and gangster movies they consumed.

world . . . That's why you should use that gun . . . No way. (*The shadow of an Attacker appears in the dark.*) I don't care how long you stand there. I'm not playing this game. Go look for someone else to shoot! (*Attacker points his gun at Woman.*) If you want to shoot me, go right ahead. That storyline will do. You can accuse me of playing Gandhi. But I'm eating three times a day. (*Gets upset because the Attacker doesn't leave.*) You're persistent, aren't you? (*Takes a gun out of the desk drawer and points it at her own temple.*) Doesn't matter how often you come. You want me to commit suicide again, don't you?[3] (*A voice says "Stop!" Girl appears from the dark; she is a ghost.*) Oh, it was you?

GIRL. Suicide isn't right.

WOMAN. I know. I'm not serious anyway. When you attempt suicide too many times it becomes really silly. Ah, I see, that's another plus of this place. People who want to commit suicide come here to lose their urge to do it. Good idea for a character in the movie. Gotta have someone like that in the script. (*Starts pounding the keys.*)

GIRL. How can you . . .

WOMAN. Hold on. Don't talk to me now. (*Continues to type but is then visibly taken aback.*) Oh, I'm sorry. Now that you've come to see me . . .

GIRL. I'll come back some other time.

WOMAN. It's all right. I can do this later.

GIRL. I'll come back.

WOMAN. No, don't go!

---

3 In 1998, Japan was confronted with a record number of suicides. For the first time since the 1980s, the number exceeded 30,000, an increase of 34.7 percent over the previous year. Especially striking was the increase in so-called economic depression suicides, suicides by men between the ages 30 and 50 confronted with problems at work or unemployment as a result of the current unfavorable economic conditions. The depression also gave rise to a visible homeless population, a new phenomenon in Japan.

GIRL. Please, don't scream at me like that.

WOMAN. I'm sorry. I don't know what happened.

GIRL. You're drinking. When you drink, your voice grows louder.

WOMAN. Well, then I'm always loud.

GIRL. Why do you drink so much?

WOMAN. I wish I knew.

GIRL. If it's because of me, please stop.

WOMAN. I'm not drunk. I'm not like all those drunkards out there. The more I drink, the clearer my thoughts become. If I don't drink, I can't come up with a storyline.

GIRL. I liked your last film.

WOMAN. That was a crappy piece of writing.

GIRL. I cried at the end, you know.

WOMAN. You can cry over that? Over a cheap melodrama like that?

GIRL. I'm cheap.

WOMAN. You're too old to talk like that.

GIRL. I'll always be like this.

WOMAN. That's right. I'm sorry. What a strange night. Not only tonight. Every night.

GIRL. Think about it. Everyone is jealous of you. You have to enjoy your work more.

WOMAN. How am I supposed to enjoy it? When I finally come up with a storyline they always tear it apart. Everyone showers me with compliments. But as soon as I turn my back, they talk about how my talent is all dried up . . . blah, blah, blah. Young writers are praised for whatever they write just because they're new on the scene. What they write isn't even original. And when I write something that's really fresh, no one even cares.

GIRL. When you started, you were like that too.

WOMAN. Tough luck! When I started, my relationship with that guy who got here today wasn't particularly to my advantage.

GIRL. I'm talking about after you took that break. After the screen-writing world changed completely. Your work was appreciated then. You were glowing from all that praise.

WOMAN. After that happened . . . It's thanks to you. But the money I got . . . after all that suffering . . . it's all gone. I hate this job. I'm forced to sell the tragedies of my private life. The tragedies and unhappiness of other people taste sweet. I suck them dry. But my own tragedies are the best. Somewhere deep down, I might even have wanted this tragedy to happen. You're my victim.

GIRL. It's fate.

WOMAN. I desired that fate, deep down.

GIRL. New plots are an illusion.

WOMAN. That's what you say.

GIRL. How can I help?

WOMAN. I don't know.

GIRL. If you're drinking because of me, please stop.

WOMAN. Shut up, will you. I'm not drinking because of you. You're so self-absorbed. You always were. Not everything is about you!

Man enters. Girl exits.

MAN (*holding back because Woman is shouting*). Oh, I'm sorry. I don't know what's going on here but I'll leave you to it.

WOMAN. Ah, that was a bit rude. She disappeared before I could even apologize. It's not like we don't get along. But I always end up behaving like the child.

MAN. Was someone here?

WOMAN. No.

MAN. I'll have some of that. (*Takes the vodka bottle and drinks.*) Then who'd you like to apologize to?

WOMAN. My little sister.

MAN. Your sister?

WOMAN. She died.

MAN. You've had too much to drink.

WOMAN. That doesn't have anything to do with it.

MAN. I don't know what has been going on lately so why don't you tell me what you are talking about?

WOMAN. Do you want a brief outline?

MAN. If you can summarize it in a few lines. The worst for me is . . .

WOMAN. Spun-out sentimentality. I get it.

MAN. You were never good at outlines. Can you do it?

WOMAN. Of course, I can do it. Stop making fun of this successful screenwriter.

MAN. Ah. (*Woman stands up. Her legs are shaking. Man takes her in his arms.*)

WOMAN. Hey, what's up with you? You only like young girls, remember? Young girls.

MAN. I got into a not-so-nice situation . . .

WOMAN. With that would-be actress?

MAN. Sometimes pure hearts are unconsciously evil. I was crushed. She broke all the bones in my body, down to the very last one.

WOMAN. Good for you. Now let me go.

MAN. What do you want?

WOMAN. I want some hot coffee.

MAN. All right. I'll get you some. (*Pulls away.*)

WOMAN. Pure hearts? What was mine then . . . dirty passion? Idiot! (*Man comes back with a mug in his hand. He gives it to Woman. She drinks.*) Two sisters. The older one just got out of a relationship with a selfish, aggressive film director. She used to be a screenwriter, but when she was confronted with her limits she started working as a waitress in an all-night restaurant. She lives alone in a flat in the suburbs. She's decided not to go to the movies ever again and only reads novels. In short, a life in which nothing happens. Then, one day, her sister comes over for a visit for the first time in a long time. The sisters have lunch together and talk about their worries and their plans for the future. That night, the younger sister stays over at her older sister's house. The older sister leaves for work. A girl on the nightshift is ill and asked the older sister to fill in for her the day before. In the middle of the night, an unknown man breaks into the apartment. The man's target was really the older sister but when the younger sister starts to scream, he becomes violent. The younger sister is raped and shot. She dies instantly. The perpetrator had been stalking the older sister for a while. He was a mad fan of her ex-boyfriend's movies, obsessed with the films she made with her ex.

MAN. But she didn't tell her ex about this.

WOMAN. No, because it seemed like such a cheap plot. Wasn't Charles Bronson in a movie like that?

MAN. Yeah. His daughter's killed by the town bully in a similar way. Bronson takes revenge. Why doesn't the older sister do that?[4]

WOMAN. No way.

MAN. In any case, you need to focus on what happens to the older sister after the event if you're planning to come up with an original storyline.

WOMAN. You just told me earlier today that there's no such thing as an original storyline.

MAN. Did I?

WOMAN. Yeah, and so did my sister.

MAN. Your sister and I have a lot in common.

WOMAN. If you make a pass at her, I'll kill you.

MAN. Seduce a ghost? No way.

WOMAN (*staring at the computer screen*). I didn't write this. Dead people are making me write this. All the characters we killed in our movies are making me write this to take revenge.

MAN. That's very sentimental.

WOMAN. I thought you were a little more sensitive.

---

4 Kawamura refers to Michael Winner's film *Death Wish* (1974).

MAN. I've already sold my soul to the devil.

WOMAN. Then you can make love to a ghost.

MAN. Nice, isn't it? That's the good thing about being a film director.

WOMAN. It's different for screenwriters.

MAN. Screenwriters lead us to the devil. (*Drinks his vodka.*) Let me take a look at what you've written so far.

SCENE 4

Another room. A table and two chairs. Men A and B approach the table with the air of having just accomplished something.

MAN A. Now, let's talk about our relationship. I need to find what's going on or I won't be able to get any sleep tonight.

MAN B. Huh?

MAN A. Don't pretend you don't know what I'm talking about. You're stealing my girlfriend, aren't you?

MAN B. I don't know what you're talking about.

MAN A. No excuses. I know what's going on. I know.

MAN B. Are you crazy?

MAN A. Who's crazy around here? Huh? I'm asking you: Who's crazy around here? I'm serious!

MAN B. All right. Whatever.

MAN A. Let's settle this. (*Takes out a revolver. Both of them sit at the table.*) There are no more bullets. I'm going to ask the chief. (*Exits.*)

MAN B (*relieved*). It's that woman's fault. She's always smiling at everybody.

Attacker A appears from the right side of the room, arms and legs tied up, and tape over his mouth. He has obviously been battered. Attacker A notices Man B and stops moving. Man A enters.

MAN A (*putting a bullet in the revolver*). He had the nerve to say there's no more stock. We've got to wait till morning. That old fart, he gave me only one bullet. This isn't some liquor store in the country now, is it? Liquor stores in the country don't sell the brand of scotch I like. You know that, huh?

MAN B. I don't.

MAN A. Well, you'd better remember it.

MAN B. Your favorite brand of scotch?

MAN A. No, you fool! About liquor stores in the country. Got it?

MAN B. I got it.

MAN A. Well, then, answer me, will you. Let's start. I'll go first.

MAN B. Go ahead.

They start to play Russian roulette. After a few rounds, it's Man A's turn. The gun goes off. He falls off of his chair.

MAN B. Bad luck. Don't be mad now. It's not my fault. But your style of dying is pretty amazing. You should cross over to the side of the attackers. So, what's the plan? I won. Does that mean that I can go out with your woman now? I'm not kidding. This was your fantasy. Hey! How long are you going to keep this up? Hey! (*Approaches Man A.*) Hey! (*Sticks a hand out to Man A's nose to check if he is breathing. Places his ear against his heart.*) His heart's stopped!

Attacker A looks on attentively. Soldier enters right behind him.

SOLDIER. How does it feel to be in the presence of a dead body? It's not enough for you, is it?

MAN B. So he's dead?

SOLDIER. This is something new. You can use it starting tomorrow.

MAN B. What do you mean?

SOLDIER. This is The Lost Babylon. This theme park will make much more money than all those dinosaurs combined.

MAN B. It's not my fault . . . he did it himself, himself . . .

Soldier suppresses his laughter. Attacker A looks up at him.

ACT II

The next day from dawn until the evening.

SCENE 1

The meeting room is empty. A door opens and Boy, blindfolded, enters the room. Behind him enters Middle-Aged Woman. She removes Boy's blindfold.[5]

MIDDLE-AGED WOMAN. Welcome to The Lost Babylon! (*Boy looks around.*) Why don't you sit down? (*Boy sits on the chair.*) What would you like?

BOY. Nothing.

Middle-Aged Woman exits and comes back with a semi-automatic rifle.

MIDDLE-AGED WOMAN. This is what you wanted, right? Go ahead, take it. (*Boy takes the rifle.*) You still feel that the rifle is an extension of your body? Here you're free to shoot. It's not a crime, no matter who you shoot. You can just relax and tell me what went on that day. How did it feel before you fired those shots, and after?

BOY. I don't know.

MIDDLE-AGED WOMAN. You have the freedom now.

BOY. What do you mean freedom? The freedom to kill people?

MIDDLE-AGED WOMAN. Freedom to be a misfit, an incomplete human being.

BOY. Can't you be a little more specific?

---

5 The Boy in The Lost Babylon is based on the 13-year-old boy who in May 1997 brutally killed an 11-year-old friend in the city of Kobe. The boy cut off his victim's head and placed it in front of the gate of the local middle school. In the victim's mouth was a note that began, "Let's start the game." About a week later, a local newspaper received a note from the killer in which he described himself as without nationality and his life as a "transparent existence." He explained his murder as revenge on the Japanese school system and Japanese society, which he blamed for his painful life. His letter also contained statements indicating that the young killer saw his actions as a game and enjoyed seeing people suffer and die.

IMAGE 2.1 **Boy tries his new weapon.**
Seiji Aito as Boy. *The Lost Babylon*, The Suzunari, Shimokitazawa and Osaka and Nagoya, 1999.
Photograph by Katsu Miyauchi.

MIDDLE-AGED WOMAN. I know that you're very mature, that you're a great reader, you love Dostoyevsky and Nietzsche. Now, give up your fantasy world for a while and be a little more realistic.

BOY. I live inside that fantasy.

MIDDLE-AGED WOMAN. So the shooting was part of your fantasy too?

BOY. Of course.

MIDDLE-AGED WOMAN. The people you killed were also characters in your fantasy?

BOY. No, those people didn't fit into my fantasy. That's why I killed them. They were the imperfect ones.

MIDDLE-AGED WOMAN. And you're perfect?

BOY. I wouldn't say perfect. I just wanted the freedom to kill people.

MIDDLE-AGED WOMAN. You've got the right to end other people's lives?

BOY. Not the right, the freedom.

MIDDLE-AGED WOMAN. What about the lives of the people you killed?

BOY. They were boring.

MIDDLE-AGED WOMAN. Do you remember how many people you shot?

BOY. Seven. Two teachers and five classmates.

MIDDLE-AGED WOMAN. Can you still shoot now?

BOY. I don't know.

MIDDLE-AGED WOMAN. Why don't you try?

BOY. I won't know until I get into a similar situation.

MIDDLE-AGED WOMAN (*points to something in front of her*). Do you see that? There! Something's moving, right? Real people. You can go ahead and shoot them.

BOY. I can shoot them?

MIDDLE-AGED WOMAN. Yes. The first person you shot was your math teacher, right?

BOY. Yeah. She was a snake.

MIDDLE-AGED WOMAN. And next was your gym teacher?

BOY. He was really stupid. He thought that all children are happy and cheerful. What a fool!

MIDDLE-AGED WOMAN. Shoot! . . . Why aren't you shooting? Why aren't you shooting? Why?

Boy gets down on the floor and grabs his head with both hands. Man and Woman enter. Man is holding the scenario written by the Woman. When they enter Boy and Middle-Aged Woman freeze, forming a tableau.

MAN. No, that's not right. That boy will definitely shoot. He's a killer. When he killed those people, it was something he absolutely wanted to do.

WOMAN. That might have been the case when it happened. But that was two years ago. He must have some regret now.

MAN. He doesn't. That's why he's still seeing a therapist.

WOMAN. This is the last phase of his treatment. He has to act out his crime.

MAN. If that's true then he has to shoot again. If he isn't able to objectively act out his behavior, then he'll never be cured.

WOMAN. This kid hasn't progressed that far yet. That's why he's been brought here.

MAN. If that's true then he'll shoot again.

WOMAN. I don't like sick movies like that.

MAN. I'm probably troubled in the head myself, but he's (*points at Boy*) the sickest one among us. Are you listening? If you want to avoid a sick movie then you shouldn't have brought this kid up in the first place. What is this, anyway? An educational movie? Leave the sick kids to the therapists and keep the action scenes coming instead.

WOMAN. I'll put those in later. First, the film director and the female producer make an appearance, right? They come to Lost Babylon to make a movie about the incident with that boy . . .

MAN. Who wants to make a movie about a miserable incident like that these days? Leave that to the Belgians.[6]

WOMAN. The film you have in your head is much more cruel.

MAN. By the way, that film director you were talking about, is he modelled after me? If he's sleeping with the producer, you should move the sex scenes up. I'm not so slow. And here you

---

6 Kawamura is referring to the Belgian film *C'est arrive près de chez vous* (1992) directed by Rémy Belvaux and André Bonzel, in which the fictitious story of a ruthless serial killer is told in documentary style.

IMAGE 2.2 **Boy stages a drive-by shooting.**
Seiji Aito as Boy. *The Lost Babylon*, The Suzunari, Shimokitazawa and Osaka and Nagoya, 1999.
Photograph by Katsu Miyauchi.

should have the boy re-enact that shooting scene. Viewers can't wait so long.

WOMAN. I'm amazed! You're a complete fool! Your excuses are as bad as those of all the worthless producers out there. I liked you better before. You've never confronted death!

MAN. That has nothing to do with it! Leave your personal crap out of it. I don't know what was done to your sister, we're working on an action movie . . . (*Woman suddenly jumps at Man and they struggle. Man holds her down. Boy and Middle-Aged Woman look surprised. Man tries to slap Woman's face and she protects herself with both arms. Man gives up and stands up. Middle-Aged Woman and Boy become a tableau again.*)

Phew! This is really Sam Peckinpah. You'll get slammed by the feminists.

WOMAN. Fucking macho!

MAN. You're the one who started it. If you decide to work with a fucking macho that's your problem. You should have known that it would become a ruthless action flick. Why would you come here after those average human melodramas of yours made you famous? If you're out to explore new territory, comedy is the way to go.

WOMAN. It must've been painful.

MAN. Deluding your audience with a humanism you no longer believe in?

WOMAN. What are you trying to tell me, jerk?

MAN. I thought you wanted to portray the dark side of human nature?

WOMAN. What a sorry excuse.

MAN. Those aren't my words. You used to say that.

WOMAN. You're evading the problem.

MAN. You can't get away now.

WOMAN. Stop analyzing everything, action-movie style.

MAN. All right. Just continue working on your plot. I'll do my part and go on the way I suggested. Let's both write to the finish and then put our storylines together.

WOMAN. What an unlucky compromise.

MAN. Better than fighting, no? (*Reads*) "Lost Babylon?" Lost Babylon? Did you come up with that name?

WOMAN. That's the name of this place. You really don't know anything. Idiot. (*Exits.*)

MAN (*follows her with his eyes*). I don't know anything? And on top of that I'm an idiot. (*Man sits down on the chair Woman has been sitting in. He takes a pen and starts working on his scenario.*)

Middle-Aged Woman and Boy start moving. Boy fires his rifle while making the sound of rapid gunfire: RATATATATAT.

BOY. Just the way you wanted. Seven people.

MIDDLE-AGED WOMAN. No one wants anything. (*To Man*) Why are you making him do this? The other version was much more realistic.

MAN. He must have wanted that.

BOY. It's useless to bring me to a place like this.

MAN. See, he still has a lot of energy.

MIDDLE-AGED WOMAN. Don't point your gun at me like that.

BOY. Didn't you say I can shoot whomever I want to?

MIDDLE-AGED WOMAN. Stop it!

BOY. Are you afraid?

MIDDLE-AGED WOMAN. Of course I'm afraid.

BOY. What are you feeling?

MIDDLE-AGED WOMAN. I ask you that. What are you feeling?

BOY. You shouldn't ask so many questions all the time. Think about yourself sometimes.

MIDDLE-AGED WOMAN. I feel like a tiny insect. I'd do whatever it takes to stay alive.

BOY. Even though you always have an answer for everything?

MIDDLE-AGED WOMAN. Yes.

BOY. I'll forgive you. You're honest. (*Puts gun down.*)

MIDDLE-AGED WOMAN (*to Man*). Don't develop the story this way. Do you have something against me?

MAN. Why don't you ask him?

MIDDLE-AGED WOMAN. Don't run away! You're not a whole person just 'cause you've fired a gun. Why do people like you want to shoot guns? Don't you really long for someone to care about you?

BOY. Don't use my case to prove your point.

MIDDLE-AGED WOMAN (*still facing Man*). We'll never solve anything this way. You can't just run away.

MAN. What am I running from?

MIDDLE-AGED WOMAN. In most cases, men's interest in guns is explained by looking at the environment in which they're raised. The cause of their behavior is a dysfunctional family, frequent fighting between the parents, and the deprivation of love that results. The urge to point a gun at someone comes from the desire to be cared for, from longing for love and affection. Were you loved by your parents when you were a child?

MAN. Yes. Much to my regret I was loved excessively.

MIDDLE-AGED WOMAN. Excessively? I see, you experienced this excessive affection as a heavy burden.

MAN. Stop analyzing the characters that kill in my films. You can't explain everything anyway.

MIDDLE-AGED WOMAN. I can.

MAN. You're a hundred percent convinced that everyone who ever used a gun grew up in a fucked-up family?

MIDDLE-AGED WOMAN. No, I'm not.

MAN. See.

MIDDLE-AGED WOMAN. But I'm not giving up on you just yet. I'm just saying that your lack of understanding is evading the problem.

MAN. What I understand is that people love watching films where the main character gets into violent confrontations and, even though bullets are flying around the whole time, doesn't get hit even once, while his adversaries, on the other hand, fall like flies. Watching this makes people feel good. Analysts make me sick. Your murder philosophy is just plain boring. There are guns here. He had a gun. What are guns for? They're designed to kill people. He picked up the gun. That's why he shot someone. That's a fact. I turn that fact into a film. In my films people shoot and get shot. The audience loves it. Is that abnormal?

MIDDLE-AGED WOMAN. Not abnormal, as long as you don't really kill someone.

MAN (*pointing at Boy*). Well, that makes him abnormal.

MIDDLE-AGED WOMAN. Not normal, in any case.

MAN. Normal? Are there really normal people in this world? Oh, I see. I, for one, was raised in a normal household. My parents believe that. I also thought that was the case. But normal just means pretending to be normal. For me that charade was agony.

MIDDLE-AGED WOMAN. There you go—family environment. Rebellion against your parents' deception.

MAN. I loved geography as a child. When I saw footage of a war zone on the television news, I looked up the country on a map and marked it. There were always a lot of border disputes. I never understood why, with so many wars everywhere around the globe, nothing was happening in my neighborhood. Why was everything around me so quiet and calm?

MIDDLE-AGED WOMAN. Awakening to the deception of society.

MAN. Once I was caught stealing. My mother got all excited and took me to the local chapter of one of those new religion groups. I was ordered to take off all my clothes and to climb into a pink tub. Their theory was that my stealing was caused by an evil spirit residing in my body and that the holy water in the pool would wash that evil spirit away. Instead, I got a hard-on looking at all the naked girls in the room. They thought that meant the bad spirit was still in me. Thank God. Around that time I decided to become an artist. I thought if I lost the bad spirit I'd never produce any art.

MIDDLE-AGED WOMAN. Skepticism about religion.

MAN. I look happy and normal but I've always hated people who look happy.

MIDDLE-AGED WOMAN. Distorted inferiority complex.

MAN. I hated happy parents pushing baby carriages or mothers with their children. Perfect homes got on my nerves too.

MIDDLE-AGED WOMAN. The luxury pathology of the well to do.

MAN. That boy is me. The only difference is that I never turned to using a gun but watched a lot of movies instead. I got some kind of fulfillment watching John Wayne, Eastwood, or Cagney do the killing for me.

MIDDLE-AGED WOMAN. Violent movies are bad for children.

MAN. That's ridiculous! I grew up watching an enormous amount of murders but I'm not killing anyone, am I?

MIDDLE-AGED WOMAN. You can never tell.

MAN. You mean you think I'm a killer? And that whatever I didn't let out as a boy is still there, smouldering inside?

MIDDLE-AGED WOMAN. There were some deficiencies in your upbringing. You lack the ability to empathize with other people.

MAN. No way. I make films for the pleasure of other people.

MIDDLE-AGED WOMAN. Your distorted films produce distorted children.

MAN. My films stave off violence. Murder's not so simple.

MIDDLE-AGED WOMAN. The problem is love. Love. The love that is disappearing from this world!

BOY. Stop already.

Middle-Aged Woman looks at Boy as if shocked.

MAN. He asked you to stop.

MIDDLE-AGED WOMAN. Why do I have to stop? I was wrong. It is my fault things turned out this way.

BOY. Stop controlling me, Mum.

MAN. What a great development for the story! (*Starts writing his scenario.*)

BOY. You shouldn't blame yourself, Mum. You're not so important.

MIDDLE-AGED WOMAN. How dare you?

BOY. Why did you leave Dad?

MIDDLE-AGED WOMAN. I had you. I was most worried about you.

BOY. That's a lie. (*Shoots at Middle-Aged Woman. She doesn't collapse.*)

MIDDLE-AGED WOMAN. That won't solve anything. Nothing . . .

Man continues to write. The TV on the wall is switched on. Something appears on the screen. Boy and Middle-Aged Woman disappear.

MAN (*stops writing and mumbles*). What am I writing? I'm supposed to be writing an action movie. An entertainment masterpiece that will bring in more money than any dinosaur or sinking ship! (*Shreds his draft to pieces. Notices the TV monitor.*)

The TV monitor shows Attacker A with his arms and legs tied up. The camera approaches Attacker A. It zooms in on his face. Even though his mouth is covered with tape, Attacker A is screaming as he faces the camera. The person holding the camera sticks out a hand to pull off the tape.

ATTACKER A. "Help! Get these ropes off!"

The camera is put on the floor and shows Young Woman loosening Attacker A's ropes. She then picks up the camera again. On the screen, Attacker A is shown in wide-angle so that we see his body. He starts shaking his arms and legs.

YOUNG WOMAN (*from behind the camera*). "Run away, quick!"

ATTACKER A. "Huh?"

YOUNG WOMAN. "You'd better run away before they come back."

ATTACKER A. "Are you kidding me? You think I can run away that easily after what they did to me? This is a war zone!"

YOUNG WOMAN. "What are you saying?"

ATTACKER A. "Nothing. I can't believe you really untied those ropes. Idiot! What about the guidelines for captives? What kind of fool lets a prisoner escape?" (*Attacker A approaches the camera. The camera backs up.*) "I'll rape you. I would only be following the guidelines." (*Close-up of Attacker A.*)

The camera falls over. Young Woman is heard screaming.

MAN. Hey, what's that? Where are you? (*Exits in a hurry through one of the doors.*)

A shot is heard. The TV monitor is switched off. Pause. A door opens and Young Woman and Man B enter, carrying an exhausted Attacker A. They drop him to the floor. Young Woman looks shocked. Man B looks as if he is suppressing laughter. Man comes running back.

MAN. Oh, you're all right! I was worried about you.

MAN B. I shot him.

MAN. He . . .

MAN B. His heart stopped.

MAN. What?! (*Checks Attacker A's pulse.*) He's . . . I think we're in trouble.

MAN B (*in blank amazement*). Now we're involved in a real murder.

MAN. Well, if we explain, I'm sure they'll understand.

MAN B. I'm not reporting this to the police. I'm not talking face-to-face with the cops. Come on, get me out of this mess!

MAN. What?

MAN B. Let's go bury him somewhere.

MAN. Wait a minute. That's easy to say, but . . .

MAN B. You don't want to do it?

MAN. We should call the police. Let's ask the soldier, okay?

MAN B. Wait. My life depends on this. Don't just stand there. Pick up the body! Live up to your murder films. You're worthless.

YOUNG WOMAN. It's all right. I'll do it.

MAN B. You can't lift him.

YOUNG WOMAN. Yes I can. I brought him here, so . . .

MAN B. We have to dig a deep hole. Hey, you can at least help with the digging. (*Picks up Attacker A together with Young Woman.*) This will follow us for the rest of our lives. (*Man B and Young Woman are about to leave when they come face-to-face with Soldier.*)

SOLDIER. What's this?

MAN B (*looks at Man*). He did it.

MAN. Hey, you, wait a minute!

MAN B. You did it and we have to get rid of the body. I've had it! You can take care of it yourself. (*Lets go of the body. Young Woman lets go too.*)

MAN. You idiots, you idiots . . . ! (*He's so angry that he can't find his words.*) Well . . . ah . . . whatever. I don't care. No, I do care.

In the meantime, Attacker A, who is supposed to be dead has regained consciousness. He raises his head and looks around.

MAN. I didn't do it, it was . . .

SOLDIER. Do what?

MAN. Kill that . . . (*Notices Attacker A.*) Huh?

ATTACKER A (*stands up*). You guys, you just made a fool out of me. I'll get you! (*Runs out.*)

Man looks at the others. They suppress their laughter.

MAN. Another zombie?

The three burst out laughing.

MAN B. This guy's face!

YOUNG WOMAN. Halfway through I started to take pity on him. He's so serious.

MAN. What was this then? Tell me what's going on!

SOLDIER. His heart stopped beating. These are new bullets. If there's only blood spurting out, then there's not much difference between this and toy gunplay. But when someone's hit by a bullet like this one, that person is clinically dead—at least for three minutes. There are individual differences. In our tests, the longest period of time before resuscitation was ten minutes. But you can't use these bullets on people with heart diseases. You've got to try these out! Here. (*Soldier gives Man a box with bullets.*) These bullets aren't all the same. There are blood bullets in here too.

MAN (*inspecting the contents of the box*). They all look the same.

SOLDIER. This is the test phase. We don't have to mark the bullets yet.

MAN. I don't get it.

SOLDIER. We're in pursuit of reality.

MAN B. It becomes more fun to shoot.

YOUNG WOMAN. It's too frightening.

MAN B. That fear is reality. There he is! The one who just experienced reality for the first time.

Man A enters.

MAN A. You're talking about me?

MAN B. You shot yourself. I was terrified!

YOUNG WOMAN. He tried to run away all by himself.

MAN A. This is really getting on my nerves! (*To Soldier.*) Hey, you, why didn't you explain all this before?

SOLDIER. Your reactions are part of the test. But I didn't expect you to shoot yourself in the head.

MAN A. This isn't funny!

MAN He's had enough gunplay.

MAN A. No joke. I feel like I'm seeing the world for the first time. A minute ago I was watching the TV news. That world is horrible! It's really bad. There are so many guys out there not worth bringing back to life. I'm more ready to fight than ever before. This is more than just a game. I'm training to make the world a better place!

MAN How did it feel to be dead?

MAN A. I didn't feel anything. Just darkness.

Pause.

YOUNG WOMAN. The night is ending.

MAN A. Let's take a nap, send out fresh troops in the morning. There's a bunch of those maniacs out there. If we don't take care of them who will?

SCENE 2

Boss appears on the TV.

BOSS. Hello everyone, how are you? Let me tell you about the city I live in. A luxurious and prosperous city. A city where people love each other, support each other, comfort each other. A city where pleasant things happen. I was born and raised in this city. I love this city. But now this city is sick. It's thirsty, suffering, gasping for air. People slander each other, deceive each other, kill each other. Children attack adults in the streets; a father comes home and smashes his son's head with a baseball bat; his wife then shoots him to death; a son randomly slashes his mother with a knife; kids quarrel and knock their siblings to death, then take the bodies to brand new housing complexes and stuff them in concrete and return to their everyday lives as if nothing happened.[7] Freaks, robbers, and homicidal maniacs are on the prowl every night. Eight years ago, I was attacked on the street and lost my wife and my left eye. When my wife was shot to death I pledged that, with the survival of the whole of mankind at stake, I would save the children, save the adults, save the cities, save the earth. To allow people to relieve stress, to teach people how to use guns, to prevent and stop crime, and to facilitate the reintegration into society of criminals, I will open Lost Babylon, the ultimate amusement park, in cities all over the world. One Lost Babylon in every city: Lost Babylon Tokyo, Lost Babylon New York, Lost Babylon Osaka, Lost Babylon Los Angeles, Lost Babylon Paris, Lost Babylon Hong Kong, Lost Babylon Berlin, Lost Babylon Seoul, Rome, Warsaw, Moscow, Manila, Bucharest, Madrid, Shanghai, Bangkok . . . (*Continues to call out names of cities.*)

SCENE 3

The desert. Soldier, Man A, Man B, and Young Woman are in a convertible. Soldier drives while the others stand and fire revolvers and

---

7 This passage refers to many recent violent incidents in Japan. In particular, Kawamura alludes to the murder of a high school student by a group of young men in 1989. Two boys lured an 18-year-old girl by staging a rescue scene: one of the boys attacked the girl while the other one pretended to come to her rescue. After torturing the girl for over a month, the boys, who upon their arrest appeared extremely detached from their crime, put the girl's body in a gasoline drum, covered it with concrete, and dumped the can at a construction site.

automatic rifles. Before long, Man A gets hit in the chest. His shirt is stained with blood.

MAN A. I've been hit! Someone made a mistake. Was it him? That black foreigner? (*Shoots.*) It serves you right! (*To Soldier*) They should miss when shooting at customers. I'll forward the cleaning bill.

SCENE 4

The common room. Girl is reading a book. Boy enters through the door, carrying a semi-automatic rifle. Girl notices Boy and looks up.

BOY. Let's start the game! (*Picks up Girl's book.*) A detective story. A novel about how people are killed. Why do you read books? For me watching movies is no longer enough. (*Displays the gun.*) This is the real deal. Join me? (*Girl shakes her head.*) You're still a child. You're afraid of the real world. Okay, cover for me. You don't have to tell people you went on a date to the movies with me. Just testify that I was very calm and cool-headed at this moment. Because I'm sure the newspapers and intellectuals will blow everything out of proportion. (*Shows her the gun again.*) No theory. It's an extension of my body. That's all, no theory. Or maybe I'm planning to take revenge on those intellectuals. They'll say I was a disturbed child, or a product of our dysfunctional society. That's ridiculous! What I'm really doing is taking revenge on all those sick people and this sick society. That's why we have these. (*Displays the gun.*) Man's best invention ever. Deep down people know they're sick. So these were invented so they could punish each other. It was just a matter of time before someone came out and did it. And that person is me. Testify that for me. You want me to kill someone for you? There must be someone you want dead. (*Girl shakes her head.*) A misfit like you? There must be some-one you want dead. (*Girl shakes her head violently. Boy suddenly hits her on the head with the rifle. Girl falls off of her chair but gets up again.*) One more time. Who do you want me to kill for you? (*Girl shakes her head.*) Don't look as if this doesn't concern you. I reached this point in the same way as all those freaks in your movies. Your movies made me do this in the first place. If it weren't for your movies, I'd still be a meek good-hearted person who wouldn't dare harm anyone. (*Boy again hits her on the head with his rifle.*) People who bring something into the world have to take responsibility for it. Get up! I said get up! (*Girl doesn't move.*) I hate cowards . . .

Boy gets his gun ready to shoot Girl but Boy gets shot. He gets shot a few more times. In a dark corner stands Woman with a gun. The stage grows lighter and Woman's fantasy vision disappears. Girl disappears. Boy is replaced by an Attacker. Man enters through the door.

MAN. You finally did it. (*Attacker gets up and runs off.*) Congratulations! Now the story's really moving along. Show me what you've got? I've been thinking about it but I gave up. Let's use your plot. (*Woman's face is expressionless.*) What's wrong?

WOMAN. A hallucination . . .

MAN. I see. So that's what opened your eyes.

WOMAN. My little sister must necessarily make an appearance . . .

MAN. You came back.

WOMAN. Then, about to be raped . . .

MAN. Who?

WOMAN. My sister. It happened in my room. The intruder really wanted to kill me. He'd been planning it for six months.

MAN. Will you stop that nonsense.

WOMAN. My sister sacrificed herself for me.

MAN. That's not true.

WOMAN. He said, "I'm doing what those psychos in your films always do."

MAN Will you stop this!

WOMAN. He hit her and kicked her and tore off her clothes . . .

MAN. Whose clothes?

WOMAN. My sister's!

MAN. What does your sister look like?

WOMAN. What?

MAN. I'm asking you what kind of person she is. What does her face look like? How old is she?

WOMAN. She is eight years younger than me.

MAN. And . . .

WOMAN. Her features don't really resemble mine.

MAN. And . . .

WOMAN. What else do you want to know?

MAN. It's a lie.

WOMAN. What's a lie?

MAN. You don't even have a sister. (*Woman looks at Man as if taken by surprise.*) . . . You don't have a sister, do you?

WOMAN. Of course I do!

MAN. No.

WOMAN. Yes!

MAN. Only in your imagination.

WOMAN. Stop it!

MAN. I'm not about to stop yet. Tell me the true story! Go on! You didn't have a sister to begin with.

WOMAN. I did have a sister. It's because of my sister that I'm still alive.

MAN. Enough is enough. You never had a sister!

WOMAN. Yes, I did!

MAN. Why don't you come back to this world now. Let's go back to the time when your talent was blowing everyone away, and you decided to put it to good use and write screenplays.

WOMAN. What are you talking about?

MAN. You, respected and praised by everyone.

WOMAN. That's a lie . . .

IMAGE 2.2 **Man is confronted by Woman who threatens to shoot him.**

Koutaro Yoshida as Man and Anna Nakagawa as Woman. *The Lost Babylon,* The Suzunari, Shimokitazawa and Osaka and Nagoya, 1999.

Photograph by Katsu Miyauchi.

MAN. No, that's no lie.

WOMAN. I got no recognition for my work.

MAN. The public wasn't ready for it, that's all. The movies we made together came out too early. Now the public has finally come up to speed. Anyway, why don't you level your gun again? Come on! You looked really good, you know, just now.

WOMAN. No.

MAN. Do it for the film, see if it makes sense or not. (*Woman raises her gun again.*) That's it. The gun looks good on you. (*Woman points her gun at Man.*) Do you want to try? There are, no doubt, plenty of reasons for you to shoot a selfish, aggressive guy like me. But I have confidence enough in myself to know that I am not just one more fucking macho. That's why it's possible for me to work with you. Our films came out too early. They weren't regular action flicks. They were reflections on killing. I know it, you don't have a sister.

WOMAN. . . . Bingo. (*Puts down her gun.*)

MAN. Go ahead and shoot me. Face your trauma. It was an unfortunate accident. I heard the news and went to the hospital but you wouldn't see me. I was already part of your nightmare. After a break of a year you wrote a very successful love story. In no time, you became extremely popular. Magazine interviews, talk shows, the star of every party. But you returned to your horrible memories. You came to Lost Babylon. Why? You don't have to answer me, but don't deceive yourself with those fantastic stories of yours. Did you think I was going to go along with your fantasy? I'm not that good. I'm a film director. Your sister is you, isn't she? But you're alive. You should shoot. The guys who come through those doors are your horrible memories, the perverts who still roam our cities.

WOMAN. I can't.

MAN. The hallucination is yours.

WOMAN. I'll make them understand.

MAN. Did you see my latest film? (*Woman shakes her head.*) You should see it. There's a character who preaches to a bunch of thugs. Tragic story.

WOMAN. That's your world.

MAN. My world? Then you should try to make me understand.

WOMAN. When I get a chance.

MAN. Oh. I'm relieved.

WOMAN. Why?

MAN. We both have our reasons to work together again.

WOMAN. No. Now that I've heard your story I've made up my mind. I'm leaving this place tomorrow. (*Interrupts Man, who seems about to say something*.) Don't flatter yourself. It's not like I was taught something. I've been thinking about this for a long time. Not about whether or not I should shoot. I have to check myself into an institution, a facility for alcoholics.

MAN. . . . I see. That's too bad. (*Woman throws the gun at Man. He catches it. Man B and Young Woman enter through one of the doors. They carry their guns. Both are exhausted*.) How was it in the war zone?

MAN B. What?

MAN. I think this set-up is a war zone close to a border. What do you think? War these days is all about atomic bombs and chemical warfare. This battlefield has too much of a nostalgic feel to it to be a war. It reminds me of *The Battle of the Bulge* or *The Longest Day*.

MAN B (*whispering*). Frogs.

MAN. Huh?

YOUNG WOMAN. I thought it was about scaring off perverts and stalkers.

MAN B. Frogs.

MAN. What are you talking about? Are you all right?

YOUNG WOMAN. I'm exhausted.

MAN B. If you look at it as a movie it's more like a Western than anything.

YOUNG WOMAN. Those new bullets are terrifying. It's too intense. Those guys look like they're really dead. Right in front of your eyes they start frothing at the mouth and then collapse.

MAN B. Frogs. They look like frogs. When I was little I killed frogs all the time. I never felt I was doing anything wrong. I am no longer a child but I still don't feel guilty—it's boring.

WOMAN. Then stop!

YOUNG WOMAN. I give up. This isn't my thing.

WOMAN. I'm leaving tomorrow. Wanna come?

YOUNG WOMAN. Yeah.

MAN B. Wait a minute! All of a sudden all the women are leaving.

MAN It's the "Lost Babylon" effect. People get sick of guns. Your scenario is right. People who commit violent gun crimes are sent here to get brainwashed until they hate guns.

MAN B. Brainwashing? You must be kidding!

WOMAN. All theme parks are about brainwashing people. Think of Disneyland.

YOUNG WOMAN. Disneyland?

WOMAN. The fantasy is that the country is clean and safe and over-flowing with friendliness.

MAN. Exactly.

YOUNG WOMAN. The two of you are seriously disturbed.

MAN. That's something coming from you, miss. Running around killing people until a few minutes ago.

YOUNG WOMAN. I've had it.

MAN. You now love mankind, do you? Where's the other one?

MAN B. He's unbelievable. He's still going at it. A real Rambo.

WOMAN. Your brainwashing theory doesn't apply in his case.

YOUNG WOMAN. I feel sick. I'm going to the bathroom. (*Exits.*)

MAN B. Frogs.

MAN. Enough talking about frogs! It's turning my stomach.
Soldier enters.

MAN B. I'm sure you killed quite a few when you were a child.

SOLDIER. Did any of you go into the weapon warehouse?
Silence.

MAN. This is the first time I've heard of a weapon warehouse.

WOMAN. What happened?

SOLDIER. Someone took the bullets. You shouldn't go in there with-out permission. None of you went in there?

WOMAN. What's the problem?

SOLDIER. No, no, no problem. Something looks funny, that's all.

MAN B. It might be him. Earlier he was going on about how there weren't enough bullets.

SOLDIER. Your pal?

MAN B. Yeah.

SOLDIER. He's getting us in trouble. The different bullet boxes were messed up and now we can't tell the difference.

MAN The ones that have the blood in them from the ones that make your heart stop, you mean?

SOLDIER. Well . . .

Sound of shots in the back.

MAN. That's coming from the bathroom.

MAN B. It must be those frogs.

Soldier runs to the back of the room.

MAN. What's with him?

Man B follows Soldier. Man and Woman are staring upstage.

WOMAN. It's an attacker.

MAN. How did he get in here?

Multiple shots are heard. Man B and Soldier come back.

MAN B (*to Soldier*). How did those frogs get a hold of the bullets? (*Soldier ignores him and leaves through the door without answering.*) Hey, answer me!

MAN. What is it?

MAN B. The girl was shot with one of those bullets that make your heart stop. Those frogs are really getting into it now.

An Attacker comes in with a gun and starts shooting. Man B shoots back and the Attacker collapses. Soldier enters carrying a box.

SOLDIER. I brought the remaining bullets. (*Walks over to the Attacker on the floor and shoots him again.*)

MAN B. What are you doing?

SOLDIER. I'm just making sure that he won't come back to life. Are you listening to me? This is an emergency situation. The girl in the bathroom might not wake up again.

MAN B. What're you trying to tell us?

SOLDIER. I'll leave it to your imagination.

MAN B. Stop pretending!

SOLDIER. They took the bullets from the warehouse. They must have a mix of three different types.

MAN. What do you mean three types?

SOLDIER. Some of them are real bullets.

MAN B. What?

SOLDIER (*points at the box*). Look, it's impossible to tell which is which. They don't know the difference either. And they don't know they're using real bullets. You should prepare to leave. Do it fast, don't panic, and don't make too much noise. I'll take full responsibility. When you're done, come back here.

Man, Man B, and the Soldier load their guns. Woman runs toward the back.

MAN B. Those frogs look more like frogs than ever!

MAN. You, shut up!

SOLDIER. It must have been a shock.

MAN. Pain in the ass.

The TV is switched on. The face of Attacker A appears on video footage.

ATTACKER A. "Hey, can you see me? Can you hear me? Listen! We had a talk, you know, and we think that being shot at all the time isn't fair. Besides, the pay is too low. We have to have some fun too. Hey, soldier, can you hear me? We got to have some fun too. Let's start the riot game!"

The image of Man A with hands and feet tied to a chair appears on the screen. His mouth is covered with tape.

SOLDIER. Hey, can you hear me? The bullets you took, there are real ones mixed in with them. Can you hear me?

People on the screen cannot hear anything. Attacker A takes the tape off of Man A's mouth.

MAN A. "Please think of what will happen next! Dammit!!" (*Attacker A points his gun at Man A.*) "Go ahead and shoot me! I'll come back to life!"

SOLDIER. Please don't shoot!

Attacker A shoots Man A. His head falls forward.

ATTACKER A. "Hell! It looks like he's really dead! Looks like real blood!" (*Woman comes back into the room with a bag in her arms.*) "Now, I'm ready to attack!" (*Screams loudly.*)

A number of Attackers enter. Violent shooting back and forth. Then the Attackers retreat.

SOLDIER. I'll call the rescue helicopter. (*To Man B*) You, come with me! (*To Man*) And you, take care of the lady.

Soldier and Man B run off through the door.

MAN. There's no need to be afraid.

WOMAN. You're the one who's afraid.

MAN. I've heard that before.

WOMAN. In my scenario.

MAN. Right. (*Suddenly bursts out laughing.*) Your script. You're pulling my leg! You see, I'm too good-natured. I was about to get tricked again. Some actors! I don't need to make movies. With games like this, we don't need movies. (*Keeps laughing.*)

WOMAN. Stop it! (*Grabs Man by his shoulders.*) Stop it! What's gotten into you?

MAN (*embraces Woman*). No need to be afraid.

WOMAN. Stop!

MAN. In your screenplay it says "they embrace."

WOMAN. You're not the one who's afraid.

MAN. As long as you can hold on to someone like this.

WOMAN. In a situation like this, you realize you're alone, all alone in this world.

MAN. But at night, after the rain clears up, the fear goes away.

WOMAN. No rain today.

MAN. This isn't real, it's just a game.

WOMAN. If that's the case, why are you so afraid?

MAN. And you're all right? (*Pushes himself away from Woman.*) You're part of it too. You're acting again, aren't you? I see. I'm on to you, you know. Hey, everyone, pull yourselves together! You can stop pretending you're dead. But why did you go through so much trouble to set me up? What did I do?

WOMAN. You made movies.

MAN. Yes, I made seven of them. In all of them people get killed. So that's my crime. I see. Then is Hitchcock in hell too? I just show what people would like to do. All I did was entertain people.

WOMAN. Yeah, many people enjoyed your movies.

MAN. Is it my fault someone couldn't tell the difference between fiction and reality and broke into your apartment? Poor you. I feel sorry for you, but this is remarkable. Are you trying to tell me that you have suffered enough and that I haven't been punished yet? I get your point. I should start repenting or this play will never end. Is that it?

WOMAN. I'm no actress. So we're in the same boat. I have no idea whether this is really happening or whether it's a game.

MAN. Then why are you so calm? Why don't you take a gun?

WOMAN. I'm afraid, always, ever since it happened. Do I look calm? If that's the case it's because simply being alive is terrifying to me.

An Attacker enters. Man levels his gun and shoots the Attacker until he runs out of bullets.

MAN. This is my movie. I am not repenting. (*Putting more bullets in his gun with trembling hands*) Look! His head's split and his brains're hanging out! Some reality!

WOMAN. I came here for you.

MAN. There, you said it.

WOMAN. Now you think you've won?

IMAGE 2.2 **Man is confronted by Woman who threatens to shoot him.**
Koutaro Yoshida as Man and Anna Nakagawa as Woman. *The Lost Babylon*,
The Suzunari, Shimokitazawa and Osaka and Nagoya, 1999.
Photograph by Katsu Miyauchi.

MAN (*his hands are shaking and he isn't really making progress*). This
is no game. We're surrounded by death. People can't seem to
say what they really think until they end up in a situation like
this one. I need you.

WOMAN (*takes a gun.*) Is this reality? Is this the truth?

MAN. I need you.

WOMAN. I need you.

MAN. If we get out of here alive, let's make a comedy together.

WOMAN. What?

MAN. Just kidding.

> *Attacker A enters from the back of the room and shoots. Man is hit and collapses. Woman shoots Attacker A but he doesn't collapse.*

ATTACKER A. Tough luck! That's fake blood, you know. (*Attacker A shoots Woman. Woman gets hit but she doesn't collapse.*) It's your lucky day too.

> *Woman shoots. Attacker A collapses. Woman pulls Man up into her arms.*

WOMAN. Don't worry, you'll be all right. In three minutes you'll come to life again. In three minutes . . . after three . . . you'll be running around again hitting people on the head with your gun, laughing out loud . . . If not three minutes, then four. If not four then five, six minutes, seven minutes, eight minutes, nine minutes . . .

> *Woman cuddles Man. The helicopter comes closer.*

SCENE 5

The common room is empty. On the table different types of guns and rifles are laid out. Two doors open. Middle-Aged Woman, dressed in fancy clothes, and Boy, dressed in combat gear, enter. Both of them look dead. They approach the table.

MIDDLE-AGED WOMAN. You can pick whatever you like, boy.

> *Boy looks at the guns on the table. Picks up the semi-automatic rifle.*

The End

CHARACTERS

THIEF

SOLDIER A

SOLDIER B

PRINCE A

PRINCE B

PRINCE C

OLD GAY PRINCE/MAN

GIRL A

GIRL B

GIRL C

GERTRUDE

CLAUDIUS

POLONIUS

HORATIO

OPHELIA

YOUNG MAN

TRAMP

LAERTES

FORTINBRAS

MAN

HAMLETCLONE

HAMLETCLONE

TRANSLATED BY PETER ECKERSALL

PROLOGUE

Large gates covered with barbed wire are strung across the stage apron, suggesting a concentration camp. When the audience enters, they discover they are on the stage proper, looking out through the wire into the auditorium.

A dog is barking at a man.

THIEF. Who do you think you are, asking me who I am? If either one of us lets on then it's civil war for sure. Is that a revolution? No! How can it be *Hamlet* unless everyone in the family kills one another?

The dream of total ruin is like a shining moon in the winter sky.

With the force of a heart attack, somewhere a vampire chants.

How could it be?

Long Live the Emperor of Japan! Banzai!

Politics! I fought in the anti-Narita airport struggle, became active in the People's Party. I hid in Osaka and on the western side of Japan. I voted for Yokoyama Knock.[1] Then I came back to Tokyo.

Dreaming of the day when we can say who we are.

Abandoned by family and company . . . Hah! The word abandoned has a tiny seed of hope. The hope that you're not going to lose anything else.

Stop! Who are you! A friend of Japan.

Bring on the civil war, I demand to play Hamlet!

---

1 Yokoyama Knock is an outspoken, right-wing nationalist politician who was a TV comedian before embarking on a controversial political career. In the 1990s, he was elected Mayor of Osaka, only to be found guilty of sexual harassment against a female campaign worker.

IMAGE 3.1 **Thief in the Prologue: "Let me find a menstruating virgin, innocent and beguiling, one who will drown in the Sumida River."**

Makoto Kasagi as Thief. *Hamletclone*, German tour, 2003.

Photograph by Katsu Miyauchi.

Can you understand? At the dawn of the new century the
curtain is drawn. But only melodrama plays.

I am Hamlet. Rough hewn and beautiful, all actors want to
be me.

To dream of acting Hamlet. I will not die before playing
Hamlet!

I am the prince. I am the prince who lives in the age of late
capitalism. To be in this age or not to be . . . that is the
question.

To be or not to be . . . that is the question. How good it is
to feel this way.

The pleasure of speech . . . the critical mass of the play
bubbles over into civil war.
Let us go and look for Ophelia now . . . Let us look among
the mass of refugees trying to cross the border.
Let me find a menstruating virgin, innocent and beguiling,
one who will drown in the Sumida River.
That's how I'll finish my civil war!

I. COLONY

Night scene in Shinjuku. Thief riding a stolen bicycle moves among the audience, singing the Japanese National Anthem (Kimigayo). An image of the 'Red Sun' Japanese National Flag (Hinomaru) is projected onto a wall. It dissolves into lurid colors as it sways in the breeze.

Two Soldiers, their rifles ready. People are lined up behind the barbed-wire. When they touch it, they realize that it is an electric fence.

A Soldier points his gun and shouts, "Stop!" Thief loses his balance and falls. As he falls his clothes catch on the barbed wire.

II. AUTOBIOGRAPHY

Prince A, B, and C and Girl A, B, and C appear as a rotating array of figures among the seats in the auditorium. Prince A is played by a male actor. Prince B is a male actor cross-dressed as female. Prince C is a female actor. All are standing, but fall at the end of each line as if shot. Their dialogue is punctuated by gunshots.

PRINCE A. I am Hamlet.

PRINCE B. I might be Hamlet.

PRINCE C. I was Hamlet.

PRINCE A. I was Mishima Yukio.

PRINCE B. I was Pier Paulo Passolini.

PRINCE C. I was Rainer Weiner Fassbinder.

PRINCE A. I was Adolf Hitler.

PRINCE B. I was Joseph Stalin.

PRINCE C. I was Pol Pot.

PRINCE A. I raped Korean women. I cut off the heads of the Chinese.

Soldier B fires his gun and Girl A reacts.

PRINCE B. I sent Jews to the gas chambers. I sentenced a political prisoner to death by firing squad.

Soldier A fires his gun and Girl B reacts.

PRINCE C. In Los Alamos I finished making Little Boy and Fat Man.

Soldier A fires his gun and Girl C reacts.

PRINCE A. I was the woman who killed my best friend.

PRINCE B. I was the woman who killed my neighbors with poisoned curry rice.[2]

PRINCE C. I was the woman who killed my child.

Soldier B fires his gun and Girls A, B, and C react.

PRINCE A. I was a bullet.

PRINCE B. I was mustard gas.

PRINCE C. I was sarin gas.

PRINCE B. As the top floors of the building collapse, the reverse course of communism is like an after-image playing on my eyelids.

Soldier B fires his gun and Girls A, B, and C react.

PRINCE A. Banzai! For the Mt. Fuji geisha girl, banzai!

PRINCE C. Banzai! For the economic animal, banzai!

PRINCE B. Banzai! For the animation and TV games, banzai!

PRINCE A. The ruins of Japan in the midst of the world. Bravo!

PRINCE B. I was Hiroshima.

PRINCE A. I was Nanking.

---

2 In the summer of 1998, at a festival in Wakayama Prefecture, local housewife Hayashi Masumi served curry rice laced with arsenic to passers-by. Four people died and 63 others suffered the effects of the poison. Hayashi was convicted and sentenced to death. Her subsequent appeal was rejected by the courts in June 2005 and she is now on death row.

PRINCE C. I was Auschwitz.

PRINCE B. I forced my way into the State funeral procession while shouting the name of the ruined city.[3] And even in the midst of all the fervor, the government gave out poisoned human flesh to the citizens.

Soldier A fires his gun and Girls A, B, and C react.

PRINCE C. The roast sirloin for the Marxists. The *karebi* joints for neonationalists. To which one should I add the *sanchu* sauce?[4]

PRINCE B. In Shinjuku Park, the homeless who ate the flesh send up smoke signals. An uprising by the homeless people. I was arrested. Meanwhile, what they saw was an empty coffin where the King was supposed to be.

PRINCE A. I took a video of my uncle and my mother having sex and sold it as part of the amateur housewives' porno collection. Thank you mother for not raping me.

PRINCE B. I looked up at the sky and saw several, low-flying passenger jets. What will they blast into next?

Soldier A fires his gun and Girl A falls.

PRINCE A. I was in the World Trade Center.

Soldier B fires his gun and Girl B falls.

PRINCE C. I lay in the empty coffin masturbating in rhythm to the world scraping against itself. I listened to the creaking squeaking world.

Soldier A fires his gun and Girl C falls.

The sound of a plane exploding. Two Soldiers climb over the barbed wire and approach Prince B. They force his arms behind his back, tie his hands, and lead him away. Princes A and C run away.

SOLDIER A. Banzai to happiness in the home!

SOLDIER B. Banzai to a healthy spirit!

---

3 Perhaps a reference to: "Something is rotten in the state of Denmark," (William Shakespeare, *Hamlet*, 1.4.90).

4 From Korean barbecue-style eating. The roast and *karebi* are different cuts of meat, while the *sanchu* is a lettuce and sauce combination in which the meat is rolled before eating.

PRINCE B. Without doubt, Hamlet's story made me gay. In the Palace, my first experience, with the buffoon Yorrick. My flower bud . . . He dribbled his saliva into my asshole and entered me. Later, a threesome with Rosencrantz and Guildenstern. As I expected, run-of-the-mill guys with mediocre technique. Oh, but distinguished Horatio. Horatio that I loved. When Ophelia found out, her menstruations went awry. That crazy old man Polonius told her. As for me, though, I was determined to have a pseudo-family.

To be sure, Polonius didn't want his daughter taken. I know this to be true. The father who never stopped wanting to commit incest.

Ah, Fortinbras, my long-distance lover in a faraway land. Polish men always cry from only one eye.[5] In my country that is full of empty laughter and complicity, Fortinbras taught us such ways of crying. A Latin man who loves pigs' trotters.

SOLDIER A. I don't want this story anymore.

PRINCE B. Well, then, what do you want?

SOLDIER A. Punishment and execution.

SOLDIER B. Hail Disney!

SOLDIER A. Hail McDonalds!

Suddenly, people surround Prince B and try to cut him into small pieces. A voice calls from a tower surrounded by barbed wire. It is Hamlet as Old Gay Prince, dressed in drag. Standing below is a political Party Leader/Woman and Prince C.

OLD GAY PRINCE. Unhealthy, unsound. A life that is finished should always be beautiful. This scene is obviously different from reality. Hatred is always lovely and the uprising is beautiful. Torture is like the cosmetics that cover a dirty body. It is always the murders on the streets that angels envy.

PARTY LEADER. That's right, Prince.

OLD GAY PRINCE. I am the only one, a Prince who conquered AIDS and continued to live a long life. My story is the drama of the

---

5 A reference to Poland, as a Soviet satellite state during the Cold War.

people. Alone, I'm a vast nothing. I haven't any dialogue or story. Everything has been left to the people. Only the people play out the drama.

PARTY LEADER. To read the drama as a history of drama.

OLD GAY PRINCE. Let the visitors through to this side.

PARTY LEADER. Yes. You, the masses. Now our country is unified.

The barbed-wire gates across the front of the stage are opened. The audience moves into the auditorium. The following texts by Old Gay Prince are projected onto the screen. Each time a text is projected thus, it signifies the voice of Old Gay Prince.

OLD GAY PRINCE/PROJECTION. This border was built as a lesson to the people of a country without borders. This lesson was unexpectedly successful. People managed to find a seed of racial discrimination even though they shared the same-colored skin. The unification of the country. Western Tokyo and Eastern Tokyo, communism or capitalism? Which blessing is suitable for the people of Tokyo to receive?

The last sentence of the previous dialogue echoes with the voice of Prince C. Party Leader and Women A, B, and C stand. They are dressed in black.

WOMAN A. This is Electra speaking.

WOMAN B. This is Juliet speaking.

WOMAN C. This is Ophelia speaking.

WOMAN A. This is Joan of Arc.

WOMAN C. This is Rosa Luxembourg.

WOMAN B. This is Marilyn Monroe.

WOMAN C. This is Scarlett O'Hara.

WOMAN A. A woman is a woman.

WOMAN B. She buries ideology in her wet crotch.

WOMAN C. Once fucked, such things no longer work.

WOMAN B. I will not wash such things as the underpants of the men of national parliament.

WOMAN A. I know no such thing as family happiness.

WOMAN C. I will not make anything like a gentleman's agreement.

WOMAN B. Long live hate and contempt, violence and death.

Prince C joins the women.

PRINCE C. I want to become a man.

Party Leader slaps Prince C.

OLD GAY PRINCE/PROJECTION. My brain is a scar that tempts destruction. Only a jumbled memory is a guide to the truth. Consciousness conspires with confusion. Half my life is strutted on stage, playing at the Imperial Theater. The last emperor of the new century. At the heart of the people's consciousness is always the desire for the last emperor. Autobiography is constantly inclined towards utopia. The turbulence of my mind gives rise to visions of civil war. I am punished for my self-loathing.

PARTY LEADER. Why?

PRINCE C. I want to ask the same question.

PARTY LEADER. Communism is invalid.

PRINCE C. How can you tell? You haven't even experienced it.

PARTY LEADER. I hate words like "proletariat."

PRINCE C. What would you know! The lowly daughter of a *tonkatsu*[6] man.

PARTY LEADER. I've got to where I am by myself.

PRINCE C. Don't you realize that unless you can give the people dreams, they aren't content?

PARTY LEADER. But you can't just say "communism" now—it's not so simple.

PRINCE C. I'm not!

PARTY LEADER. Well, then, do you have any other bright ideas?

PRINCE C. We must tell the people how fortunate they are not to be bothered by visions and dreams.

PARTY LEADER. Prince.

---

6 Pork cutlet dish, often cheap and eaten on the run.

PRINCE C. What?

PARTY LEADER. Nothing, I just felt like saying your name. Prince, Prince, Prince . . .

III. FAMILY PORTRAIT

A godlike and mythical photographic tableau of the Emperor's family doubles as Shakespeare's characters. Claudius and First Son, Polonius and Second Son, Horatio and Third Son, Gertrude and Mother, Ophelia and First Daughter. Old Gay Prince reflects on his life.

OLD GAY PRINCE/PROJECTION. The age of hope is coming to the suburbs. Happy thoughts grow inside me and wipe out the memory of bad dreams. Trees grow and the leaves spread thickly. The scent of the forest fills my senses, encasing my entire consciousness. I am the Prince of the Suburbs. In the city built after the bomb, I lost my father. At a wild orgy, mother got-it-on with my uncle.

CLAUDIUS. It is the privilege of a young man to have a gloomy face.

GERTRUDE. Do you think I brought him up badly?

HORATIO. Mothers always speak like that because they are animals wanting to affirm their own identity.

CLAUDIUS. The problem is that he (*Hamlet*) doesn't even look for work.

POLONIUS. It's the fault of society.

CLAUDIUS. How about him training at your company, Polonius?

POLONIUS. If you don't mind a girl like this. What do you think, Ophelia?

OPHELIA (*in a wheelchair, her whole body wrapped in bandages*). I won't be able to get married.

POLONIUS. That's why I'm telling you to.

OPHELIA. But I won't be able to.

GERTRUDE. What's so funny, Horatio?

HORATIO. One can live without working. Look at me. I'm living but I don't work.

POLONIUS. What is going to happen to this country?

HORATIO. Sometimes I talk about it with the Prince.

CLAUDIUS. I'd like to listen in on that.

HORATIO. The main point is to overthrow all existing conditions.

OPHELIA. Ha ha. I won't be able to get married.

CLAUDIUS. Education. The problem lies with school education.

Thief appears reading Shakespeare's Hamlet.

GERTRUDE. Here he comes.

HORATIO. Shush!

THIEF. Then I gave roles to the family. The reason that the family is so divided is that everyone was demanding a role to play. I finally realized that. I am Hamlet. My wife is Gertrude, the eldest boy is Claudius, the second is Polonius, the third is Horatio, and the eldest girl is Ophelia. Just now, I went to a lecture on Shakespeare at my local public theater. The lecturer, who is also a theater director, was arguing that theater contributes to the recovery of the human spirit. "In the world of today, everything is out of alignment." This is a gloomy story but I was born to make things right! So let's get going.

OPHELIA. Where are you going?

POLONIUS. To Hello Work, the job center, of course.[7]

GERTRUDE. Do you have your lunchbox? You know you can't afford to eat out when you don't have a job.

THIEF. I only had a bowl of plain soba noodles at the train station.

GERTRUDE. So you can save money.

THIEF. Denmark is a prison.

CLAUDIUS. This house is a prison.

GERTRUDE. Why don't you leave, then?

CLAUDIUS. It'll cost me too much money.

GERTRUDE. Well, if everyone's going to speak so plainly . . .

---

7 Haroowaku (Hello Work) is a chain of employment agencies in Japan.

CLAUDIUS. It's because you brought so many of us into the world. This is the age of one child per family, you know. But this household always wants to go against the norm.

THIEF. That's not what it's about.

POLONIUS. What isn't?

THIEF. Hamlet.

POLONIUS. Hello Work, right?

THIEF. To be or not to be, that is the question.

GERTRUDE. That's exactly right. It's pitiful.

THIEF. Um, somehow, I think we're being too realistic here.

POLONIUS. Don't you think that's good?

THIEF. No, it's not!

OPHELIA. What isn't? And don't talk so loudly.

CLAUDIUS (*opening a book and reading*).

If it were done when 'tis done, then 'twere well
It were done quickly: if the assassination
Could trammel up the consequence, and catch
With his surcease success; that but this blow
Might be the be-all and the end-all here,
But here, upon this bank and shoal of time,
We'd jump the life to come. But in these cases
We still have judgment here; that we but teach
Bloody instructions, which, being taught, return
To plague the inventor: this even-handed justice
Commends the ingredients of our poison'd chalice
To our own lips.[8]

Unnoticed, Thief walks behind Claudius and stabs him. Claudius falls to the ground.

THIEF. Those lines are not written here. (*Hits Ophelia on the head with a golf club. Hits Polonius with a baseball bat. Ophelia and Polonius fall.*)

GERTRUDE. What! A baseball bat?

---

8 William Shakespeare, *Macbeth* (1.7.1–12).

THIEF. Dumb sow! You probably didn't notice, but I knew. The moment they realized this bat was a weapon . . . (*swings the bat.*)

GERTRUDE. Is that your memory?

THIEF. Yes.

GERTRUDE. It's so sad. . .

THIEF. Because I'm a father. (*Removes the leather belt from his pants, puts it around Gertrude's neck, and begins to choke her. Gertrude goes limp.*)

OLD GAY PRINCE/PROJECTION. *Inside my consciousness, a forest sways in the wind. I become a featureless person. I am bored with the pleasures of being seen and speaking. To be socialized is to become bland and nothing. I am nowhere. The sound of breath at birth and its absence at death is the only truth.*

THIEF. The play was a failure. (*Runs away.*)

Everyone killed by Thief get to their feet again.

CLAUDIUS. Then what happened?

POLONIUS. Then what happened?

OPHELIA. Then what happened?

GERTRUDE. Then what happened?

HORATIO. The people left.

IV. LEADERSHIP STUDIES:
HOW TO BE A SUCCESSFUL IMPERIALIST

Enter Prince A and Horatio. Various photographs are projected onto the wall. Horatio starts to put make-up on Prince A's face. Thief rides by on a bicycle.

OLD GAY PRINCE/PROJECTION. I become a woman, amidst the destruction of war, the US occupation forces behind me.

The taste of Hershey bars remains as a memory on my gums. Mickey Mouse raped me. My cock wet with McDonald's ketchup, Donald Duck sucked me.

Wearing a suit and tie, my father worked in the public service built from the ruins. The country prospered from public works. There is little doubt that the first images seen by the children who flooded the subways with sarin were images of the Nazi gas chambers.

HORATIO. What a mess contemporary history is.

PRINCE A. My play won't happen anymore.

HORATIO. True, but they're demanding that we play it out no matter what.

PRINCE A. Who is?

HORATIO. The play that was not part of the contemporary history of this country. A premonition of civil war.

PRINCE A. There was, I was there.

HORATIO. Was a national boundary ever created?

PRINCE A. That was a bad dream.

HORATIO. You just put the people to sleep, you drug them.

In the midst of a peace that they didn't win by themselves, the people just want to be idle.

PRINCE A. They're intoxicated by a bad dream.

HORATIO. More than cool-headed understanding, what is needed now more than anything else is a clear ability to calculate.

PRINCE A. In what way?

HORATIO. Well, that is what we should try to learn. I'm totally disgusted with suffering this emptiness.

Horatio kisses Prince A. Prince A leaves. On the way out, he bumps into Thief. Thief picks up a piece of paper that Prince A has dropped and runs after him.

HORATIO. You, are you OK?

YOUNG MAN. This country is rotten.

HORATIO. Tell me something I don't know.

YOUNG MAN. I saw the Prince . . .

HORATIO. Don't worry. I let him go.

YOUNG MAN. How about me?

HORATIO. I didn't say anything.

YOUNG MAN. When are you going to tell him?

HORATIO. All in good time. He's still being trained.

YOUNG MAN. I wrote out a plan.

OLD GAY PRINCE/PROJECTION. The metropolitan self-defense ground forces and the armored division of the Kanto region are the main forces directed by the authorities to put the plans into action. The metropolitan defense forces should immediately take control of the following upon their dispatch: The police and the police communications center, the main branches of the Bank of Japan and other banks inside Tokyo, the financial calculations centers, the Tokyo Stock Exchange and computer center, the Tokyo electrical distribution center, the communications and telephone company NTT, the national broadcaster NHK, Japan Rail, all private rail lines, the Tokyo underground lines, and switching center.

  After the arrival of the armored division, when the defense force has successfully taken control of the above-mentioned utilities, comrades and sympathizes of the *coup d'état* occupy the Imperial Palace, Nagatachō, the Prime Minister's residence, and the surrounding Akasaka area, and declare the establishment of a new political order.[9]

HORATIO. Of course, I see. And then?

OLD GAY PRINCE/PROJECTION. Installing the head of the liberal opposition party as the head of Cabinet, who proclaims a national state of emergency and a one-year suspension of the Constitution. After a year, a national referendum is held on the rights and wrongs of the new political system. The dissolution of political parties is effected by drawing attention to the country's security. The success of the coup depends on the approval of America.

---

9 This quotation, about an imaginary overthrow of the post-war order in Japan, is from the right-wing critic and neonationalist, Fukuda Kuzuya. Japan's parliament is located in the Nagatachō area.

HORATIO. We'll need money.

YOUNG MAN. We'll need some weapons too.

HORATIO. We'll be busy.

YOUNG MAN. Please do your best. I am relying on you and your skills of persuasion.

HORATIO. This is for the good of the country. You make it sound like I'm bluffing people. People must know they have a responsibility.

YOUNG MAN. Don't worry. This is history in the making.

HORATIO. The masses are like a woman.

V. TRAINING BRIDES FOR HOME-MAKING DUTIES
(Or Classical Arts that Every Good Woman Should Know)

The Head of the political party and an armed Female Soldiers appear late at night in a drinking club. (No speaker nominated in the text.)

> I dreamed that in the month of October a general election and a state funeral were held at the same time.
> I dreamed that in the month of October a *coup d'état* and a revolution broke out at the same time.
> I dreamed that in the month of October both the land war and racial purification act was discussed at the same conference table.
> I dreamed that in the month of October Tokyo City separated into East and West.
> I have this cunt, which is the one thing in the entire world.
> I was raped.
> In a coffin-shaped bed, I cry out in a gasping voice, a voice as mighty as the world's inheritance, as I smell the body of an old man.
> A national treasure, I pissed on the street that is marked by the blood of a recent murder.

I plucked my pubic hair at the request of the male capitalist machine. I took off my underwear at the request of the Stock Market.

I was raped.

Just before the start of the rainy season on my way back from school, I was raped in the woodlands near a suburban sprawl.

I was raped as I traveled on the Chūō line in the morning.

The rapist threw himself on the tracks at Kokubunji.

So, whenever the train stops because of an accident or a suicide, I remember the smell of sperm.

I was raped in "Yaruki Jaya, Takanobaba shop."

I was raped in a karaoke bar in Nakano, on the Broadway side.

I got to know the word rape when I was raped.

The meaning of the word is painted on the wall that divides Tokyo into East and West.

Because you don't know the sweet taste of revenge.

Because you don't drink expensive wine with the young madams of Shiroganedai.[10]

Because you don't throw underwear stained with menstrual blood at middle-aged men at the street stalls.

Nausea, nausea, nausea. My nausea is the most beautiful in the world, the dirtiest thing in the world is I, and the smelliest thing is my cunt.

Inside my underwear it is even filthier than a middle-aged man who has piles.

Venereal disease or Chlamydia, which is truly the most lonely disease?

I didn't go to Egoist.[11] But I was raped and became a true egoist.

Nausea, nausea, nausea. My nausea, full of chocolate, the most proud.

At dusk, I buried my family in the woods near the suburbs.

There was a TV broadcast of the state funeral when I returned to my house.

---

10 A wealthy suburb of west Tokyo.
11 A beauty salon franchise.

The King's coffin moved along the street and passed the masses.

In the startling glare, I saw the Prince . . . a memory of a group attack.

Vulgar pedigree although high born.

Prince, I want to commit adultery with the memory of your murderous desire.

There is some more time yet.

It would have been OK to stop the story.

Don't be arrogant, there was never an age when things were not out of whack. You middle-aged diabetic!

But I don't hate that smell because I was always surrounded by it, full of rotten things, and the smell of decomposing things is the normal smell for me. Being rotten is my everyday existence.

So there is no assassination or betrayal.

Here, I opened up my legs as you wished! For the happiness of the people! After burying my family there was no role left for me, except for memories. Although, I knew that the memory was already written down.

A wave of racial purification marched towards the city following the state funeral and the election. The porn video that I acted in was confiscated.

In order to erase my memory, I drew lines in the city.

I formed a line that was like a border.

To escape from the kidnapping and entrapment, acts interpreted this way and that.

That was the beginning of our beautiful civil war.

I hate men . . . men who are worried about the state of the country.

For the first time I threw myself into political activities.

Ophelia, Polonius, and Gertrude enter. In a prison surrounded by barbed wire, the women change into girls' school uniforms.

POLONIUS. I will take care of all the expenses for the wedding.

GERTRUDE. Of course. It's the wedding of your own daughter.

OPHELIA. Ha ha. I won't be a bride.

GERTRUDE. I was a wife, the wife of Hamlet. King Hamlet, the great masturbator. Washing, cleaning, putting out the garbage, sucking cock. I was a good wife. It was just a fancy of mine to start thinking about killing my husband.

POLONIUS. You just want the insurance money.

OPHELIA. I won't be able to get married.

GERTRUDE. The only thing that men couldn't destroy is women's power to give birth to children. And the child loves the mother unconditionally. Husband. My husband. My honorable husband. All the wives in this country are slaves and chattel. But even these honorable men couldn't cut the bonds of love that slaves and chattel have. The married man soon realized that he must acquire the love of a child for himself.

POLONIUS. So that's how you women make men useless and vain. You say such things knowing their cruel effect.

GERTRUDE. I gave birth to a baby boy. I bought him up to be a real boy. Courageous and masculine. No matter what, he ran to my side whenever I faced peril.

POLONIUS. I feel like throwing up.

GERTRUDE. I have no luck with men whatsoever. My first husband was an army fanatic. He loved to play shooting games in army camouflage and collecting GI Joe dolls. My second husband was the younger brother of my first. He was an animation freak. He dressed me up like an action figure while he wanked into his underwear and masturbated me. My partner in fidelity . . .

POLONIUS. A man who wasn't a man.

GERTRUDE. No. A father who sexually abused his daughter.

POLONIUS. You misunderstood.

GERTRUDE. The lowest form of man, fucked-up men, completely hopeless luck with men. This is the reward I get, the so-called satisfying deal . . . cleaning, washing, cooking, and putting out the rubbish, sucking cock. . . . The only real man among you is my son!

POLONIUS. But that child was homosexual.

OPHELIA. Ha ha, tee hee.

POLONIUS. It's okay. I've given him extensive jerking-off training.

Gertrude and Polonius embrace each other (with sexual overtones).

OPHELIA. After forty years my father said he loved me. Then he went into the bathroom and locked the door, put up photographs of the children on the basin next to the black stockings and garter belts. He masturbated looking at those photographs and then hanged himself in the shower. It was his ultimate, final erection. And final orgasm. When my father died, a huge earthquake occurred and sarin gas was scattered in the subway. I could not hope for a better death if I tried. Because I feel guilty for having an abortion after being raped by a family member . . . you don't have to worry . . . I'm not going to say your name. The reason why my father committed suicide is that he thought I was no longer attractive.[12]

GERTRUDE *(to Polonius).* Do you want to sleep with my husband?

Ophelia gets up from her wheelchair and removes the bandages wrapping her body. Underneath, she is wearing a Japanese school-girl uniform.

Women appear dressed as Japanese schoolgirls. Their mobile phones start ringing in a variety of tones. The girls leave as if haunted by some spectre. Only Ophelia and Girl A remain.

Horatio appears.

HORATIO. Who are you?

---

12 Adapted from texts by Karen Finley with additional material by Kawamura.

Thief opens a piece of paper dropped by Prince A. In the distance Tramp is listening to the horse races on the radio with a vacant expression.

Horatio, Girl A, and Ophelia approach Tramp. Horatio takes a video camera from his bag and films Girl A and Ophelia. (Tramp has paid the girl to masturbate him.)

TRAMP (*to Girl A*). Don't you know who I am? (*Girl A is silent. To Horatio*) Why did you bring this useless prostitute along?

GIRL A (*protesting*). Don't call me that!

TRAMP. Don't play dumb. I know you're thinking things through, always calculating the margins. Hey (*to Ophelia*), how about you? You know me, right?

HORATIO. Please forgive her, she's new.

TRAMP. It doesn't matter. My name is Ishida. I was the Vice-Minister for Self-Defense. I was . . . always thinking about . . . the good . . . of the country. Those underground, left-wing scum destroyed this country. They destroyed the pride of the nation's people. Yes, it is I, Ishida the patriot, who went to Senkaku Island and planted the flag of the rising sun.[13]

OPHELIA (*suddenly*). I know, I know.

TRAMP. You know, ha! You (*to Ophelia*) swap with her (*Girl A*).

HORATIO. I said she's new.

TRAMP. Even better.

HORATIO. Now, no hitting or punching.

TRAMP. When did I ever smack anyone around?

HORATIO. You know full well that you often bash people up. That's why all the girls run away from you.

OPHELIA (*approaching Tramp*). Phew! You stink!

---

13 A reference to an event when right-wing neonationalists, including Tokyo Governor Ishihara Shintarō, visited Senkaku Islands (Senkaku Shotō, also known as Diaoyu Islands) to plant the rising-sun flag and thereby claim them as Japanese territory. The Senkaku Islands are a contested territory under claim by Japan, China, and Taiwan.

HORATIO. Of course he does.

OPHELIA. Yes, you really smell bad.

HORATIO. So?

OPHELIA. I'm upset.

HORATIO. About what?

OPHELIA. That a person can be this smelly.

HORATIO. What do you want to do?

OPHELIA. I want to see the Prince.

Tramp suddenly slaps Ophelia roughly. She starts to weep quietly.

HORATIO. There, you've done it again!

TRAMP. Don't speak of that family in front of me.

HORATIO (*to Girl A*). Get to work. Do your job.

TRAMP. You think my cock's so cheap that it'll get hard with this kind of stuff? Do you want to hear about my cock?

HORATIO. I don't care.

TRAMP. I was sued for sexual harassment.

HORATIO. By a secretary or someone . . .

TRAMP. It doesn't work unless it's in the rough hands of a labourer or soldier. You need big hands.

HORATIO. Now I know. That explains it. Is that why you always gave me a hard time?

TRAMP. I always feel like vomiting when I smell young women. You should praise me for having done a good job.

HORATIO. Shit. Revolutions aren't easy.

TRAMP. So suffer, young man.

HORATIO. I'll hand-job you. (*Reaches for Tramp's cock.*)

TRAMP. Oh no. No. Your hands are the hands of an artist, so it's no good.

HORATIO. Shit! Oy, old man. (*Whispers to Thief standing beside him with a blank expression.*) Can I borrow it?

THIEF. You know I don't have any.

HORATIO. Not money. Can I borrow your ass?

THIEF. Oh, ass. OK.

HORATIO. Fuckwit.

THIEF (*approaching Tramp*). You stink.

TRAMP. Too old.

THIEF. But I think he's firm enough. He's never done it before.

TRAMP. Now listen here. You should value life!

THIEF. Ha ha ha. Hey, I've heard something like that before. From the sex worker. After so many times. Ha ha ha ha . . .

TRAMP. Are you kidding me?

THIEF. No no no no.

TRAMP. You're just a dirty old man.

THIEF. That's a bit much, coming from you. God, you stink!

HORATIO. Oy. Get your clothes off, quickly now!

Thief and Tramp take off their clothes. Tramp rapes Thief.

TRAMP (*to Girl A*). I might get hard if you strangle me. Do it and see. (*Girl A strangles him.*) Yes, more. You're really good at this. That's the spot. That's the spot.

As the sound of the horse races stops, Tramp falls dead.

HORATIO. Is he dead? I'll make a video. Let's take him somewhere and you can pose like you're fucking him.

GIRL A (*pointing at Tramp*). With him?

HORATIO. Yes. While he's still warm.

Horatio carries Tramp on his back and leaves with Girl A. Left alone, Thief shakes the radio next to him, hoping to get some sound out of it. The horse races start again. He puts on the clothes that Tramp earlier removed and sits calmly.

THIEF (*to Ophelia*). Stop crying. It's never any good being sorry for yourself. Come here, young lady. Don't worry, I'm not going to do anything. This old man can't even get it up.

OPHELIA (*standing up*). Hey nonny nonny.

THIEF. Ophelia!

OPHELIA (*reading the text in a dead flat monotone*). Oh the heart that was so kind has become so cruel! This beautiful country, the revolution of this country, the coup was a perfect war, civil war personified. All the tramps rejoiced. But everything, everything is finished! I am a very unhappy and pitiful girl. Everything, everything is finished! Ah, how sad. Everything, everything is finished! (*Repeats and exits.*)

THIEF. Get thee to a nunnery, to a nunnery go! (*Sees her off.*) . . . We did it, what a great scene!

Claudius enters.

CLAUDIUS. What sort of life is this?

THIEF. Your Majesty!

CLAUDIUS. I am in the midst of inspecting how the people live. Don't you have a job for me?

THIEF. No, I'm afraid not.

CLAUDIUS. There's going to be a compulsory evacuation. I'm only telling you this because it'll look bad if you get hurt. You should go somewhere else. (*He looks at Thief whose expression is uncertain, anxious.*) I understand the feelings that you have towards me. But there is no relation between the changes now and your former military associations. It is only your sexuality that is of concern. Do you understand?

THIEF. What?

CLAUDIUS. Please be quiet for now. If you do, you'll be able to rejoin the Party later. The people here are forgetful, in time they'll forget . . . But you won't be able to be a parliamentary vice-minister like before . . .

THIEF. Sorry for all this trouble . . .

CLAUDIUS. You have a Japanese sword, right?

THIEF. What?

CLAUDIUS. Please be quiet! (*Finds a Japanese sword underneath the mattress in a cardboard-box shelter and exchanges it for his own.*) This is good. You're neither a spy nor an informer. You just didn't know. Let's have a drink sometime soon. We can talk all night about when the Japanese were real Japanese. (*Exits.*)

Thief picks up the sword from the mattress and removes the blade from the scabbard. He examines the blade. Young Man enters, looking harassed.

YOUNG MAN. Don't. Ishida. What are you doing?

THIEF. What?

YOUNG MAN (*snatching the Japanese sword*). There are police everywhere. (*Swings the sword as he speaks.*)

THIEF. You'll be seen too.

YOUNG MAN. Hide it. Hide it! Don't let it go out of your sight—whatever happens. Promise me. Soon the civil war will begin. As Ishida hoped and prayed, soon the inner city will become a battle zone. Here, the morning paper for you to read. I've already read it. Sell it and keep the money for yourself. (*Runs away.*)

Thief holds the newspaper. His family is visible in the background.

GERTRUDE. Papa.

CLAUDIUS. Dad.

POLONIUS. Father.

HORATIO. Old man.

OPHELIA. Father, Sir.

THIEF. You OK?

GERTRUDE. I've joined a new religion.

CLAUDIUS. I've joined a sect.

POLONIUS. I've joined the rightists.

HORATIO. I've become the owner of a brothel.

OPHELIA. I've started to appear in sex videos.

THIEF. You're all wrong. It's time you all lived more morally.

POLONIUS. This is the right balance. The story goes more smoothly if you aren't around.

OLD GAY PRINCE/PROJECTION. Destruction is blind. I won't make you dance anymore. Nothing remains. So what are you going to do? Are you going to fill up your disgusting daily life by looking for a miracle cure that doesn't exist? Will you overlook the street battles as you mumble on about wanting to help and be good? How about if you make a clone? Let's give the people something from the past.

No, I'm not going to do this. If I'm going to make a clone, I'm going to make my own clone. I want to make my DNA live long. Piece by piece, I want to carve the hatred and apathy of the world into a clone.

Papa, there is no drug, no miracle cure for this time. All that remains is the certain death of those who keep on looking. The shock of death gives people the hope for a miracle cure. It makes them feel they've taken a wonderful drug. I'm a clone of my clone. That's it. When the time comes, that's the only thing for it.

Two Soldiers appear.

SOLDIER A. Banzai to happiness in the home!

SOLDIER B. Banzai to a healthy spirit!

The Soldiers beat Thief with batons.

VII. A PERFECT MASSAGE PARLOR

OLD GAY PRINCE/PROJECTION. When I went outside, the moon was hazy with a green fog. Thinking about the new century I started to reflect on a new system for society, a new political structure. I became excited by thinking about the things that could connect the loneliness of communism with the solidarity of capitalism. My fecund state was cause for caustic comments from high-school girls as I walked to Kabukichō. I wanked, spraying my cum over the ruins of the wall dividing Tokyo into East and West. Two young soldiers came by and kicked my feet out from under me.

A group of high-school girls are in the barbed-wire prison. Ophelia moves among them.

GIRLS. Therefore I took a lot of sleeping tablets but nothing
    happened.
Therefore I slit my wrists with a cutting knife but nothing
    happened.
Therefore I thought about my life but nothing happened.
Therefore I fucked you for a whole night but nothing
    happened.
Therefore I went on a diet but nothing happened.
Hey nonny nonny.
Therefore I appeared in an adult video but nothing happened.
Therefore I went to the funeral of a famous rock singer who
    committed suicide but nothing happened.
Therefore I went to Shibuya and then went to Ikebukuro
    west-side park but nothing happened.
Therefore I beat up a thirty-eight-year-old language teacher
    but nothing happened,
Hey nonny nonny.
When I stopped going to the Egoist beauty parlor I became
    a true egoist.
I was raped.
Hey nonny nonny. Nonny nonny.
I live in an age of dead ends, a dead culture, and a dead-end
    world. With a dead-end job. My home is a dead end, my
    children's future is a dead end. A long, long street that is
    a dead end. Long, long street that is a dead end.[14]
Hey nonny nonny.

OPHELIA. I was Ophelia.

Horatio enters carrying a video camera.

HORATIO. Are you ready? (*Focuses the camera on Ophelia.*)

Ophelia pulls down her underwear and urinates.

PARTY LEADER. You slept with the Prince, didn't you?

---

14 Adapted from texts by Karen Finley with additional material by Kawamura.

Party Leader slaps Ophelia. Girls spread out. Dropping their underpants and crouching, they each urinate.

VIII. OVERSEAS RESEARCH REPORT: FROM THE LONDON STUDY VISIT

Claudius wears female underwear and talks to a female sex doll.

CLAUDIUS. I am embarrassed, don't look. This is my interpretation of the overseas research report from the London study visit.

Horatio aims the video at Claudius.

HORATIO. I got you on tape. (*Runs away.*)

CLAUDIUS. Stop that!

OLD GAY PRINCE/PROJECTION. Horatio goes on living thanks to the existence of the secret videotape.

PRINCE B. It wasn't Horatio to whom I gave the real instructions for dressing in drag, but Ophelia's big brother Laertes. I made him up to look like the prostitutes who hang out in St Dennis in Paris.

LAERTES (*in drag*). Do you want to eat my heart, Hamlet? Ha ha ha.

PRINCE B. That's not your line, is it?

LAERTES. I don't hate you.

PRINCE B. I don't blame you if you do. I made you go crazy, after all.

LAERTES. She was a terrible anorexic before you met her. She read all these suicide manuals. And who was it who decided that such books were dangerous?

PRINCE B. Your father.

LAERTES. I see. And who that declared "Kimigayo" the national anthem?

PRINCE B. My father.

LAERTES. Well, now, let the duel begin.

Claudius and Polonius enter carrying swords. Gertrude stands between them.

PRINCE B. This disagreement between these two men over my mother—it is not possible to resolve this. They refused the TV stations' proposal to stage the bout and are determined to fight this battle themselves. This is the true story of Hamlet. Laertes and I have no swords, though.

I was forced to fight duels countless times and countless times I and was killed. I'm tired of dying for the sake of people whose only sense of drama is the *Titanic*. I've seen this already.

LAERTES. I've seen it too. Want to buy some popcorn?

PRINCE B. No.

Claudius and Polonius begin fighting a duel. Horatio films them. At the end of the duel, Claudius, Polonius, and Gertrude are dead.

PRINCE B. And so the three of them die. Horatio sold the video for a lot of money to the TV station and used the money as a down payment for the forthcoming civil war. It was broadcast as a special program and the ratings where high. People declared it an important record of the twentieth century. The new leader of the country was Fortinbras. A young and spirited man, a man among men.

I retired from political life and opened a gay club with Laertes. And while it has been a rocky road, at times we've managed to make a happy life. Hamlet went on living. Even so, we never forgot politics.

Several gunshots are heard and Prince B holds a gun in the firing position.

LAERTES. You shouldn't waste bullets.

PRINCE B. It is necessary to prepare for the civil war.

LAERTES. You're so cool-headed about these things.

PRINCE B. Yes. I can't believe it myself, it's like I won the lottery.

LAERTES. You've become a nihilist without even realizing it.

PRINCE B. That's absolutely necessary in terrorism.

LAERTES. Let's agree on that. And re-read *Das Kapital*.

PRINCE B. We should work towards achieving a committed and full exchange with the public.

LAERTES. You're going to be terribly busy, aren't you?

PRINCE B. We should practice. Let's go to the park.

They approach a cardboard-box shelter. Inside they find Thief, wounded and covered in bandages.

PRINCE B. You've suffered a bad beating. Who did this to you? (*Thief is silent.*) Was it the Tokyo city workers? The local toughs? (*Thief is silent.*) Or was it a fight among yourselves? (*Thief is silent.*) Aren't you dissatisfied with society? (*Thief is silent.*) Let's fight! (*Holds out his right hand. Thief stays silent but also holds out his right hand. They shake hands.*) The working classes have lost the ability to speak.

LAERTES. We have to do something about that.

PRINCE B. Yes.

They leave. A Young Man appears and approaches Thief.

YOUNG MAN. Mr. Ishida, just a little longer. Please be patient.

Horatio appears.

YOUNG MAN. You should stop making fun of them.

HORATIO. Well, aren't you a man of the times!

YOUNG MAN. That's me for sure.

HORATIO. Is that so? You weren't so certain a little while ago.

YOUNG MAN. That was then, that was not me.

HORATIO. The principle of uncertainty should be strategic planning enough for this country. There's no point in deciding left or right.

YOUNG MAN. Has anything changed? Do you think there's any future to be had in Fortinbras's policy?

HORATIO. It's surprising you say such things. Although of mild temper, I think Fortinbras is a true patriot.

YOUNG MAN. It's sickening to think he has such fame without having any proper policies. What is needed is a strong country.

HORATIO. I don't think so. As long as we have a wise and adaptable nation.

YOUNG MAN. Although the target is still the same. It's you who has changed.

HORATIO. Shit! It's the current political order that is the most uncertain thing. But you're thinking about re-examining the framework, aren't you?

YOUNG MAN. No way. It's business as usual.

HORATIO. You sure about that?

YOUNG MAN. The glories of the past . . . give me the guns and we can overthrow all existing conditions.

Horatio hands the Boston Bag to Young Man. Fortinbras appears.

HORATIO. This is not good.

Young Man throws the Boston Bag at Thief.

FORTINBRAS. Oh dear oh dear, the video maker.

HORATIO. What! You're going out without a guard?

FORTINBRAS. Eating at *yakitori* stands and drinking *chūhai* under a bridge . . . it's the best way to experience life among the common people.

HORATIO. I see. I can well see the reason for your popularity.

FORTINBRAS. If you have any suggestions, please tell me. I'd like to consider them. Have I met you before?

YOUNG MAN. No.

FORTINBRAS. What are you doing here?

YOUNG MAN. We're a club in support of the Hinomaru and "Kimigayo."

FORTINBRAS. I see. That's good. That's good.

HORATIO. I take my leave. (*Exits.*)

YOUNG MAN. As do I. (*Exits.*)

Left alone, Fortinbras approaches Thief.

FORTINBRAS. I've looked everywhere for you, Ishida-san. I'm sorry you've had such a hard time of things. Could you please come back? You're the hero of the moment, of the new regime. You were a political prisoner, a refugee in this country. You show us the inhumanity of the past. I promise to give back what was taken from you. I will guarantee to give you back your twentieth century as it should have been. (*Exits*.)

Thief looks in the Boston Bag: it's full of guns and hand grenades. Thief is surprised, closes the bag, and moves away. Unable to resist, he finally takes out the weapons and arranges them in front of him.

THIEF. Over here! Over here! (*As if hawking his wares.*)

Man A enters, takes a gun, and starts shooting at random.

IX. PREMONITION OF CIVIL WAR

The middle of the night. Heavily armed women are talking in a lesbian club.

WOMEN. Diabetes! Gout! High blood pressure! Cirrhosis of the liver! Enlarged liver! Stroke! Cerebral hemorrhage! Subarachnoid haemorrhage! Let's stigmatize people with these diseases of old age. Let's brand them. Carers of sick people, brand them with failure.

We are a rash. A rash and menstruating!

All power to the rash and menstruating!

Cancer, cancer, cancer. Breast cancer and cancer of the womb are the symbols of the battle.

Wait. Don't you want to add HIV-AIDS? Let's think about that.

That's what the people who are ill say. We should have discussions right away!

What shall we do? Shall we add AIDS?

Before we discuss this, I have an objection to the theory of diseases of old age. Subarachnoid haemorrhage happens to young women too!

Diseases of aging are diseases of discrimination! Down with discrimination!

Let's not get bogged down by incidentals and small details
here!

But let's be frank and have a free discussion!

Freedom with responsibility!

Stop talking about morals and ethics. There is no freedom
with responsibility. Freedom will only come when we are
free of responsibility!

Let's destroy!

No, let's not! No no no no no! Smash and ruin, it's
so-o-o-o phallocentric. One ejaculation and everything's
over and done with.

What can be done? Cut it off? Standing up to cocks just
makes the cocks stand up!

Fight libido! Don't sew yourself up, don't sew your womb!
But fight!

Penetration means both conquest and subordination!

Libido, libido, libido, the core is hot, even as desire cools!

There is something rotten in this age of hope!

The last pathetic jokes of capitalism!

Okay, okay, let's put AIDS into the group!

OLD GAY PRINCE/PROJECTION. Hollow ringing and empty talk has never
produced any grand theories. Better that talk grows by practical means. The girls've already stopped talking about stories
of vision and hope after the revolution.

PARTY LEADER. Group Number Three to the electric company, Group
Number Four to the phone company.

OLD GAY PRINCE/PROJECTION. The girls stuck their thumbs in Marx's
asshole. They love reading the books of Ezra Pound. They
chew off the cocks of the fascists.

PARTY LEADER. The railways control center is Group Five.

OLD GAY PRINCE/PROJECTION. The ex-high schoolgirls learned that people realize latent homosexual desire only when they are
removed for the determinations of history and culture.

PARTY LEADER. To gain approval, the new government installs as its
mouthpiece a collaborator with a hotline to the White House.

OLD GAY PRINCE/PROJECTION. Politics, politics, politics, politics and women, women and politics, gays and politics, women and gays, perverts, perverts, perverts, perverts, perverts and women, gays and perverts, politics and perverts, politics and perverts, and women and gays.

PARTY LEADER. The emperor system should continue unchanged.

OLD GAY PRINCE/PROJECTION. I want to be rid of my story.

The women start to dance, and freeze only when Fortinbras appears. Prince B and Laertes continue dancing.

FORTINBRAS. Hamlet!

PRINCE B. Fortinbras!

They kiss passionately.

FORTINBRAS. What's with the get-up?

PRINCE B. Why? Something wrong with it?

FORTINBRAS. I don't like it. I told you before I don't like it. The Joan of Arc look. The Drag King thing.

PRINCE B. So?

FORTINBRAS. I don't like Drag Queens either.

LAERTES. You shit!

FORTINBRAS. I heard you, you queer!

LAERTES. Your cock's covered in shit.

FORTINBRAS. Grab the queer.

Soldiers appear and take Laertes away.

PRINCE B. But I don't understand?

FORTINBRAS. Horatio's been arrested. He's been charged with hiding a camera in an official residence. He wanted to blackmail me with a videotape of my life. I heard Claudius was also being blackmailed. Claudius's weakness was also discovered by the same method. So they're not partners, after all.

PRINCE B. Laertes isn't part of it?

FORTINBRAS. Horatio confessed everything. From the plans for a coup to everything else. But you're not a part of this, right?

PRINCE B. Let Laertes go.

FORTINBRAS. I can't. If I'm going to let anyone go it will just be you, Hamlet. Only you.

PRINCE B. That's unacceptable.

FORTINBRAS. Why do you care what happens to Laertes? It is because you feel guilty for leaving Ophelia.

PRINCE B. What happened to Ophelia?

FORTINBRAS. Didn't you know? She died. Shot by a stray bullet in some drive-by shooting.

PRINCE B. Who did it?

FORTINBRAS. A fifty-two-year-old unemployed man. Ophelia just happened to be there. The women are insisting she was assassinated. It's given them a cause—suddenly, women power is on the rise.

PRINCE B. When did it happen?

FORTINBRAS. Just recently. On a street in the second district.

PRINCE B. . . . I think it might be me who shot her.

FORTINBRAS. What makes you think that?

PRINCE B. I don't think I'm a complete woman, after all. Ophelia has done well to extract her revenge. I'm not a perfect woman yet.

FORTINBRAS. Exactly. You are simply a man, that's all.

PRINCE B. Arrest me.

FORTINBRAS. Are you sure?

PRINCE B. Yes.

> *Two Soldiers take Prince B away. We see Laertes and Horatio standing with their hands tied behind their backs and their eyes blindfolded. Prince B is made to stand in a plastic, children's bathing pool. The Soldiers shoot at the three of them. Young Man —upon seeing the failure of the coup—commits seppuku, i.e. ritual suicide.*

X. AS THE SHIP SAILS ON[15]

OLD GAY PRINCE/PROJECTION. The attempted coup by the National Defense Force organized by the young man was a failure. Of course, the agitation and disruption never reached even a single soldier in the inner circle. History was repeated as comedy. Even so, his act of hara-kiri was not a meaningless one. In the confusion over his death, the women's White Stalk Party started a civil war and took over the government. At their command I survived and lived through the troubles. The new government planned to have the Gay Prince as a symbol of the people. Everyone thought it would be a combined government of women and gays. The women were not stupid, they weren't a single cell of feminist separatists. They even invited Fortinbras to join them. By including a man who was popular with the public they made a pragmatic decision. That a lot of politicians, bureaucrats, and financial power brokers from the old system were arrested gave the people hope. The women carved lines from Shakespeare and Müller on my body. I became a perfect woman.

A souvenir photo of government officials is about to be taken.

PARTY LEADER. This way, Prince.

Prince C enters and joins the group for the photograph.

FORTINBRAS. Wait a minute. Ishida's not here. He's the director of the environment agency. He's the hero of the day who stopped the *coup d'état* planned by right-wing forces. A young man tried to attack him with a sword. Director Ishida got wind of their plan and swapped the rightists' steel sword for a bamboo one.

PARTY LEADER. So the attacker committed seppuku with a bamboo sword.

FORTINBRAS. Exactly.

PARTY LEADER. It must have hurt like hell.

Thief enters quickly, putting a tie on as he rushes to join the group.

---

15 The title of a 1983 film by Federico Fellini.

THIEF. Excuse me, I'm not used to this.

Thief joins the group and a photo is taken. They disperse as they leave.

THIEF. So, you're Hamlet are you?

PRINCE C (*stops*). Yes.

THIEF. I always admired you. A cheap, proletarian fuck-head like me, I always wanted to act like you. I wanted to be you.

PRINCE C. The time for class struggle has already passed.

THIEF. That's not true. Throughout history, there's never been a time when I could be a hero.

PRINCE C. Do you want to act?

THIEF. Oh yes. That's but a tiny hope of the people.

PRINCE C. What's so tiny about that?

THIEF. If you say so . . .

PARTY LEADER. Prince, I want to talk to you alone.

THIEF. I'll take my leave.

PRINCE C. Wait. He's one of us.

PARTY LEADER. Really?

THIEF. Yes. I'll do anything for Prince Hamlet.

PARTY LEADER. Really?

THIEF. I'll do anything, then my name will go down in history.

PARTY LEADER. You want to be a player?

THIEF. Yes, yes.

PARTY LEADER. Then kill Fortinbras.

PRINCE C. Party Leader, your beard's growing longer.

PARTY LEADER. Prince, I want you to be part of this plan too.

PRINCE C. Are you planning to make me act again?

PARTY LEADER. You can't just sit back and watch. I won't let you.

PRINCE C. Not that boring play again!

PARTY LEADER (*to Thief*). I'll give it to you. (*Hands a gun to Thief.*)

PRINCE C. At the end of the twenty-first century?

THIEF (*receiving the gun, he announces in a clear voice*). To be or not to be, that is the question.

PARTY LEADER. You're doing so well. Keep up the good work.

THIEF. Everyone, look at me. Your father's doing an excellent job.

PRINCE C. Ophelia!

THIEF. Ophelia is you. Hamlet is I. Get thee to a nunnery. A nunnery.

Fortinbras enters.

FORTINBRAS. Well now, the Communications Intercepts Bill exists for this kind of purpose. Tapping phones, eavesdropping, it's not illegal anymore.

Two Soldiers appear.

PARTY LEADER. Hamlet, shoot!

A short battle ensues. The Soldiers collapse. Party Leader runs away.

FORTINBRAS (*shot, breathing softly*). You repay good with evil. Although I made you one of us, on this side. The proletariat is in the end the proletariat. There is no story. (*Dies.*)

Thief runs away. Prince C cuts his wrists with a knife and holds his arms high in the air. Blood drips down his arms.

PRINCE C. This is Ophelia. I love the emptiness of the world. I love its hollowness. I love nothingness. Facing the city that has destroyed the entire world, I send out e-mails in the name of the victims. I bury the emptiness in my face. I bury the hollowness in my breasts. I swallow the void in my womb. I choke between my thighs the province of interpretation and stories. The main point is to overthrow the happy ending, overthrow hope and the subordination of capital. When she walks through your bedrooms carrying butcher knives, you will know the truth.

OLD GAY PRINCE/PROJECTION. Even with all this, I didn't die. I was put under house arrest. From my life in prison, my body changed back to a man.

IMAGE 3.2 **Prince C commits suicide.**
Sonoko Soeda as Prince C. *Hamletclone*, German tour, 2003.
Photograph by Katsu Miyauchi.

XI. THE BIRTH OF A NATION[16]

Thief appears with the Boston Bag. He takes out a gun and shoots.

THIEF. Don't think I'm a fool. No more am I a cheap Thief. I'm the
Minister. Minister! I've become a great man. I'm going to tram-
ple over all the people who looked down on me. Company men.
High-school girls, boys with long hair. I am going to triumph
over you, I am going to triumph over you, I am going to triumph
over you, I am going to triumph over you. (*Continues to shoot.*)

---

16 The title of a 1915 film by D. W. Griffith. Considered a masterpiece of the early
American cinema, the film is also explicitly racist. Based on the story *The Clansman*
by a white supremacist church minister named Thomas Dickson, it has been report-
edly used as a recruitment film for the Klu Klux Klan.

IMAGE 3.3 **After the Old Gay Prince's last monologue.**
Hamletclone, German tour, 2003.
Photograph by Katsu Miyauchi.

OLD GAY PRINCE/PROJECTION. This is the story of my people. Ten days that shook the land. History sped up. The lecture on drama given in the new public theater was the beginning of the revolution and civil war. A moment of hope for the people of the suburbs. Clear felling of the trees was terminated. The leaves on sway in the gentle breeze of early summer. Happiness is only born when the word itself has been forgotten. Just mention the word and the suburban civil war will go on and on. I dreamed of cram school as I slept in the backyard.[17] From

17 *Juku* or cram schools, specializing in preparing students for competitive entrance exams, are common in Japan. Students attend *juku* in the evening after regular school and can be as young as five years old. Many educational specialists are critical of *juku*, where students rote-learn subject material and also suggest that such intense pressure on students who succeed gives rise to social problems.

resting on my bare feet, an ant climbed into my nose and pierced my heart. A heart that beats between the sentiments of ill will and reconciliation. I was Hamlet. A prince of depravity and corruption who was born of depravity and corruption. The ruins of Japan lay at my feet. The women reach out in anticipation. In the streets, random massacre. Having lost the ideal of politics, to take part in the massacre is to take part in history. Political asylum and refugees . . . these things won't end. But the new century will begin when the dishonest look for the hatred and love within themselves. Again, the happy ending is suspended at the end of the twenty-first century. I don't want to be cured. I don't want to be saved.

Civil war breaks out on the street. Thief shoots Old Gay Prince in his tower.

OLD GAY PRINCE/PROJECTION. Then I collapse. Shot by a nameless assassin. The bullet penetrates my left lung and a new emptiness is born. My autobiography is now complete. The title is *The Birth of a Nation.*

The barbed-wire cage is opened by the hands of dead people.

The End

IMAGE 4.1 **Rokujō, as a ghost, returns to express her love for Hikaru**

Rei Asami as Rokujō and Hiroki Hasegawa as Hikaru. *Aoi*, Setagaya Public Theater, Tokyo, 2007.

Photograph by Katsu Miyauchi.

AOI

CHARACTERS

TŌRU

AOI

HIKARU

ROKUJŌ

AOI

TRANSLATED BY AYA OGAWA

An indistinct space. A room that seems to exist out of time. A human-sized doll, devoid of any features, sits on a chair facing downstage. The doll has a head of long hair, and Tōru is practicing cuts on it. He senses a shift and stops his work.

TŌRU. What . . .

> *As if to test his intuition, he executes another cut with his scissors. The snipping sound reverberates. Aoi appears.*

AOI. Is Hikaru here?

TŌRU. Miss Aoi . . . Are you all right now?

AOI. Yes. It turned out to be nothing. I guess I must have a really sensitive disposition. Hikaru's always scolding me about it.

TŌRU. I'm glad to hear you're well. We should celebrate your release from the hospital.

AOI. Thank you. You're always so kind to me, Tōru, you give me the strength to go on.

TŌRU. You've got Hikaru too.

AOI. No. It's not like that with Hikaru.

TŌRU. . . . Don't worry. Hikaru's always thinking of you.

AOI. Hikaru cares only about my hair.

TŌRU. Your hair? The hair on your head?

AOI. Yes.

TŌRU. It's only natural for Hikaru to be drawn to your hair, Miss Aoi. You have the most perfect blue-black hair. The best for someone who cuts hair.

AOI. Even you admit it. That's what I said: Hikaru loves only my hair.

TŌRU. That's the same thing as his loving you.

AOI. I wonder.

TŌRU. It's true.

AOI. Do you really believe that?

TŌRU. Of course, Hikaru has his own idiosyncrasies. But people with extraordinary talent are all like that.

AOI. . . . Um, is Hikaru here?

TŌRU. Oh, didn't you know? It's his day off.

AOI. That's right . . . I'm so stupid.

TŌRU. Should I give him a call?

AOI. That's all right. Please don't worry about me, Tōru. Don't let me interrupt your work. I'm sorry to have bothered you.

TŌRU. Don't worry, Miss Aoi. I'm just practising.

AOI. Practising?

Tōru removes the wig from the doll. Aoi cries out in surprise.

TŌRU. What's the matter?

AOI. Oh my god, I just thought it was a real person.

TŌRU. This is just for practice.

AOI. I didn't know you had anything like this.

TŌRU. Yes. But it doesn't compare to human hair. Hikaru's right. You've got to practice on hair that is alive. Cutting dead hair doesn't give you the feel of it at all.

AOI. Is this person dead?

TŌRU. . . . I'm going to call Hikaru. (*Takes out his cellphone.*)

AOI. Use me for your practice, Tōru.

TŌRU. I couldn't.

AOI. Why not? Are you saying I'm already dead?

TŌRU. . . . What are you talking about?

AOI. Please cut my hair. I came all the way here for a haircut.

TŌRU. Hikaru will be angry.

AOI. I'll tell him I begged you to.

TŌRU. Then I guess I have no choice.

AOI. Do you think I'm being selfish?

TŌRU. I wonder?

AOI. I'm selfish.

TŌRU. Not really . . .

Tōru removes the doll from the chair and Aoi sits. Tōru stands behind her.

TŌRU. How do you want it?

AOI. It's up to you, Tōru.

TŌRU. Tell me something, even if it's just a feeling, of how you want it.

AOI. I can't. I just let Hikaru have his way with me.

TŌRU. All right . . . (*Begins to cut, but stops himself.*) I can't do this. I'll call Hikaru. (*Takes out his cellphone and leaves.*)

AOI. Wait . . . (*She is left alone. She remains facing downstage.*) It's you again. We're friends by now. You look so blurred on the other side of the mirror. Are you under water? What are you doing there? You keep beckoning me. Is it so comfortable over there? Perhaps you actually are me? I can tell exactly what you're thinking. I can read you as easily as if you are thinking my very own thoughts. I don't want to be defeated by you. Ugly? You're talking to me for the first time. Ugly? Me? Of course, I know that. Anyone can see that I'm ugly. Liar? Me, a liar? Give back your hair? Why? You already have such gorgeous jet-black hair. Please stop it, stop pulling my hair. You're hurting me, stop it. Stop pulling my hair! Stop! Daddy! (*Faints.*)

Hikaru enters, approaches Aoi.

HIKARU. Aoi . . . (*Picks up the hair fallen on the floor.*)

Tōru enters.

TŌRU. Oh!

HIKARU. Did you cut this?

TŌRU. That . . . No, it wasn't me.

HIKARU. You shouldn't have done that.

TŌRU. But I didn't do it. That's dead hair.

HIKARU. Don't talk back to me.

TŌRU. No, you misunderstand me. There's no life in that hair.

HIKARU. There's no such thing as lifeless hair. You've completely forgotten what I say all the time.

TŌRU. No, that's not . . . Just forget it.

HIKARU. Forget it? If there's one thing I've taught you, it's that hair, even when it's been severed from its roots, still bears life.

TŌRU. I know, but you misunderstand me. I was practicing on a mannequin when Miss Aoi arrived and asked me to cut her hair. The hair in your hands is from the mannequin.

HIKARU. . . . How idiotic.

TŌRU. It seems Miss Aoi has been released from the hospital. Congratulations.

HIKARU. She escaped from the hospital and came here. She hasn't been cured. She's only getting worse. (*Tōru is silent.*) . . . So, you didn't cut her hair?

TŌRU. Whose?

HIKARU. Who do you think? Aoi's.

TŌRU. Of course not!

HIKARU. You really are a boring man.

TŌRU. Sometimes I don't understand you at all.

HIKARU. You should have said you cut her hair, even if it was a lie.

TŌRU. I don't get it. Why would I lie about that?

HIKARU. To make me jealous. It would have made this tedious world just a little bit amusing.

TŌRU. . . . I'll sweep the floor. (*Begins to leave.*)

HIKARU. No need to clean up right away. It's all dead hair anyway. Now listen to me, because I'm not done yet.

TŌRU. Miss Aoi belongs to you.

HIKARU. Belongs? Like an object, hm? Then I can trade her in for something else, or even throw her away, right?

TŌRU. Is it really like that?

HIKARU. No. She isn't an object. She doesn't belong to me. Aoi is Aoi. She doesn't belong to anyone. In fact, if anything, that girl's a kind of disease.

TŌRU. Disease?

HIKARU. She's a sublime sickness that no one can cure. I'm not talking about her recent attack. Long before that, ever since I met her, she's been a glorious sickness.

TŌRU. So, you do love Miss Aoi, after all.

HIKARU. I'm amazed you can utter such embarrassing words.

TŌRU. If that's not love, what is?

HIKARU. All you commoners try to sum up everything with that word. My relationship with Aoi is not that simple.

TŌRU. . . . As a commoner Joe Schmoe, may I venture to say something?

HIKARU (*laughing*). Go ahead.

TŌRU. Don't you think that it is precisely your bizarre attitude that is making Miss Aoi's illness even worse?

HIKARU. You don't understand, do you? That girl's always been sick.

TŌRU. When you brought her here for the first time, she was the very picture of good health.

HIKARU. Health? That's evidence of your own limitations right there. You weren't capable of recognizing her illness.

TŌRU. Miss Aoi was a very cheerful woman, straightforward and smart.

HIKARU. You'd better return to your backwoods.

TŌRU. To be honest, I was shocked to hear that someone who seemed so healthy had just come out of hospital.

HIKARU. What, you're still harping on about her seizure? You're saying it was my fault she had her attack? I see. I didn't realize you were talking on such a superficial level. Listen closely to what I'm saying. You must try to understand that I was thinking on a level far deeper, on a cosmic scale. If all of your thoughts are grounded on your standing here in this room, imagine that I am suspended in zero gravity in outer space. There's no point in us trying to have a conversation from such different standpoints. So let's not even bother. All I'm going to say is that you're wrong about one thing: Aoi's recent seizure and hospitalization have nothing to do with me. Her condition's been worsening from half a year ago. And I know why. Don't you? It's the hair. How many times have I said so? Even the strands that fall to the floor have life in them. Every strand—immersed in the memories and lives of the women it's cut from—is still alive. That's why, when we sweep the floor we have to be extremely careful and not miss a single hair. Because if each hair were to war with another, the matter would be out of our hands.

TŌRU. Are you saying that Miss Aoi's sickness stems from someone else's hair?

HIKARU. It's the price of failing to clean carefully. I'm not blaming you.

TŌRU. No. If that's truly the case, then it is my fault.

HIKARU. No, it's me. I wasn't good enough.

TŌRU. You do love her, after all. You love Miss Aoi.

HIKARU. It's no use talking to a country bumpkin like you.

TŌRU. "Country bumpkin" suits me just fine.

HIKARU. Your skills are never going to develop.

TŌRU. I'll sharpen my skills in my own country-bumpkin way.

HIKARU. You'll never get anywhere. (*His cellphone rings. He takes it out and looks at the screen. It stops ringing. He stands there in silence. Then leaves.*)

Tōru watches him leave, then brings out the cleaning supplies and sweeps the floor. Aoi regains consciousness.

AOI. Tōru . . .

TŌRU. Miss Aoi, are you all right?

AOI. This time you'll really cut my hair, won't you? Promise me.

TŌRU. . . . I'll get Hikaru. (*Exits.*)

Aoi walks to the far end of the room and leans against the wall. Hikaru appears suddenly and leans against the wall in a similar manner.

AOI. Where were you?

HIKARU. I could ask you the same thing.

AOI. I was inside a water tank.

HIKARU. An aquarium, huh?

AOI. Probably. It wasn't the ocean or a lake.

HIKARU. You must have been swimming. Was it fun?

AOI. I was dragged into the water, by a woman. I know her. Her name is—

HIKARU. Don't say it! Think about something happy. Only about things that make you happy.

AOI. Then I'll think about you, Hikaru. My executioner. Tell me: Where were you?

HIKARU. Just as you wished, at the execution grounds. How do you want to die?

AOI. I don't want to be hanged. I'd like to be a beautiful corpse.

HIKARU. Injection?

AOI. Boring.

HIKARU. Electrocution?

AOI. No.

HIKARU. Bullet?

AOI. They'd shoot my face, right? I don't think so.

HIKARU. I'm stuck . . . Guillotine? Not likely.

AOI. Yes. That sounds lovely.

HIKARU. But if your head is severed from your body, I won't be able to embrace you. Let me think of something better.

AOI. Have you given any thought to my funeral?

HIKARU. Yeah.

AOI. Where will I be buried?

HIKARU. Behind a small church at the foot of a dormant volcano.

AOI. That sounds lovely. Don't cremate my body. You'd forget me quickly if I became a pile of ash.

HIKARU. That's not true.

AOI. I still want my flesh and blood, even in death. I want to feel my body rotting. Hikaru, promise to make love to me even when I'm dead. Come to me, once a week. But there's no way you could make love to my decaying corpse.

HIKARU. Didn't you know? There's nothing better than a decomposing pussy.

AOI. Where did you learn that?

HIKARU. I discovered it myself. When we're alone, just the two of us, it feels as if we both cease to exist in this world. (*Grasps Aoi's hair in both hands and embraces her violently.*)

Aoi swiftly walks forward, escaping his clutches, and sits on the chair. Hikaru chases her.

AOI. Could I get a haircut, please?

An enormous mirror descends. Aoi looks into it.

HIKARU. How would you like it cut?

AOI. You want to make me your corpse, don't you Hikaru? As you please. (*Hikaru begins cutting her hair.*) Do you like hair, Hikaru?

HIKARU. Yeah.

AOI. Do you like my hair?

HIKARU. Of course.

AOI. What about my hair down there?

HIKARU. I love it. But I prefer the hair on your head.

AOI. Perhaps you love only my hair, Hikaru.

HIKARU. . . . Well, it is my profession.

AOI. That's not what I'm asking.

HIKARU. The feel of your hair is unbeatable.

AOI. Does it make you hard?

HIKARU. Yeah. I'm hard right now. Feel . . . See?

AOI. But Hikaru, it's not only my hair that you like, is it?

HIKARU (*stopping*). What are you trying to say?

AOI. I found it. Your collection of hair, Hikaru.

HIKARU. . . . . I told you not to go into that room. Just forget what you saw. You shouldn't have.

AOI. Are they all from different women?

HIKARU. Yeah.

AOI. So you can remember each and every one.

HIKARU. No. They're just to test my sense of touch from time to time. It doesn't matter whose hair it was. I'm just interested in the varied textures. The people, their faces and bodies, that I'm sick of. Do you understand, Aoi? That's the kind of man I've become.

AOI. Are you sick of me, too?

HIKARU. You've still got a face and body. You're the only one, Aoi. As long as you've seen my collection, I might as well tell you what I've never told anyone else.

AOI. Is it something scary?

HIKARU. Perhaps, depending on who you are.

AOI. I'll listen to anything you have to say.

HIKARU. All right. The secret of my sex life: I fondle, stroke, and indulge in all the hair I've collected while I pleasure myself.

AOI. Whose hair?

HIKARU. I told you, it doesn't matter. And it's a different person's every time. I don't remember who they are. I have no such memories. I only care about the way the hair feels.

AOI. You must be having that woman's hair in your collection?

HIKARU. That woman?

AOI. That woman. She told me her name from inside the mirror.

HIKARU. Aoi, stop it.

AOI. That woman, she said she'd curse me. She said she wanted to kill me. Her name is—

HIKARU. Don't!

AOI. Her name is—

HIKARU. If you say her name, you'll be doing exactly what she wants you to do.

AOI. Her name is . . . Rokujō. (*The moment she finishes her sentence, her face and body are frozen.*)

HIKARU. Aoi! Aoi!

Tōru runs in.

TŌRU. What happened?

Hikaru's cellphone rings. He looks at the screen and quickly answers it.

HIKARU. It's you, isn't it?

AOI. H-E-L-P M-E!

TŌRU. Hold on, Miss Aoi!

HIKARU. You're very close, aren't you? I know you are. I can tell everything you're thinking and doing. Stop acting like a stalker. It's fine if it were just me, but you have to stop disturbing Aoi. Aren't you ashamed of yourself, doing things like this? Hello? Are you listening to me? If there's something you're unhappy about, why don't we meet somewhere and sort it out, once and for all? Hello? Why don't you say something? You're the one who called me, don't keep me on the line with your silence. Hello? Hello? (*Meanwhile, Aoi, her arms frozen in a strange position, rises out of the chair, and floats through the air, parallel to the ground. Tōru watches her, stunned, as she disappears. Tōru runs after her. Hikaru realizes Aoi has disappeared from the chair.*) Aoi, where are you?

Rokujō stands on the other side of the mirror, talking into her cellphone. Hikaru seems not to see her.

ROKUJŌ. I'll never forget. How could I forget.

HIKARU (*into his cellphone*). Hello? You just said something. Can you repeat it, please?

ROKUJŌ. It's Rokujō. I have a two o'clock appointment.

HIKARU. So it was you. What did you do with Aoi?

ROKUJŌ. That chair was reserved for me.

HIKARU. You're close, aren't you? Hello? . . . Hello? . . . If you're close by, please come into the salon right away.

Rokujō puts her cellphone away and slowly appears from behind the mirror. Hikaru is suddenly aware of her presence.

HIKARU. We're finally here.

ROKUJŌ. It's been a long time, Hikaru. My, how you've grown!

HIKARU. And you, you haven't changed a bit.

ROKUJŌ. That makes me happy, even if you are lying.

HIKARU. Let's talk things out, calmly.

ROKUJŌ. Calmly? Aren't we both calm enough? Do you really find it necessary to say that?

HIKARU. What do you want?

ROKUJŌ. What do I want? What an exaggeration. I just came here to get my hair cut by you, that's all. (*Picking up the hair from the floor*) That girl's hair. So young. Such resilience and gloss. (*Tries to sit on the chair on which Aoi was sitting a while ago.*)

HIKARU. Don't sit there.

ROKUJŌ. Same attitude as six months ago. Is she that good? (*Blows Aoi's hair into Hikaru's face.*) What an awful salon. Treating a loyal customer like this. Where is it you want me to sit, then?

HIKARU. Bring her back to me.

ROKUJŌ (*laughing*). "Bring her back," he says. Certainly. She's not an object. The way you talk. I can't keep listening to you, Hikaru. I never taught you to carry yourself like that.

HIKARU. I am not yours anymore.

ROKUJŌ. You, mine? Was there ever a time that were true? I may have taught you how things work in this world, but turning you into an object? Don't make me out to be a disgusting woman.

HIKARU. Please stop torturing her. If you have to harm anyone, let it be me.

ROKUJŌ. You don't understand. That girl's pain is something that was within her from the beginning. Stop making such desperate faces. It doesn't suit you. That's an expression that girl forced upon your face. I know it. That kind of girl always turns men into boring soft things. Don't worry, Hikaru. Your precious little girl is fast asleep on the other side. (*Points to the mirror.*)

HIKARU. The other side?

ROKUJŌ. Yes, the other side, where all your hidden emotions appear as flames or water. If that girl spends some time there burning herself on her own emotions, she might come out the other side as a sophisticated woman.

HIKARU. She's not like that. She doesn't exist in the realm of emotions that translate into fire or water.

ROKUJŌ. That little shit, she's just a brat. She's afraid of having such emotions. Hikaru, you must be fed up, dealing with that brat's world. That's probably it. That's why you called me.

HIKARU. Always putting things in terms that are convenient to themselves. That's why I can't stand old women.

ROKUJŌ. How dare you!

HIKARU. I didn't call you here.

ROKUJŌ. Then why am I here?

HIKARU. I don't know!

ROKUJŌ. You summoned me, that's why. I wouldn't have come unless you called. I'm an extraordinarily busy woman. So, Hikaru, tell me. Why are you so concerned about that girl?

HIKARU. Because I love her . . .

ROKUJŌ. You love her? Give me a break! I can't believe you've begun using such words.

HIKARU. No, no! It's not love, I can't stand love!

ROKUJŌ (*smiling*). You're wonderful, Hikaru. That face you just made, just like the way you were before. You were a nobody back then, and even more disdainful for it.

HIKARU. What exists between me and that girl cannot be expressed in words.

ROKUJŌ. What you're referring to is quite different from love. You recognize that yourself, don't you? To tell you the truth, I was in love with you. Did you love me?

HIKARU. Yes.

ROKUJŌ. You see?

HIKARU. But you liked me for being the kind of man who wouldn't so easily utter the word love, didn't you?

ROKUJŌ. That's right.

HIKARU. So which is it? Make yourself clear.

ROKUJŌ. You should have loved only me.

HIKARU. You're too obvious. That story's long been over. Now, Rokujō, please go to the other side. And return that girl to me.

Rokujō, after a long silence, starts moving toward the mirror but then stops midway.

ROKUJŌ. It's not over . . . Do you truly believe that it will ever be over? Ensnaring me by labelling me as too obvious? (*Her eyes are glued on Hikaru.*) You're the one reduced to being such an obviously grown-up man.

HIKARU. You turned me into this.

ROKUJŌ. No. I'm disappointed with you. You never used to be like this. Let's talk about how we used to be.

HIKARU. If it'll make you happy.

ROKUJŌ. You speak so coldly to me. When you were my accomplice . . .

HIKARU. I don't know what you're talking about.

ROKUJŌ. When I first met you, you were twenty-two. Cherry blossoms should have been in full bloom, but it was a very cold spring that year. He took you to a restaurant famous for it's view of the flowers, but you sat by yourself with your back to the windows. Looking at you I thought the cherry branches were sprouting out of your body. You had wrapped that trunk of a cherry-tree body of yours in an Italian suit.

HIKARU. Italian suit? More like a plain suit off the rack. The master was certainly stingy. He never wasted money on anything. Rich folk are all alike . . . . Don't get me wrong, I was grateful. I'll never forget what he did for me. The master was the man who opened the door to my current success.

ROKUJŌ. Stop calling him "the master!" What does that make me, his maid? His slave?

HIKARU. That's not what I meant. You're a completely independent adult woman.

ROKUJŌ. You have a way of saying things that sound so inconsiderate . . . When I met you, I became free. First cherry branches, then wings. I could see the wings unfolding from your back. Wings that were yet to completely unfurl, the feathers that looked so charmingly naive. That's how you were when you first flew down to perch beside me. Just a young man burning with wild ambition. But in your eyes a kind of empty look. You'd have such a knowing expression on your face at times, a look of such deep understanding of everything. It was that expression that I couldn't endure. I knew the reason behind that look. It was because, sexually, he had you completely under his control.

HIKARU. What are you saying?

ROKUJŌ. And I thought, if I don't liberate you from him then your wings would rot away. Even though I couldn't bear that empty expression on your face!

HIKARU. Let's stop this trip down memory lane.

ROKUJŌ. You belonged to my husband.

HIKARU. There you go again. Please just stop it.

ROKUJŌ. No, I won't. This is very important. He was the master. You and I, we were both his servants, his slaves. We bore that role, you and I. Slaves to that jiggling body of his, the fat swollen . . . to his lust for control. Isn't that so?

HIKARU. That's absurd. I don't want to answer that. Why don't you go ask your master?

ROKUJŌ. Silly, how could I?

HIKARU. The master merely recognized my innate talent, that's all.

ROKUJŌ. My master. A man. A man of strength. A man of wealth. A man among men, who basked in the admiration of the world. And his manner of controlling others was always the same. He was the kind of man who couldn't sleep unless he'd drawn everyone around him into submission. I was determined to save you from him. Why do you think that was? It happened when I went to your salon. You came and stood behind me. In the mirror I could see your wings spreading. And the moment you put your fingers in my hair . . . Put them in. Now. (*Hikaru puts his fingers in her hair*.) Good. It still feels the same. A sublime sensation that only a nobody possesses.

HIKARU. That's enough now. Please go home. I won't ask for her back. I'll find Aoi myself.

ROKUJŌ. . . . The time we spent together, were you happy?

HIKARU. Yes. I'm grateful to you for it.

ROKUJŌ. Grateful?

HIKARU. You made me into a fine man.

ROKUJŌ. What do you mean?

HIKARU. You made me into a social entity.

ROKUJŌ. I don't understand what you're talking about. Social entity?

HIKARU. It's awkward for me to say this myself, but I'm now considered a man of charisma. And it's all because of our relationship. You groomed me into an adult man who now possesses money and power.

ROKUJŌ. That's not true! That I made you into such a man. Money and power? That's just like my husband! I cherished you for the anonymous non-entity you were. I only taught you how to remain who you were and live proudly.

HIKARU. That's what you say, but in the end what you taught me was how to grow up into a man.

ROKUJŌ. Stop it! "Make into a man," "turn into a man." You ought to keep living without any of those constructs.

HIKARU. In this world, it's impossible for a non-entity to retain its essence.

ROKUJŌ. You're saying you've become a man, in the end.

HIKARU. I'll amend what I said before: You made me into a fine human being.

ROKUJŌ. Not a man?

HIKARU. That's right.

ROKUJŌ. Good. So, you still have the qualities of a non-entity.

HIKARU. No. I'm a bona fide man.

ROKUJŌ. No!

HIKARU. I saw many women before I met Aoi. If I'm a man now, it's probably due to all the time I spent with those women.

ROKUJŌ. I know that, darling. Even when you were with me you were seeing several little girls. Don't think I didn't know it! I only pretended to not know. I thought it was part of an important lesson for you, so I didn't say anything. To think that you would end up like this! Tell me, how many did you sleep with?

HIKARU. I didn't keep count.

ROKUJŌ. So many that you couldn't keep count, you fucking slut!

HIKARU (*surprised, dumbstruck*). . . . What did you just say?

ROKUJŌ (*continuing without realizing what she said*). You think there is another woman like me? A woman who will shut up and let her lover play around? I was able to bear it. Because I knew what you were doing had nothing to do with love. Even if you told me that it was love, I would know with certainty that it was a love that would serve you no purpose.

HIKARU. But I don't have any regrets. Although I don't feel grateful toward any of them.

ROKUJŌ. They don't deserve any thanks from you, you ought to spit on them! Those little girls didn't give you anything, they only stole from you. They stole your nobility. And that Aoi is just one of them, nothing more.

HIKARU. Leave me alone!

ROKUJŌ. "Leave me alone?" You sound just like a stupid man. I knew I would have to set you free one more time. In order for us to be free, we need to forge a complicit relationship in crime, again. Search our memories and re-visit that night.

HIKARU. I can't understand what you're saying.

ROKUJŌ. I'm talking about that night.

HIKARU. Which night? I spent thousands of nights with you.

ROKUJŌ. I liked the way you said that. Makes me hot all the way up to my uterus.

HIKARU. I don't have time to dilly-dally with a nympho like you.

Rokujō comes up to Hikaru and slaps him.

ROKUJŌ. That night! Of course! That long, hot night in August, when that terrible heat wave hit the resort.

HIKARU. Was there such an August?

ROKUJŌ. You're afraid to remember! I'd been with him at the lakeside resort for two days, waiting for the right moment. I remember, there was an eerie glow in the sky since the afternoon. Looking up from the terrace, the air was yellow as if it were filled with a toxic gas, and the light reflecting off the water's surface made the lake look like a desert. A desert of water. As the day grew longer, the colour grew darker. And by the time the sun was setting, the sky was stained such a deep red it seemed as though a neighboring town had been bombed and was on fire. I was terrified and hid myself in the bedroom. He was completely unaware of my fear and kept checking the stock market on his computer. I could see the night sky through the skylight. Such a deep blue that I felt it would suck out my insides. Imagine—after that bombing, everyone living like empty shells. Perhaps at the beginning of the world the sky was that colour. As I was thinking this, I felt an intense desire to be with you. Before I knew it, the temperature had risen drastically, even the air-conditioning couldn't take the edge off the heat. I was fine, because I had nothing inside. I was just a human-shaped vessel. A tall slender glass that burned with desire for you. I walked into the den and found him unconscious from the heat. I made sure he was not responding and called you. Come . . . Hurry, come, I said.

HIKARU. Please don't do this.

ROKUJŌ. There in the dim light, this man who controls so much power and wealth is lying prostrate, just from the heat. Can't you see?

An image of the husband appears: the lower half of a male mannequin with elaborately formed genitals.

ROKUJŌ. Hikaru, Come . . . Hurry, come. He's saved us the trouble of giving him sleeping pills or whatever else we'd have had to use. See, I can be this close to him and he won't budge.

HIKARU. What are you thinking of doing?

ROKUJŌ. There's no turning back, Hikaru, now that you've come here.

HIKARU. Leave me out of this.

ROKUJŌ. You can't escape, Hikaru. You owe me. I pretended to be fooled while you were cheating on me with all those other women. Now it's payback time. I gave you your freedom but I am not free. And you aren't actually free either. (*Winds an invisible rope around her husband's neck.*) Help me, Hikaru. Look, he's thrashing about so violently. (*Hikaru tries to leave.*) Hikaru! (*Hikaru comes back, steps toward the mannequin.*) Here, hurry, take the other end of the rope and pull!

HIKARU. If I do this, will you let this be the end of it? (*Rokujō nods. Hikaru takes the other end of the rope and pulls. Both of them, pulling. Gradually Rokujō and Hikaru let go.*) . . . That's enough.

ROKUJŌ. You promised to see this through to the end.

HIKARU. End?

ROKUJŌ. Why do you look so surprised? You think we can just leave him here like this and the world won't care? . . . Such a carefree expression on his face. Serves him right. This is your punishment for keeping me tied down.

HIKARU. Perhaps he loved you too much.

ROKUJŌ. . . . Why are you saying such a thing? . . . Why did you say that, darling? Come on, take the other end.

The two pick up the mannequin.

HIKARU. Where are we taking him?

ROKUJŌ. To the bathroom.

HIKARU. Where is it?

ROKUJŌ. Over there.

The mirror rises, revealing a bathtub. They throw the mannequin into the tub.

HIKARU. I know. You're going to cut him up, right?

ROKUJŌ. That'll take too much work. There's a much better way. Bring that over here. (*There is nothing there.*) It's too heavy for a woman, so you carry it. (*Hikaru moves to where she points, picks up something with one hand, and carries it back to her.*) Didn't I say it was too much work for a woman? Why don't you do things the way I tell you to? (*Hikaru grasps at the imaginary object with both hands and struggles to bring it to her.*) Pour it in here.

Hikaru mimes pouring something into the bathtub.

HIKARU. What is this stuff?

ROKUJŌ. Sulphuric acid . . . It'll dissolve right to the bone. (*Hikaru is silent, astonished.*) Look. Our empire is melting away . . . Melting away, our empire . . . Hikaru, make love to me. (*The two grapple with each other. Hikaru grows aggressive, breathing heavily atop Rokujō.*) And then, you and I headed for the lake, still naked. The night sky was a deep blue. The colour of the beginning of the world. Far away, the noises of explosions. We had survived. It was as if our internal organs suddenly returned to our bodies, and with them the heat. The two of us dived into the water. A transparent blackness. Our naked bodies brushing against one another in the weightlessness of water, we were creatures who had transcended gender. Do you know what I mean? At the lake at sunrise, you and I drifted lazily together, like clione—sea angels—swaying between glaciers. We were perfectly formed transcendent creatures. Since that day, I've remained in the water of that lake. You have too, only you don't realize it. We experienced that water together. Reality is nothing but a delusion . . . (*Stands up.*) Time to work. (*Carries something over.*)

HIKARU. Wha—?

ROKUJŌ. We're going to take the remains out. With this bucket. There're the remnants of an abandoned bomb shelter behind the house, we'll pour him in there and bury him. Then we'll be finished. Done. All right, Hikaru? You have to help me. (*Approaches the bathtub and gags at the odour.*) What an awful smell! That's not going to stop me. (*Begins scooping. Again, she gags, coughing.*) You're not going to stop me. (*Continues. She hits something heavy.*) Here we go, hup two, hup two. Oops! (*Slips and falls. Everything splatters out of the bucket.*) Oh no, what do we do? What do we do now? I've got to clean this up. (*Flustered, she grabs an invisible mop and makes cleaning gestures. Then, again, with an "oops" she slips and falls.*) What should I do? What should I do? Help! Help me, Hikaru!

HIKARU (*placing his hands on her shoulders*). That's enough now.

Rokujō stops weeping.

ROKUJŌ. . . . Before I knew it, without my knowing, I'd made you into a man. And when you became a man, you flew away from my side. I'm still in the lake. I've been watching you and that girl from the water, all this time.

HIKARU. I'm going to look for Aoi.

ROKUJŌ. I don't understand. Is that girl so special?

HIKARU. Aoi is sick.

ROKUJŌ. And is that so unusual?

HIKARU. Shall I tell you about how Aoi and I met?

ROKUJŌ. Aoi! Aoi is all you can talk about.

HIKARU. If you don't want me to, I'll stop.

ROKUJŌ. Tell me.

HIKARU. It is different from any other kind of romantic relationship. Within a few moments of meeting, we were laying our bodies on top of each other. That's how it was. You might think that indecent. And it was. We had an indecent first encounter in an indecent place. But what I experienced with Aoi was something I'd never felt with any other woman. I thought it was what suited me best, to feel such fondness and lewdness at the same time. Everything I had ever said to a woman, every gesture I'd ever made, had been a lie. My world turned upside down in that one moment. We met countless times after that. The more I slept with her, the closer I felt to the filth so deeply entrenched in her. That white body of hers is filthy. I understand this. When I held her in my arms, the memory of every man she'd slept with would emerge as a stain on her body. But instead of repulsing me, I found them emblematic of her nobility. That girl is beautifully tainted. Her filth has a lovely aroma. I couldn't tear myself away from her. What shocked me was that she genuinely believed she was ugly. So many times I'd said to her: To be defiled is not the same as being ugly. You are beautiful. But she could never be convinced. After a while I came to learn that it was her father who'd ingrained that belief in her. Growing up, her father kept telling her she was ugly. Her mother left home when she was still young. Her father abused her as a child. Sexually, that is. When she was seventeen, he tried to kill himself. He was dressed in her underwear and high-school uniform, and wearing make-up. She sensed something strange and ran to the bathroom. She held up his dangling body. Thanks to her, he managed to stay alive. But who knows if that was a blessing . . . The blood had stopped flowing to his brain, and he never recovered. He is still alive, in that brain-damaged condition. When she told me all this, I finally understood why I felt so drawn to her . . . Aoi is me.

ROKUJŌ. You?

HIKARU. I'll tell you something I've never told anyone . . . I was ten years old. A college student who lived next door. He . . . how can I say this . . . I guess he played some tricks on me. You understand what I'm trying to say? It was the first sunny day after the monsoons. He stopped me on my way home from school . . . After that day, he hanged himself. When I heard about it, I thought I'd killed him. That's where I'm different from Aoi. I killed, but Aoi saved. But, even now, the fact that she saved her father still torments her. It would have been better to have killed him.

ROKUJŌ. No wonder . . . I knew it all along. You think I'm surprised by your confession? I knew it, I knew something like that had happened to you. But you've got a long way to go. (*Laughing*) Hikaru, you've still got a long long way to go.

HIKARU. What do you mean?

ROKUJŌ. Darling, you've been so gorgeously taken in by that girl.

HIKARU. Taken in?

ROKUJŌ. She's lying. All lies.

HIKARU. Lies?

ROKUJŌ. Everything that girl says is a lie. When you started seeing her, I looked her up. She's just an ordinary girl. The ultimate in mediocrity, just a baddish girl from the suburbs. A brain-damaged father? That girl's father is doing just fine. He's retired and living a boring life in a house in the suburbs. (*Hikaru is silent. Rokujō picks up Aoi's hair.*) I knew it. You just fell in love with her lies. (*Burns Aoi's hair with a lighter.*) That's the last I'll speak about it. So, how about a haircut? It's all right if I sit here, is it? (*Hikaru is silent.*) I'm sitting. (*Sits.*)

HIKARU. . . . Liar. (*Rokujō is silent.*) You looked her up? You could be lying about that.

ROKUJŌ. . . . You can believe that if you wish.

HIKARU. This is what women are like. I don't mean that disdainfully, I say it with all respect.

ROKUJŌ. Give me a haircut. A last haircut. (*Hikaru stands behind Rokujō.*) You want to make me a hateful woman. All I wanted was to live with you in a world without any jagged edges. You never knew yourself, you were always unaware. You come from a world without jagged edges and wound up here by mistake. With the feathers of an angel and the wings of the devil. You rode the wind with your wings and set my suspended time in motion. I was already exiled from my empire. I loved to breathe in your scentless sweat. I loved to taste your semen on my tongue. It was summer. At night when the insects by the lake would start crying, you'd hold that alcoholic novelist's favourite cocktail in your hand and tell me about the land you came from: "In my country there are no jagged edges. There are too many jagged edges in this world, that's why there are wars. Because people are born rich or poor, master or slave. If all the jagged edges were rubbed away, everyone would live happily. Without its sharp edges, our world would be completely smooth and blank, all our suffering would disappear. There'd be no need for tall buildings. Trees would take root wherever they wished. So, for the sake of the plants and the trees, we ought to make the whole world a complete blank. Even people's faces. It's because we have noses and eyes and ears that the concepts of beauty and ugliness take hold. If our faces were a complete blank, then there'd be no need for plastic surgery." I must have answered you, laughing: "Oh, but if that nose of yours suddenly disappeared, how sad would it be?" But the landscape of the world you described was spectacular. The great earth wrapped in blankness. You and I can meet there, laugh and play in a verdant lush place full of fresh pure water. We'd not be bound by age or gender. You would not be man, I would not be woman. All of our edges and our features would be gone. Even then

I'd want you to make love to me. It was summer. Yes, summer. The time in which I existed began to move again, and the summer heat matched its pace. By the time it's fall, the color of the blood we bathed in in August will have faded. The dry fall sunlight will rid us of the smell. And winter will be a time of reflection. By spring I'll meet you again, renewed and reborn. I'll always be with you. If I'm not, my time will come to a standstill. It was summer then. It was also summer when I first grew suspicious of you. Sooner or later, I knew you'd take flight from my side. And that thought made me begin to hate your feathers, your wings. That was when my jagged edges came back. There was a reason I always caressed you between your shoulder blades. I was looking for my chance to rip out your wings. But thinking like that was like wrestling with myself. By then you'd already formed edges and become a man. A fine adult man. You had no need for your wings and feathers. And I was nothing but a mumbling old lady who was trying to rip out those wings that had already long since disappeared . . . Come back to me, Hikaru.

HIKARU. . . . I'm going to start cutting. (*Begins cutting her hair.*)

There is a bizarre sound and huge amounts of hair fall from the sky and obscure the two. Darkness. When the lights come up, Hikaru is on the ground. He comes to and looks around. Huge heaps of hair surround him. He picks up a broom and begins to sweep it into one pile, gradually forming a mountain of hair. Tōru enters.

TŌRU. Oh, Hikaru.

HIKARU. Hey, where've you been? What is this mess? You've got to keep this place tidy.

TŌRU. Uh, sorry, sir. Um . . .

HIKARU. I don't get it, my head's in a daze. Hey, have you seen Miss Rokujō?

TŌRU. Well, yes, so . . .

HIKARU. Did she go home?

IMAGE 4.2 **Rokujō decides to leave Hikaru and announces that this will be their last haircut.**

Rei Asami as Rokujō and Hiroki Hasegawa as Hikaru. *Aoi*, Setagaya Public Theater, Tokyo, 2007.

Photograph by Katsu Miyauchi.

TŌRU. No, she's just arrived.

HIKARU. Where?

TŌRU. When I got here, she was just stepping out of her car . . .

Rokujō appears, an elegant and refined woman.

ROKUJŌ (*toward the wings*). Could you park it nearby? I'm sorry, I'll just be a minute. (*Turning back*) Long time no see, Hikaru. How have you been? (*Hikaru is silent.*) What's with the long face? Is something wrong? Did something bad happen? Should I not have come?

HIKARU. Um, you, where have you been?

ROKUJŌ. Where? What are you asking me? I just got back two days ago. Half a year going back and forth between Paris and Milan. And these last two days spent recovering from jetlag. I've been in such a daze, I couldn't tell if I was awake or asleep! Here, just a boring little souvenir. I have something for Aoi too. Is Aoi doing well?

HIKARU. Yes . . . she's all right . . .

ROKUJŌ. I'm so glad to hear it.

HIKARU. Miss Rokujō, weren't you . . .

ROKUJŌ. Hikaru, you seem so happy.

HIKARU. Weren't you here just now?

ROKUJŌ. What are you saying? I just got here, didn't I? I was traveling all this time, with my master. My master is so silly, he just can't do anything without me. He can't even make a pot of tea on his own . . . It was a lovely trip. (*Touching the chair*) I've missed the feel of this chair.

HIKARU. Miss Rokujō, do you know where Aoi is?

ROKUJŌ. What?

TŌRU. Miss Aoi went back to the hospital.

HIKARU. Oh! Oh, is that where she went?

ROKUJŌ. Hikaru, you look so pale! Are you ill? Are you all right?

TŌRU. I . . . I saw Miss Aoi to the hospital myself.

ROKUJŌ. Aren't you Tōru?

TŌRU. Yes.

ROKUJŌ. My, what a fine young man you've become. Back then, you seemed like you'd just come to the city from the country. Won't you cut my hair next time?

HIKARU. I'm going to the hospital.

ROKUJŌ. What about the souvenir?

Aoi enters when Hikaru begins to walk off.

HIKARU. Aoi . . . (*Grabs her hair and rips it off her head. It is a wig. Aoi's head is shaved, without a single strand of hair. Hikaru is dumbfounded.*)

AOI (*staring at Rokujō*). I'm ready for my execution, Hikaru.

ROKUJŌ. Oh, is this the fashion here these days?

AOI. Hikaru, how do I look?

HIKARU. Who did this to you?

TŌRU. I did.

HIKARU. You?

AOI. I asked Tōru to do it. He promised he'd cut my hair.

TŌRU. . . . I'm sorry.

HIKARU. Why did you do that? (*Lunges at Tōru and hits his face with incredible force.*)

ROKUJŌ. Wait, you two, what in the . . . Why are you . . . What is this?

AOI. I knew it! (*Tries to leave.*)

HIKARU. Aoi, wait! (*Runs after Aoi and holds her tight.*)

Rokujō approaches Tōru.

ROKUJŌ (*holding him up*). Are you all right, dear?

TŌRU. Yes . . . Dammit.

AOI (*struggling with Hikaru*). Daddy, stop it, just stop, Daddy.

ROKUJŌ. You people . . .

AOI. Daddy, stop pulling my hair!

HIKARU. Aoi, it's all right. I'm not your father.

AOI. Stop pulling!

HIKARU. It's all right, it's all right.

ROKUJŌ (*to Tōru*). Darling, let's get out of here. You know, I can see wings unfolding from your back. Wouldn't you like to spread those wings and fly away?

TŌRU. Wings?

ROKUJŌ. I'm joking, it's a joke. Come, come with me. I promise you nothing bad will happen. Hikaru, you take care now. Goodbye! (*Takes Tōru by the hand and exits.*)

Aoi has calmed down.

AOI. . . . Is she gone?

HIKARU. Huh?

AOI. Did that woman leave? (*Stands up.*) Good. All right, Hikaru, shall we begin? I'm feeling great. I've been reborn. And it feels wonderful. (*Hikaru is silent. Aoi sits on the chair.*) You can cut my hair now.

Hikaru stands behind her.

HIKARU. How do you want it?

AOI. However you like. (*Hikaru begins to rustle through her non-existent hair.*) Hikaru, do you love me?

HIKARU. Yeah. Of course . . . I'll never let you go . . . Your hair, it's so beautiful . . .

A gentle breeze blows through the mountains of hair.

The End

CHARACTERS

MAN

OLD MAN

OLD WOMAN

KOMACHI

KOMACHI

TRANSLATED BY AYA OGAWA

I. A MOVIE THEATER

Autumn. Far away, the sounds of war. Man sits on a chair, splayed out as if dead. After a while he gathers himself up.

MAN. . . . So that's what happened. Of course, there is a banal story connected to why things happened the way they did. I don't even think I should bother telling it. The world is already bursting with banal stories, and anyway, stories are fundamentally banal. But I was bored as hell with going around pretending like I knew something. I wanted to become savage. To be savage means to imagine you exist in a world in which not a single story has yet been born. As you can see, I am not young nor am I old. Unemployed. Some people call me a film director, but give me a break—a film director's someone who makes films, right? I haven't made one in eight years. I can't tell if eight years is a long span of time or not. But think, if I had had a kid back then, that kid would be old enough to be wearing a schoolbag right now . . . Anyway, to get back to the story: At the time, I was wandering around in search of a new story. I hardly came home to my apartment. To tell you the truth, I was also able to keep my landlord and creditors off my back this way. The reason I set foot in this town was because I'd never gotten off at this train station before. I might discover a fresh story in a town I'm visiting for the first time. Looking back, I think I must've been a bit sentimental then. The area around the station was desolate, with a stand-and-eat noodle joint, a sushi-go-round place, and a chain coffee shop. On the other side of the street was a library commemorating all the neighborhood writers. The most famous was a writer who'd committed suicide at the age of thirty-five . . . Suicide. For me, being completely financially bust was reason enough for suicide, but I wouldn't have wanted that to be my motive. If you have enough energy to kill yourself, you ought to buckle down and live . . . As I walked along the main road flanked by narrowing railroad tracks, most of the stores along the shopping area were shuttered closed. It seemed like years since anyone had visited the bars; their doors were stained by exhaust fumes and the half-broken windows were boarded up. The road gradually came to a hill. The slope reached its peak at a crossroad, and I wondered which way to go. I ended up turning back and ducking into an alleyway off the hill. A little way in, side by side, there was a noodle shop and a restaurant specializing in eel. They seemed decent and I thought I'd go into one of them for a late lunch on my way back. The narrow alley grew even narrower. The walls around private homes and trees blocked out all sunlight. The air was humid and none of the traffic noise from the main road could be heard. Just as I imagined, there was a shrine with a small statue of a fox deity along the way. I patted the fox head, tossed in a penny, and brought my hands together sweetly in prayer: Please let me make a movie next year. I went further down the alley and suddenly it was gone. I found myself on a bigger road, but different from the one I'd taken from the station. Perhaps because I was suddenly thrust into the sunlight, I thought I felt a dizzy spell coming on so I looked for a place to rest. But there wasn't a park or a cafe in sight. Instead, I found a movie theater. Well, how about that, it was one of those theaters that screened double bills of great films. But this was no time to get excited. I needed to take a break, so I walked into the theater without checking what was playing. (*Sits back in the chair.*) In other words, this was it. My story begins here in this movie theater. At this moment, I am sitting in this movie theater. The film hasn't begun. The vinyl-covered seats are terrible, their springs jut out. There's a mustiness emanating from the walls and floor, and for some reason *Rhapsody in Blue* is playing through the poor speakers. I'm the only one in the house. I close my eyes. The melody of

Rhapsody in Blue lulled me to sleep. I don't know how much time I spent sleeping. When I wake up, content, the movie's begun. It's an old Japanese film, black and white. The Nazi flag flutters alongside the Japanese. It seems like a terribly old movie. I've never watched it. The story goes something like this: The hero has just finished his studies in Germany and is about to go back home, to Japan. He has a German lover on the side but a fiancée back in Japan. Influenced by Western values during his stay abroad, once he's home he can't help but think of all his relationships as the remnants of a feudal system. The Japanese girl who is his fiancée is shocked by how much he's changed. Even his own family has grown apprehensive of him. But the more time he spends back home, the the stronger his Japanese sensibilities resurface. Around the same time, his fiancée, despairing at her man's change of heart, tries to commit suicide by throwing herself into a volcano. He goes after her and rescues her in the nick of time. They marry and spend their days farming a new tract of land. The two, who toil and harvest over their expansive fields, are blessed with a child. The man holds his baby up above the great earth. Smiling Japanese soldiers with rifles safeguard the couple and their child.

I couldn't move a muscle after it was over. I just sat there in the dark, staring at the screen. It wasn't that I was moved by the plot but that I had finally remembered the title of the film. I couldn't even remember when, but I must've come across it in some film-history book. The glorious stretch of earth in the last scene had to be Manchuria. This was *Graceful Nation*, a film that hadn't been let out of the can since the war. The heroine was none other than the legendary actress Komachi, the mysterious star who suddenly disappeared from the silver screen shortly after the war. How was it that I was able to to watch this movie here . . .

Suddenly Old Man appears by Man's side.

OLD MAN. How long have you been here? (*Man is surprised.*) Where did you come from?

MAN. Um . . .

OLD MAN. Have you got legs? . . . Or are you a ghost?

MAN. Huh? I didn't realize. What have I done?

OLD MAN. Please go home at once.

MAN. The movie . . . just now . . . was it by any chance . . .

OLD MAN. You saw it?

MAN. Yes.

OLD MAN. Then you must be satisfied. Please, go home.

MAN. All right. Thanks for this rare opportunity. (*Stands up and then realizes something.*) I wasn't the only person in the audience. In the darkness, I could smell a strong scent of perfume. I tried to head straight toward the exit but that scent was making me dizzy . . . (*Stumbles toward the source of the smell. Old Woman is sitting on a chair. Man gazes at her face.*) Excuse me . . . I felt as if time has stopped. It was that old woman's face that stopped time. The horror and cruelty of age. And yet, that scent is so bittersweet, nostalgic . . .

OLD MAN. Please go home. My Lady does not see anyone. As I mentioned over the phone, we refuse any and all requests for interviews. We've had enough of you journalists.

MAN. But I'm not.

OLD MAN. You didn't call?

MAN. No.

OLD MAN. Then, who are you, sir?

MAN. Well, I used to make movies.

Old Woman reacts to the news.

OLD MAN. You made films? So, you are a film director?

MAN. I guess you could say so . . . But say, how is it that you have that film here?

OLD MAN. This is my Lady's private space. Come now, my Lady. The sun has set. The night mist is not good for you.

Old Woman gets up from her seat and leaves, accompanied by Old Man. On her way out, Old Woman casts amorous glances at Man.

MAN. As soon as I got outside I realized for the first time that the theater was shut down. That old woman he kept calling "My Lady" must've been a tremendously wealthy heiress to be able to buy the place and use it as her own private theater! What a luxury! He said something about an interview. I wonder if it was about the theater. Or maybe word had gone around that they had gotten hold of *Graceful Nation* . . . Well, whatever. I'm not a scholar or a fan. Anyway, I really lucked out unexpectedly. As I recall, that film was shot by a German filmmaker, a Nazi sympathizer. The first Japanese–German movie to be made after the Japanese German Alliance Convention. The final scene must have been symbolic of the Nazi's recognition of Japan's agenda for Manchuria at the time. This was a film that some people wanted to forget. It was in the can the whole time, hardly ever screened. Or so I read once. Right, there was a time when I couldn't make movies so I'd spend all my time at the library, poring over film books . . . That autumn evening, I went back down the streets I came. The shadows in the alleyway were echoed with the cries of insects. The smell of moist earth. The scent of a fragrant olive. For some reason, I was in high spirits. I went into the noodle shop as planned but then I remembered that I hadn't a penny to my name. But I no longer cared. I'd fallen head over heels for the young Komachi in the movie. The noodle shop was dark; darkness clung to the walls and floor, and the kitchen in the back was completely enveloped in black. I order a hot sake and an egg roll. No answer. But five minutes later my order was brought out to me. The yellow wrinkled hand of a man placed my bottle in front of me. I looked up at him but his face was blurred. The alcohol soaked into my body and I was getting drunk quickly. Why was I sitting there all alone? . . . Because I'd never loved anyone. I'd only ever loved actresses on the silver screen . . . I'd like a bowl of noodles, please, soba.

Music is heard from far away. Man drinking sake is half-conscious. In his stupor he sees Old Woman with a parasol. She begins to dance to the images and representations of various film actresses. For example:

> The concept and the sensuality of the Actress
>
> Lillian Gish's eyes
>
> Garbo's profile
>
> Dietrich's sunken cheeks, smoke exhaled from a cigarette
>
> Woman of Destiny (*Las Abandonadas*)
>
> Veronica Lake is a Gun for Hire
>
> Lana Turner Always Rings Twice
>
> Leave Her to Heaven Gene Tierney
>
> Simone Signoret's lips
>
> Rita Hayworth as Gilda, swaying her hips
>
> The world has changed
>
> Whatever Happened to Baby Betty Davis?
>
> Joan Crawford can't sleep at night
>
> The Vamp
>
> Lauren Bacall's flat chest
>
> Under the gaslight Joan Bennett's face appears. The woman by the window is covered in blood.
>
> The women sitting behind their decoration windows.
>
> Angie Dickenson wielding a machine gun
>
> Anna Magnani runs through a vulnerable city
>
> Or Ingrid Bergman in Stromboli
>
> A woman who faints
>
> Hitchcock films
>
> Grace Kelly plants the stolen money on Joan Fontaine standing on a cliff and runs North by Northwest with Eva Marie Saint when Tippi Hedren is attacked by The Birds

Silver Screen, Silver Screen, Silver Screen, Silver Screen

Film Actress, Film Actress, Film Actress, Film Actress

The smell of women

Sweat and perfume and jealousy and ambition

Utter loveliness

Old Woman vanishes.

MAN. After a long wait my bowl of noodles arrives. (*Eats*) Strange noodles. The noodles squirm in my mouth. These aren't noodles but an enormous bowl of earthworms. (*Spits them out.*) Hey, what the hell is this? Come out here. I know you're back there! (*Old Man appears.*) Wha—?

OLD MAN. Oh, are you here? My Lady wanted me to detain you.

MAN. What's going on with this noodle shop?

OLD MAN. Is something the matter with your noodles?

MAN. Here, look, this mound of . . . (*sees nothing but noodles in the bowl.*) Huh? (*Eats.*)

OLD MAN. The noodles here are hand-made—delicious. We, too, frequently come in the evenings to enjoy their noodle dishes, hanamaki soba we eat often. Now, let's get going.

MAN. Where?

OLD MAN. Not to worry. I'll take care of your bill here.

MAN. That's awfully kind of you . . . But where are we going?

OLD MAN. You saw that film earlier, did you not?

MAN. I saw the film starring Komachi.

OLD MAN. So, to Komachi.

MAN. Huh?

OLD MAN. Miss Komachi is waiting for you, Sir.

MAN. . . . Please stop joking around. Just because you think someone's penniless. I'm going home. Thanks for dinner.

Man tries to leave but Old Man moves behind him and presses a cloth over his nose and mouth.

Man is seated in a chair, blindfolded, his arms bound behind him.

MAN. I could tell immediately from the feel of the chair that I was in that movie theater. It was a very uncomfortable seat. I hadn't realized it during the films but the seat was freezing cold, like a block of ice . . . There was another film playing. Not *Graceful Nation.* This one too I'd never watched. *Morning Bugle Call.* Sounds of a fighter-plane engine. Explosions. Overwhelming sounds of war. Komachi's passionate text knits the shots together. I knew immediately that it was a war propaganda film starring Komachi and shot during the war. Ah, I want to watch the movie. Take off my blindfold. I was watching the film with my ears. The first film ended and the next one began . . . This one I have watched. No doubt, it's *Portrait of a Glorious Adolescence.* A coming-home-from-the-war film. A suffering Komachi appears. Between her liberal father and a lover who's thrown himself into the leftist movement, she is victimized and oppressed during the war. Defeat for Japan means victory for her. Here's the final shot. She's lifted onto an Occupation flatbed tractor by some other farmers. She's become a leader of the agricultural reform movement. Thus she's transformed from the Madonna of a warring state to the Goddess of Liberty . . .

Suddenly Old Man is beside him.

OLD MAN. How do you feel?

MAN. Hey, don't you think you're being a little rough for an old man?

OLD MAN. I'm very healthy for my age.

MAN. You're not healthy, you're violent!

OLD MAN. If you say so.

MAN. You won't get anything out of kidnapping me. Just try and get a ransom for me—my family's long since forsaken me.

OLD MAN. Are you really a film director?

MAN. I haven't made a film in eight years. But if you want to call me that, go ahead.

OLD MAN. What are your best-known works?

MAN. I haven't made them yet. Um, could you take the blindfold off?

Old Man takes off Man's blindfold.

OLD MAN. Which films have you made?

MAN. I was assistant director for some soft porn and then I shot three of my own. *Hot for Teacher: She's Wet, She's Wet* was my debut film. The second was *Explosive Virgin: Nympho on Fire*, then *Horny Housewife: I'm on Super Sale*. No, wait, there was another one. *Horny Housewife* was the fourth and *Pervert Trance: I'm Cumming on Sundays* was the third. Oh, no, *I'm Cumming on Sundays* was the fourth. That's right, I'm forgetting *Husband in Pearls: I've got Four Inside* . . .

OLD MAN. Enough, that's enough.

MAN. Wait, hear me out. I made one film that wasn't porn. Not that I've got anything against porn. That last one I made—*The Owl's Bet*—was a commercial film.

OLD MAN. Oh-ho. Now, was that a comedy or a melodrama?

MAN. . . . Neither.

OLD MAN. It must have been one or the other.

MAN. I guess it was more a melodrama.

OLD MAN. I see.

MAN. It created quite a buzz. I got a little arrogant from all the attention and I began doing film reviews. That was the beginning of the end.

OLD MAN. Oh-ho. And why was that?

MAN. I didn't realize how quickly you lose favor when you start spouting crap like film theory and blah blah blah. It's been eight years . . . I'm exiled from the entertainment industry.

OLD MAN. Eight years is nothing. I have been pottering about for almost a hundred.

MAN. Really? You're in awfully great shape. Oh yeah. The films you were screening just now. I recognized *Portrait of a Glorious Adolescence* right away, but what was the first one?

OLD MAN. *Shanghai Suicide Squad.*

MAN. I've never heard of it.

OLD MAN. It was a film that was squelched by history. There was nothing that could have been done. We lost the war.

MAN. Are you a Komachi-film archivist?

OLD MAN. I suppose you could say that. There's no greater fan of Komachi than me.

MAN. This theater's a cultural asset.

OLD MAN. It was built before the war. The memories of many films are buried within these walls. And these seats, aren't they cold? It's because they're made out of gravestones. Before, during and after the war. All those of the film industry who died without achieving their life's ambitions—these are their gravestones. And the only one who is permitted atop them is my Lady.

MAN. And why am I here?

OLD MAN. For defiling these gravestones, I'd say.

MAN. I'm not here because I want to be. Could you please undo the rope or string or whatever? Then I'll be more than happy to get out of your way.

Old Man unties him. Man stands.

OLD MAN. Are you really a film director?

MAN. Aren't you persistent? Didn't you kidnap me because you didn't believe me?

OLD MAN. You have no proof.

MAN. How do you want me to prove it? Oh all right, why not make me shoot a film? Then you'll see.

OLD MAN. Do you want to make a movie?

MAN. I'm a film director, aren't I?

OLD MAN. Can you read a screenplay?

MAN. Are there any film directors who can't? I suppose there are . . . In fact, most of them probably can't.

OLD MAN. And you?

MAN. I believe I can. I write screenplays myself, so . . .

OLD MAN. You're a screenwriter as well?

MAN. Yes. Most everything I've shot I've also written.

OLD MAN. Marvellous.

MAN. What is?

OLD MAN. My Lady! This man is a Film Director!

Old Woman enters, dragging a huge ancient trunk. She sits in the chair, and, as if bringing forth pieces of her own memory, takes worn-out manuscripts out of the trunk and hands them to Man. Man hesitates and then accepts them.

MAN. What are these?

OLD MAN. Screenplays.

MAN. Did you write them?

OLD MAN. No, these were written by Major General Fukakusa.

MAN. Major General Fukakusa? Never heard of him.

OLD MAN. His name is not known in the history of cinema. He was supposed to shoot this film, starring my Lady. He left this screenplay with my Lady and went off to the battlefields. He fell ill and died. If only he had made this film, my lady's career as a star-actress would have been quite different . . .

MAN. Wait a second. Ma'am, just who exactly are you?

Old Woman is silent.

OLD MAN. She is Komachi. The legendary actress, Komachi.

MAN. Um . . . You know what, I need to get home after all.

OLD MAN. Why?

MAN. It's not important. Can I just go home now? (*Tries to leave. Old Man pulls out a military sword from the trunk, unsheathes it, and points it at Man.*) . . . You're a violent old geezer.

OLD MAN. Just healthy. You must answer my question.

MAN. All right, then. I'm not so compassionate as to waste my time entertaining you two senile old fogies. You've miscast me in the role. Try finding someone a bit more gullible next time.

OLD MAN. You are disrespecting Komachi.

MAN. Komachi? This old hag? Komachi from *Portrait of a Glorious Adolescence* and *Tsukuda Island Story*? She's disappeared from public life and been a recluse for the last forty-odd years. Surely this isn't her! Choose a younger director who knows far less cinema history. And if you really want to fool someone, find a woman who at least looks like her.

OLD MAN. You are a disgrace to this country!

Tries to attack Man, but Old Woman comes between them. Old Man puts the sword away. Old Woman takes out numerous photographs from the trunk and gives them to Man.

MAN (*looking at the photos*). All right. Every single one is of the young Komachi at the height of her stardom. But this doesn't prove that you are Komachi yourself.

Old Woman takes one last disintegrating photograph and gives it to Man.

MAN (*looking at the photo*). This is . . . This guy looks exactly like me . . . or, rather, this *is* me.

OLD MAN. That is Major General Fukakusa. When I first saw you, I thought I'd seen his ghost.

MAN. Oh, so now you want me to indulge your little trip down memory lane.

OLD MAN. We'd like you to make this film. For Komachi.

MAN. . . . All right. If, just if this old lady actually is Komachi . . .

OLD MAN. What do you mean "if!?"

MAN. OK, OK. Let me ask you something: Are you two married?

OLD MAN. How could Komachi, known as "the eternal virgin," be married?

MAN. You didn't fall for it, huh. I was hoping you would.

OLD MAN. I am just a fan.

MAN. All right. I understand. I've got one more question for you: Why do you want to make a film with Komachi, now, after all this time? I thought she'd gotten sick of facing the camera. I thought she'd retired. She must have been in her teens when she shot *Graceful Nation*. It was a Japanese–German collaboration, directed by a German. About Germany's support of Japan's foundation-building measures for Manchuria, and Japan's ode of complicity with the Nazis. I seem to remember you actually went to Berlin for the premiere. Even met Goebbels. You embodied it all: the mother of the militaristic nation before the war, the goddess of post-war democracy, the symbol of nostalgia for the humble Japanese woman, the epitome of Japanese beauty. A flawless, shining acting career. You said a moment ago that her acting career could have been different, but how could it have been any better?

OLD MAN. You're absolutely right. And to tell you the truth, I am opposed to relaunching Komachi's career. Never mind that Major General Fukakusa left his screenplay behind. Komachi's stardom should just continue to breathe on the silver screen. However, never-fading youth and beauty will not forgive us.

MAN. Youth and beauty, eh?

OLD MAN. Major General Fukakusa fell in love with Komachi. He visited her studio almost every day. "Please star in my film," he begged her, ninety-nine times. And every time, Komachi would only smile silently at him. For the longest time I thought she was silent because he was someone who had no track record in films, but I was wrong. Komachi was actually deeply in love with the Major. But it was a love that could never be, for Komachi was the eternal virgin. Komachi died when she first heard news of the Major's illness and death. She died the eternal virgin. She has been but a corpse ever since. And that is precisely why, decade after decade, she has been able to play such prominent roles. After retiring, she was finally able

IMAGE 5.1 **Old Woman and Man looking at a photo: "This guy looks exactly like me . . . or, rather, this *is* me."** Akira Kasai as Old Woman and Touru Tezuka as Man. *Komachi*, Setagaya Public Theater, Tokyo, 2007.

Photograph by Katsu Miyauchi.

to be at peace. All she has left to do is to sit quietly with the gravestones, like a true corpse. But alas, her ever-glowing skin, her blue-black hair, her soft supple body will not let her go!

Old Woman takes a clapper board out of the trunk and gives it to Old Man.

MAN. What is she trying to do?

OLD MAN. What an unfortunate fate awaits film actresses.

MAN. What's going on?

OLD MAN. You are going to shoot a movie!

Old Woman starts to pose as if standing in front of a camera.

MAN. Shoot a movie?

OLD MAN. Everything is ready. Come, we would like you to hear you speak the words of the director, as soon as possible.

MAN. . . . And . . . Action!

Old Man claps the clapper board.

IV. BEFORE THE DEFEAT

Old Woman dances
She dances extending her wrinkles.
Her gray hair flows through the air as she dances
The young Old Woman dances
Over the earth
In that moment, everything collapses. Before the war, during the war, after the war
Everything melts.
Darkness in a pre-war house. Shoji sliding screen-doors. Lanterns. Latticed gate.
Eastern-style toilet. The head of the household is anxious.
Tatami room, making love in the darkness.

Sounds from the shadows
Air raids.
The darkness in the light
The darkness of this shelter
Your profile faintly visible in the fluorescent light.
The darkness speaks
The darkness chatters in favor of democracy
Manchuria
Nazi Party grand procession
New soil
Triumph of the Will
Darkness folds around history
The darkness in the stain on the portrait in Manchuria
The darkness in the gaze hidden by the army cap.
The darkness of the shadows cast on the road by marching
      soldiers
The darkness of Goebbel's cheeks
Actress
Actress
Actress
The scent of the Actress
Dictator
Dictator
Dictator
The body odor of the Dictator
The anti-Semitism of a film director

(*Old Woman turns into a young Japanese soldier.*)

The daughter of a Chinese girl
Wanderer of the continent
Pistol
Bandits
Dust clouds
Gun smoke
The smells of all of these

No, how embarrassing to receive such things from a Japanese
    soldier!
The horizon of the continent
The heavy dot of the setting sun
The darkness of the falling military sword
The aroma of the earth
The smell of emptiness

V. REUNION

*Old Man, dressed as a Japanese soldier brings his sword down on Old
Woman's neck. Man is startled:*

MAN (*screams*). My head! (*Old Woman is silent.*) Komachi! (*Old
Woman turns to look at him.*) That's right. That's what happened. Komachi, can you see me? Can you see what I am
now? (*Old Woman nods.*) I'm just a head now. The sixteenth
regiment where I was stationed set off from Shanghai, via
Talin, two hundred kilometers, and arrived here in Nanking.
Here on this earth I was executed by the hands of my own
countrymen. Because I let a Chinese girl escape. That girl, she
looked exactly like you. When I showed her your photograph,
even she was shocked at the resemblance. I'm sorry, Komachi,
I fell in love with that girl. She looked too much like you. But
perhaps it's a mistake to call this love. Because the truth is I
had raped a girl who didn't put up a fight. And as punishment
I've been reduced to being just a head. It's a relief. No lower
body, one less thing to be bothered by. (*Old Woman is silent.*)
This way, you truly can remain the eternal virgin. (*Old Woman
is silent.*) Or, maybe you have already . . . (*Old Woman remains
silent.*) It doesn't matter even if you have. Now that I've been
reduced to this, I know this with certainty: The body and the
spirit are completely separate. The spirit alone is capable of
making a film. Did you read my screenplay? What did you

think of it? (*Old Woman is silent.*) I'm so glad. I've been so worried about your opinion. Do you remember? The path you and I often strolled along? We would have plenty of distance between us, we would pretend not to know one another. When I thought no one was looking, I'd turn back to see if you were following me. It was a dusty path, smelling of orange osmanthus. We would always walk at dusk. We could watch the sunset on the other side of the telephone wires. We'd climb up a hill and turn into an alley and catch an American film at the cinema. We both loved Chaplin. Often, at the studio, you'd make me laugh by doing Chaplin imitations. My dream was that one day they would screen our movie at that cinema. Once that dream came true, I wouldn't care if my spirit died . . . We're going to lose this war. There's absolutely no question about that. That's even more reason we have to shoot this movie. We must burn onto film a record of the graceful darkness we lived in together. Then my spirit will disappear. But you'll keep on living. You must continue to live. Because you know the darkness we lived through, you have to continue to breathe life with the film that we made together. Your spirit is never-ending, I know. There will be countless obstacles across your path. Countless crowds and movements promulgating all kinds of ideas and principles will use your beauty for their causes. There's no need to resist them. No one will be able to truly use you. Japan will lose this war. This graceful darkness will be consumed by an insipid light and disappear forever. But your spirit and our film will live on. I don't care what anyone says. I know, I am now just a head, I can see into the future . . . The people of this country will wander from illusion to illusion, living a mediocre existence, and they will come to vilify you. Let them say what they want. The horror of patching together higher principles can only be known to those who have done so. This film we're shooting now will be proof of that. Our Garden of Eden, full

IMAGE 5.2 **Old Woman strangles Man with film.**
Akira Kasai as Old Woman and Touru Tezuka as Man.
Komachi, Setagaya Public Theater, Tokyo, 2007.
Photograph by Katsu Miyauchi.

of the graceful darkness. . . . Komachi, get ready for our final shot. (*Old Woman prepares.*) . . . Once I've shot this scene, I'll finally be released . . . (*shaking his head*) No, wait. My . . . my head is still attached to my body. I'm not Major General Fukakusa. You tried to trick me again . . . But . . . Komachi . . . How graceful you are. Graceful, to the point of cruelty . . . I want to touch you. I want to film you. I want to project you onto the screen. A gentle touch across your eyelids. The empire within your retina. A slave to the passion and resignation that you reap, I drown in shadows and blossom in the light. I want to shoot the film not to record you but because you are made of light and shadow. The essence of film. Your skin on the screen. There's nothing of you up there. There never was, from the beginning. That's why I can say without any embarrassment, that you are graceful. Komachi, we're going to the next shot . . . And Action!

Komachi dances. A dance full of beauty for the world, for film and empire. Soon she takes out a real reel of film, and winds it around her body. Then she draws Man in, winding the film around his neck and begins to strangle him. Man sits on the old chair and dies. Komachi sees Man's corpse and cries out loud. When she finally calms down, she seems bright and cheerful. Embracing the clear emptiness of the sky, she exits.

VI. RE-RELEASE SCREENING

Old Man appears and investigates the corpse.

OLD MAN. She's done it again. Which means this one had no talent either. Not much hope in the young these days . . . Perhaps it's for the best, yes, for the best. Now, let's get rid of all the evidence. (*Unwinds the film from Man's neck and leaves.*)

MAN (*as a corpse*). So that's what happened . . . An unlucky guy, as always. In the end, I never figured out who that old woman was. No use trying. Anyway, I died. I wonder if the old man's going to cut up my body and throw me into the ocean, or bury me deep in the forest. I hope I don't disappear into the countless missing persons cases—I hope they find my body and that my death makes the news, even as a tiny article in the corner of a page. Anyway, it's too late now, I'd better stop dwelling on my own misfortunes. Maybe they'll re-release some of my films and my name will be remembered as one of the many film directors who died young . . . What a pathetic life . . . I wish I'd been able to finish that bowl of noodles, I wish I'd had enough time to read that screenplay by Major General Fukakusa . . . I wonder what it was like. No doubt it was a banal story written by a total amateur. And I took a spin on that banal story and died. That's why you can't let your guard down when it comes to stories. I wonder if my spirit, swept away on the flow of that story, is now doomed to wander the Manchurian landscape, like the last scene of that movie. And there, finally my spirit will be buried in graceful darkness . . . How idiotic . . . But I suppose it's not impossible, stories seem so ordinary but something always happens that is beyond ones imagination . . . a graceful darkness . . . How far do I have to go to find that? Among the films that have been erased from the history of cinema, or in an incomplete story? And the film-maker that tries to shoot the last scene will, no doubt, die, the same fate as mine. This has nothing to do with talent . . . Who am I even talking to right now? If there's anyone out there listening to me, let me warn you (after all, I am dead, so allow me to make some grand statements): Beware of anyone who calls herself an actress. Don't take it lightly, don't start a conversation. I can't believe . . . and . . . Action!

Behind him a projection of the seats in a cinema. Among the seats, Man sits alone, facing forward, enjoying a film. Old Man and

Old Woman appear. Old Man drags Man's corpse down to the ground and pulls him off the screen. Old Woman poses like an actress in front of the camera. Blossoms like a flower.

The End

THE WHITE HOUSE IN
THE HILLS OF ARGOS

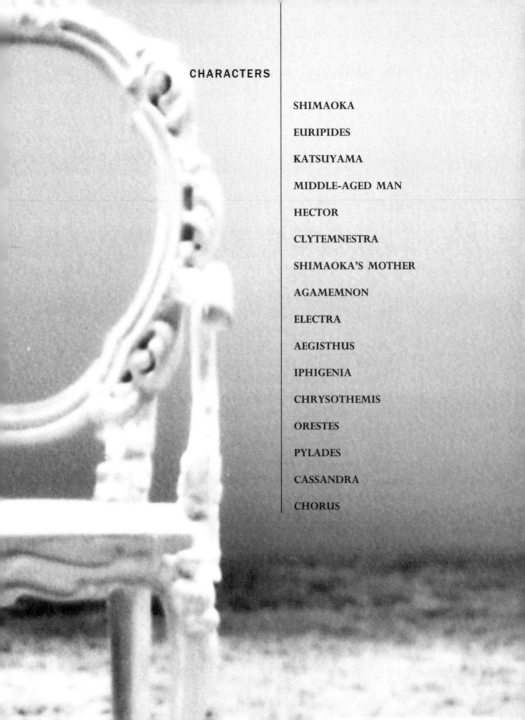

CHARACTERS

SHIMAOKA

EURIPIDES

KATSUYAMA

MIDDLE-AGED MAN

HECTOR

CLYTEMNESTRA

SHIMAOKA'S MOTHER

AGAMEMNON

ELECTRA

AEGISTHUS

IPHIGENIA

CHRYSOTHEMIS

ORESTES

PYLADES

CASSANDRA

CHORUS

THE WHITE HOUSE
IN THE HILLS OF ARGOS

TRANSLATED BY PETER ECKERSALL

ACT I. At the Place of the Gods

SCENE 1

Brilliant sparkling music. Electra and Orestes are on stage. Orestes holds a kitchen knife. They sing.

ELECTRA. Our Fate, our destiny lies in the stars,
    And circumstances bring ill times.
    We were born in this house,
    Cursed to kill our mother.
    Adoration, cruelty, hating one another,
    Jealousy, desire, quarrelling,
    Evil blood courses through our veins,
    A family destined to kill one another.

ORESTES. Killing our mother, I am a murderer,
    From before I was born, a murderer,
    A fate decided in my mother's womb,
    Decreed by the Gods, a murderer,
    A murderer, in the White House of Argos.

ELECTRA. Tantalus. A family fated to live in eternal conflict.
    Tantalus. A vengeful family.
    Who started this bitter turn?
    Who struck with hate's vicious blow?
    Atreus . . . cast out?
    The bloody house of Atreus.
    No one can stop,
    This pitiless blow mandated from heaven.

ORESTES. Everyone kills.
    Our grandfather is a murderer,

Who loves dismembered corpses.
Twenty-first century Tokyo has become deadly pale.
Decapitation.
A family of murderers. Even the Gods recognize this.
The destroyers of the White House of Argos.

ELECTRA. Atreus. Our grandfather.
Atreus. The King of Argos.
Sly and cruel.

ORESTES. By cutting into tiny pieces,
Everything except the head and hands.
He cooked in a pot,
And fed to Thyestes,
My children's flesh, my own flesh and blood.

ELECTRA and ORESTES.
Tantalus. Our ancestor.
Atreus. Our grandfather.
Agamemnon his child.
Our bloodline.
The blood of killers.
The foul wretched blood of beasts,
In this White House of Argos!

They continue singing.

ELECTRA. Come over here, Orestes.

ORESTES. Electra?

ELECTRA. What.

ORESTES. I feel like I'm in a dream.

ELECTRA. If you say this is a dream, then it is a dream that we share.

ORESTES. Come. Together with me, my elder sister.

*Electra bows her head to say yes. Orestes and Electra run offstage.
Enter Katsuyama.*

KATSUYAMA. As I expected, Shimaoka. This doesn't work. This musical style just doesn't suit Greek tragedy.

SCENE 2

Euripedes is drinking sake from a small serving bottle and reading a newspaper.

EURIPIDES. It's started, it's started. The war has started again. It's amazing how much humans love war. Even if it's just a play about war everyone's interested. I wonder what I can write about this war? A melodrama? A comedy? What about an anti-war musical? That's another way to do it. What about an experimental play? Earnest, sour, and dark. Well, no one's going to ask me anyway. (*Drinking sake.*) Ahhh, delicious! The taste of sake is better now that the war has begun.

Shimaoka enters.

SHIMAOKA. Are you Euripides?

EURIPIDES. Do you recognize me?

SHIMAOKA. Just about.

EURIPIDES. How do you think I should look, then?

SHIMAOKA. You should be wearing a toga, like an ancient Athenian.

EURIPIDES. You think so?

SHIMAOKA. Yes . . . But I wonder why I'm here.

EURIPIDES. You don't know the answer?

SHIMAOKA. I got lost in the plot somewhere.

EURIPIDES. Young man, you could be a playwright.

SHIMAOKA. So you know?

EURIPIDES. I can tell by looking at you. We're in the same game. What circumstances bring you here?

SHIMAOKA. I seem to remember being very drunk. Just a short while ago. I was drinking in a bar in Shinjuku and then I went to another bar. Then, I don't remember . . .

EURIPIDES. Have some sushi?

SHIMAOKA. No thanks. But more important . . .

EURIPIDES. I don't know how, so don't ask. I can't tell you how to write a play.

Shimaoka is about to leave.

EURIPIDES. Are you leaving then?

SHIMAOKA. You told me to.

EURIPIDES. Don't you think it's too easy to leave?

SHIMAOKA. I guess you've had enough of dealing with the problems of other playwrights. I'm going.

EURIPIDES. Where to? (*Shimaoka is silent.*) And it's no good going to see Aeschylus either. He's already certified for Level Three nursing care. I've heard he just wanders through the hospital corridors in the middle of the night, muttering to himself: "Tragedy, tragedy." And you can forget about Sophocles. He's menopausal and depressed. He has no energy to do anything.

SHIMAOKA. I know. Writing tragedy drives you insane.

EURIPIDES. Not me, I'm fine.

SHIMAOKA. Why?

EURIPIDES. Who cares. I'm just fine. Have a drink?

SHIMAOKA. Thanks, I don't mind if I do.

EURIPIDES. What is it that you want to ask me?

SHIMAOKA. How to write a tragedy.

EURIPIDES. Umm . . . well, then, you can go.

SHIMAOKA. Oh go on . . .

EURIPIDES. Fuck off.

SHIMAOKA. I'm sorry. I'll take my leave.

EURIPIDES. Hang on. Wait a minute. You give up too easily. You're too detached.

SHIMAOKA. But you said to go . . .

EURIPIDES. Yeah, yeah. Because I'm one of the great playwrights, there are many procedures to follow. If you ask me to teach you something, if you want to learn something, you need to show commitment. Stand in front of the gate for one week or something.

SHIMAOKA. But I don't have time.

EURIPIDES. Does the play open soon?

SHIMAOKA. The rehearsal schedule will be ready very soon. I think it's impossible for me to write a tragedy now. I'll have to make a formal apology and cancel the play. (*Runs away.*)

EURIPIDES. Oiii, wait a minute. That's the wrong direction for the theater . . . (*Talking to himself about playwriting.*) What a stupid question. Maybe I've forgotten. Maybe I need someone to teach me. But . . . no, all I need to do is my work. I'll work now. (*Opens a big book with blank pages for writing kanji and starts writing characters with a quill. Shimaoka returns.*) I'm surprised you've come back.

SHIMAOKA. I got lost.

EURIPIDES. Everyone does.

SHIMAOKA. Would it be all right if I stayed for a while.

EURIPIDES. You can stay if you like but I can't teach you.

SHIMAOKA. Let me just rest here for a short while. (*Euripedes continues writing.*) It's amazing that you can write after drinking.

EURIPIDES. *Electra* and *Orestes* were written while drinking too.

SHIMAOKA. Is that a new kind of tragedy you're working on?

EURIPIDES. Don't talk about tragedy. If you love tragedy so much, why don't you marry it!

SHIMAOKA. It's not tragedy?

EURIPIDES. I'm copying the names of the war dead.

SHIMAOKA. The war dead?

EURIPIDES. The names of all the people who died in all the world's wars. This work takes time.

SHIMAOKA. Is that your new play?

EURIPIDES. And what's wrong with that? War, war, and more war. War gives birth to tragedy. We teach something to stupid human beings with tragedy. And then the story ends. But, in real life, the war starts again. I'm fed up with this endless game—a cat chasing it's own tail. I'm bored by these tragic stories. Dead people are something new. Death is the new living. We don't need to write the stories anymore. Naming the dead suffices. When you write the names of the dead, their stories come forth. All we have to do is wait.

SHIMAOKA. That must take a long time. You're very patient.

EURIPIDES. Don't you want to say something? What's wrong with that? (*Shimaoka tries to take a look at what Euripedes is writing.*) No looking!

SHIMAOKA (*pointing at the big book*). . . . what's that?

EURIPIDES. The list of the names of the war dead.

SHIMAOKA. According to whom? Who recorded this?

EURIPIDES. The Gods.

SHIMAOKA. The Gods? . . . That's another thing I don't understand.

EURIPIDES. Well, it's not something you have to think deeply about. The Gods are very inaccurate, irresponsible, they'll say anything.

SHIMAOKA. But we can't write tragedy without the foresight of the Gods.

EURIPIDES. You don't have to think about these things in complicated ways. Drink. Please, have a drink.

SHIMAOKA. Don't mind if I do. Cheers!

EURIPIDES. Have some sushi too.

SHIMAOKA. I don't eat when I drink.

EURIPIDES. That's bad for your liver.

SHIMAOKA. Eating clouds the taste of sake.

EURIPIDES. Ummm. You're a quite a drinker! Drink to your heart's content. (*Shimaoka drinks.*) . . . Ahh good! I like how you drink. I am pure a child of Edo. You know, real salt-of-the-earth. You drink like an Edo person. Let me offer you some advice.

SHIMAOKA. Are you really Euripides?

EURIPIDES (*ignoring the question*). So, what are you going to write about?

SHIMAOKA. The tragedy of the family of Atreus.

EURIPIDES. So . . . good . . . the family of Atreus. Young man, it must be about Agamemnon then.

SHIMAOKA. Yes.

EURIPIDES. So you want to write about Agamemnon.

SHIMAOKA. And about his wife, Clytemnestra. And his son Orestes and . . . his daughter Electra . . . and Aegisthus and Iphigenia . . . And who else? . . . There are so many variations—it's confusing, a tangled web.

EURIPIDES. Just keep it simple, will you? (*Speaking to someone offstage, distracted.*) Hey old man, give me my usual . . .

SCENE 3

A large cloth backdrop lowers and opens. The family tree of the House of Atreus is printed on it.

SHIMAOKA. What's this?

EURIPIDES. I sometimes use it in a lesson to teach new Gods.

SHIMAOKA. New Gods?

EURIPIDES. Yes. I run workshops for young and emerging Gods.

SHIMAOKA. I thought you were fed up with tragedy.

EURIPIDES. I still have to earn money.

SHIMAOKA. Yes. It's a hard life.

EURIPIDES. Look at this family tree. (*Speaking in the style of a carnival spruiker.*) This bloody House of Atreus. (*Pointing to the names*) But why is this house called so? It all began with Tantalus, son of Zeus. He was so arrogant and jealous that he cut his own son Pelops into small pieces. He cooked his flesh in a pot and tried to get the Gods to eat this diabolical meal. Such an evil thing to do! But why was Tantalus so cruel? Because he was spoiled rotten by the Gods. The Gods were not thinking clearly. They did not preach their message of love and peace. Crimes and chaos resulted from such moodiness and lack of care.

Everyone, please remember this! Bloodlines of the meaty, cannibal chef Tantalus lie in this house of Atreus. And more than that! Lying hidden in this lineage, love and hate blow back and forth like a tornado. Yes, this family is a family of pernicious murderers. And yet, one might well ask about the cause of this insidious stain. A constellation of begrudging, jealousy, and forbidden desire. A curse is on the House of Atreus. Victims of the evil ways of Tantalus and Pelops. Apprehensions of evil rise from the mist of their past deeds. A divine justice no less. One gets what one deserves in this world and the heavy hand of divine justice will descend upon you. For the descendants of the House of Atreus, evil begets evil.

SHIMAOKA. Please, I have a question.

EURIPIDES. Uh? What's your name?

SHIMAOKA. I am Shimaoka, a playwright.

EURIPIDES. Mr. Shimaoka. Please, what is your question?

SHIMAOKA. Wasn't it the son Pelops who was killed by Tantalus? Then why did what happened to Pelops become a matter of divine retribution?

EURIPIDES. Well, that's a good question, Mr. Shimaoka. The Gods stitched Pelops' arms, legs, and head together. They brought him back to life. But then he went on a killing spree: murdering his father, committing all manner of crimes of passion, brawling over women. In other words, he became just like his father.

SHIMAOKA. I really don't understand what the Gods are doing.

EURIPIDES. Yes, well, I'm not interested in your opinions here. Only your questions . . . which I will try to answer as best I can. Well, now, here we have Atreus, grandson of Tantalus. At that time, there was a golden sheep meant as an offering. But as soon as Atreus saw the sheep he wanted to keep it for himself. Instead of offering it to the Gods he secretly killed it and hid it at his place. Imagine hiding such a thing! How bad it must have stank! How rank he was.

More than that. I don't know if it was the God's anger about the sheep or a curse from a past life, but the younger brother Thyestes had a relationship with Aërope, the wife of Atreus. This relationship was not a superficial thing. To cut a long story short, they slept together.

SHIMAOKA. I know. I understand.

EURIPIDES. Not only that, but Aërope was quite a woman. She gave the golden sheep, hidden by her husband, to Thyestes. That sheep was important: a messenger from the Gods had said that whoever possessed the golden sheep would become king. Naturally, there was a struggle among the brothers over their rights to the crown. Then many things happened and finally Atreus became the king and Thyestes was banished. It's a common story. Brothers usually fight over the spoils of family property. However, this is not the end. Greek mythology is without end. Things always get worse. That is the nature of Greek mythology. I guess Atreus couldn't forgive Thyestes. Even after banishing him, whenever Atreus drank, he would remember how his younger brother had slept with his wife. His anger rising, he would plot another revenge . . . Seriously, I say to you, don't drink too much. Two days a week, give your liver a rest. If you drink every day, just have the one glass.

SHIMAOKA. Please continue the story . . .

EURIPIDES. In an evil mood, Atreus pretended to reconcile with Thyestes and asked him back to the country. Secretly, he murdered Thyestes's three children. He cut them into small pieces and served them as a dish at Thyestes's welcome feast. Exactly as his grandfather Tantalus had done! How much this family loves to cook food in a pot! Unknowingly, Thyestes ate the flesh of his children until he was completely full. So delicious, he said. This is the true taste of tragedy. Tragedy with MSG. Here, indeed, we witness the birth of the mythology of the hotpot. As Thyestes was speaking, Atreus took one of the children's heads from the pot and said, "Look at yourself." Then, once again, he banished Thyestes from his house.

SHIMAOKA. Truly, a twenty-first century crime, a deathly pale-face crime.

EURIPIDES. Aegisthus, who later becomes involved with Clytemnestra and murders Agamemnon, was the son of Thyestes. Agamemnon was the hero who defeated the Trojans in the battle for Troy. Indeed, the story of the Trojan Horse is famous. Agamemnon defeated the Trojans with the help of Odysseus and the famous warrior Achilles. He made a tri-umphant return with Cassandra as his hostage and lover. Aegisthus was killed while playing in a soap-land with Clytemnestra—there was a fire of forbidden fruit that burned between them. But they both also held a grudge against Agamemnon. Aegisthus's father was killed by Agamemnon and the son wanted to avenge his father's death. For Clytemnestra, it was the fact that Agamemnon had killed her daughter, Iphigenia. When Agamemnon was sailing to Troy to join the battle, his ship was caught in a storm. Taking this as a sign from the Gods, he made a sacrifice of Iphigenia by pushing her overboard. Clytemnestra could not forgive her husband's cruel deed. So she invited Agamemnon along with Aegisthus to play in the soap-land.

SHIMAOKA. Stop making things up.

EURIPIDES. I'm sorry. But the part about the killing in the soap-land bathtub is true. And that's not all. Then, the other sister and brother, Electra and Orestes, felt aggrieved and could not for-give Aegisthus and their mother Clytemnestra who killed their father. So, they planned to murder them. Can't forgive . . . can't forget . . . each one of them had a reasonable excuse for revenge. But what a family! Such a blood-soaked family tree! Now do you understand my friend, Mr. Shimaoka?

SHIMAOKA. Yes, I understand.

EURIPIDES. What do you understand, young man?

SHIMAOKA. Obviously this family is cursed. But I can see another possibility. There must be such experiences in my own life as well. Me, Kiyoshi Shimaoka. My very existence comes from those unthinkable stories of my ancestors. If I think in this way, the tragedy of the family of Tantalus and of Atreus is nothing special. Even now, in the twenty-first century, there was a boy who killed his mother and cut off her head. After a couple of thousand years, is it possible to know our fate? Perhaps we are all descended from murders. There are hundreds of millions of ancestors . . . so the chances are that one or two of them could be . . .

EURIPIDES. Ha ha ha.

SHIMAOKA. What's so funny?

EURIPIDES. You're not so bad, young man.

SHIMAOKA. Then teach me how to write tragedy.

EURIPIDES. I've forgotten.

SHIMAOKA. Please read this. (*Passing him a manuscript.*) I've started writing a tragedy for the twenty-first century.

EURIPIDES (*takes the manuscript*). So you can write, eh?

SHIMAOKA. It's not even half-finished. It's just a list of scenes.

EURIPIDES (*reading*). Oh, I see that you have Agamemnon as a film director and Clytemnestra as an actress.

SHIMAOKA. "Troy Wars," the best spectacle in the history of tragedy, with Agamemnon in the director's chair.

EURIPIDES. But this "block-buster" description is so old fashioned.

SHIMAOKA. Movies like this haven't gone anywhere since the time of Cecil B. deMille.

EURIPIDES. I really can't be bothered, but if you insist I'll read it.

SHIMAOKA. Sorry to take up your time. I really appreciate this.

EURIPIDES (*reading the manuscript*). "Scene One: Family Portrait."

The backdrop with the family tree falls to the ground. Agamemnon, Clytemnestra, Iphigenia, Chrysothemis, Electra, and Orestes stand in a line, posing for a family portrait. The photographer (actor who also plays Aegisthus) looks into the viewfinder of his camera that rests on a tripod.

PHOTOGRAPHER. Ready, everyrone?

AGAMEMNON. Everyone, big smiles now.

PHOTOGRAPHER. Here we go.

SHIMAOKA. It's a family portrait. They were still a happy family back then.

PHOTOGRAPHER (*looking over his shoulder*). I'm not sure there ever was a time when this family was happy. The image in the viewfinder shows all their secrets, reveals what they try to hide. It's an image of doom.

SHIMAOKA. Don't speak like this, Aegisthus. Your dialogue comes later.

EURIPIDES. Let him speak. He's going be killed soon, anyway. It doesn't matter what he says.

AEGISTHUS. I won't be killed so easily.

EURIPIDES. You want to argue with me? Do you know who I am?

SHIMAOKA. Cool it, will you? Aegisthus, please go backstage at once. Orestes, you go backstage too, you've already left home in this scene. Electra, you . . .

ELECTRA. I know. Don't tell me what to do. (*Leaves.*)

AGAMEMNON. So you said I'll come on later?

SHIMAOKA. Yes, King Agamemnon. Please take a break.

EURIPIDES. So the war for Troy is over?

AGAMEMNON. Not yet.

EURIPIDES. Quickly, you'd better register the trademark for the Trojan Horse.

AGAMEMNON. Yes, you're right.

EURIPIDES. Achilles and Odysseus are also trying to get the patent.

AGAMEMNON. Ahh, I see. Thanks for the tip, old man. (*Exits.*)

SHIMAOKA. Don't mix everything up.

EURIPIDES. I wrote all of those people. There are so many memories. I can't help it.

CLYTEMNESTRA. Don't make me come out just for this.

SHIMAOKA. I'm sorry, Queen Clytemnestra.

CLYTEMNESTRA. Also, can you do something about my name. Cly–tem–nes–tra: it's so difficult to say.

EURIPIDES. That's right. That's why Electra and Andromache always get the heroine roles. Electra . . . sounds so good. When I hear that name it gives me a hard-on. Andromache, it sounds so fresh, like eating a hamburger in one bite.

SHIMAOKA. Wait a minute, please don't say anymore. I'll think about it.

Clytemnestra exits, Iphigenia and Chrysothemis remain.

IPHIGENIA. What about us?

SHIMAOKA. You two stay here.

IPHIGENIA. Which of us is the eldest? I forget.

SHIMAOKA. It's you, Iphigenia.

IPHIGENIA. I heard we were three sisters.

SHIMAOKA. Yes. Iphigenia, Electra and Chrysothemis.

CHRYSOTHEMIS. I thought we were doing a Chekhov play . . .

EURIPIDES. Don't be so stupid.

SHIMAOKA. It's all right for Chrysothemis . . . she can think that.

Cassandra enters.

CASSANDRA. Wait a minute! What's going on here?

SHIMAOKA. What do you want, Cassandra?

CASSANDRA. Why am I not invited? Why didn't you call me? What's wrong?

SHIMAOKA. Because you're not family.

CASSANDRA. But I used to sit here.

SHIMAOKA. Cassandra can't come in now. Please wait a while.

IMAGE 6.1 **Euripides (left) discusses the art of writing with the playwright (center background), while Clytemnestra (center front) ponders her fate.**

Katsuya Kobayashi as Euripides, Akio Nakamura as Shimaoka, and Yoshiko Sakuma as Clytemnestra. *The White House in the Hills of Argos*, New National Theatre, Tokyo, 2007.

Photograph by Masahiko Yakou.

CASSANDRA. Can you give me a hint when? I need to prepare for my role. What kind of mistress am I supposed to be?

EURIPIDES. Read Watanabe Jun'ichi's novel, *A Lost Paradise*.

SHIMAOKA. Don't listen to him. I'll give it some thought.

Cassandra exits in a huff.

EURIPIDES. Is this a comedy?

Shimaoka is silent. Katsuyama enters.

KATSUYAMA. Shimaoka, why are you taking over the rehearsal? Who said you could?

SHIMAOKA. This is not a rehearsal, it's a *theatrum mundi*. The theater of my world, incomplete, a work in progress. Everything is mixed-up at the moment.

KATSUYAMA. Because you haven't finished the script. Go home and write. And no musicals.

SHIMAOKA. I know, I know.

EURIPIDES. Who's this?

SHIMAOKA. This is the director, Katsuyama.

KATSUYAMA. And who's this old man?

SHIMAOKA. Euripides.

KATSUYAMA. What?

SHIMAOKA. I said it's Euripides.

KATSUYAMA. Are you insane? This old man stinks.

SHIMAOKA. Please, Katsuyama, please leave now.

KATSUYAMA. Why?

SHIMAOKA. If you come on now it'll be completely messed up. I promise I'll finish the play.

KATSUYAMA. When?

SHIMAOKA. Two or three days.

EURIPIDES. Whew. Who does this guy think he is?

KATSUYAMA. What did you say, old man. You talking to me?

SHIMAOKA. All right, cool it, Katsuyama.

Katsuyama exits.

EURIPIDES. It's so hard, you have so much trouble. Everything's piling up. You'd better get away from everything. Go to a spa resort.

SHIMAOKA. Please keep reading.

EURIPIDES. Anyway, my opinion's not going to help.

SHIMAOKA. Things are gradually becoming clearer.

EURIPIDES. Clearer?

SHIMAOKA. Please continue.

EURIPIDES. OK. (*Reads.*)

The stage is set like a living room of a house where a family of entertainers live. Iphigenia and Chrysothemis sit.

CHRYSOTHEMIS. Finally, it's your debut, elder sister

IPHIGENIA. Yes. I don't quite know what to say.

CHRYSOTHEMIS. Congratulations.

IPHIGENIA. Wait until it's over.

CHRYSOTHEMIS. Ever since we were children I always knew it would happen one day. Our debut in our father's film.

IPHIGENIA. I don't want people to think that we're just riding on his coat-tails.

CHRYSOTHEMIS. Elder sister, just show people what you're capable of.

IPHIGENIA. I wonder what our mother's doing.

CHRYSOTHEMIS. She's still asleep.

IPHIGENIA. Ahh.

CHRYSOTHEMIS. Is this part of the script?

IPHIGENIA. Yes.

CHRYSOTHEMIS. Can I have a look.

IPHIGENIA. Yes. But make sure your hands are clean.

CHRYSOTHEMIS (*reading*). Helen of Troy. She was the most beautiful woman in the Greek mythology picture book—beautiful! Someone bought this for me when I was a child. Do you remember, elder sister?

IPHIGENIA. That picture book was handed down from me.

CHRYSOTHEMIS. No, it wasn't. Father bought it for me.

IPHIGENIA. But I read it before you were born.

CHRYSOTHEMIS. That was an old one. Father bought me a new one.

IPHIGENIA. Ah, yes, that's right. Electra was reading my book almost every day until it fell apart.

CHRYSOTHEMIS. Electra's always enjoyed reading. I'm very happy for you, sister. I'm proud of my sisters. Electra made her debut as a novelist and now you're going to debut as an actor. If my friends ask for your autograph, please don't say no.

IPHIGENIA. I wonder if I can really act the role of Helen.

CHRYSOTHEMIS. You can, you can.

IPHIGENIA. Chrysothemis, please give me your honest opinion.

CHRYSOTHEMIS. What?

IPHIGENIA. Am I ugly?

CHRYSOTHEMIS. Why do you ask such a thing?

IPHIGENIA. Answer me truthfully. Am I ugly?

CHRYSOTHEMIS. Not ugly but . . .

IPHIGENIA. I'm really worried.

CHRYSOTHEMIS. What are you worried about?

IPHIGENIA. Don't you think I am miscast?

CHRYSOTHEMIS. You can do your own Helen, you'll be fine.

IPHIGENIA. Actually, I have many questions for Mother.

CHRYSOTHEMIS. Then ask.

IPHIGENIA. I can't . . .

CHRYSOTHEMIS. Why not?

IPHIGENIA. She'll be my mother now but in the next moment she'll become an actress. When I figure out she's being an actress, she suddenly switches back and becomes my mother. It's always been like that since I was little.

CHRYSOTHEMIS. I know what you mean. But she loved us equally.

IPHIGENIA. Of course. But since this is my first role, I should find my way on my own. If people knew I was worried, then they might say something. You should be careful, too, outside the house. You can't trust people, you know.

CHRYSOTHEMIS. Mother's often said so too.

IPHIGENIA. Mother says so?

CHRYSOTHEMIS. Yes.

IPHIGENIA. I wonder if she said it as a mother or as an actress?

Aegisthus enters.

CHRYSOTHEMIS. Good morning.

AEGISTHUS. It's too late for good morning.

IPHIGENIA. Time for my appointment at the hairdressers. Can you give me back the script?

CHRYSOTHEMIS. OK.

AEGISTHUS. The script might change again. We're getting a lot of complaints from the maestro. So if you learn your lines now it might be a waste of time.

IPHIGENIA. I don't take orders from you.

AEGISTHUS. I'm counting on you, "Helen." It's a role of rare beauty.

IPHIGENIA. Don't expect too much. (*Exits.*)

AEGISTHUS. For some reason I always feel this house is cold.

CHRYSOTHEMIS. It's because of you, old man.

AEGISTHUS. Me?

CHRYSOTHEMIS. Because of the way you behave.

AEGISTHUS. Stop calling me "old man."

CHRYSOTHEMIS. Then what should I call you?

AEGISTHUS. "E-gee".

CHRYSOTHEMIS. Ugh!

AEGISTHUS. Everyone hates me in this house, so it doesn't matter what you think. Just a little kindness, please.

CHRYSOTHEMIS. You drank too much yesterday too.

AEGISTHUS. Yes. I'll have a "hair of the dog" as well. But I'm not drunk. It's my daily constitutional. If I drink water I get drunk. So I drink alcohol instead. People misunderstand my drinking but no one blames me here. This is a good house. I don't care if people don't like me. I like it here. And because I like it here, I can deal even with the maestro. I can wake up anytime, day or night . . . no one says anything. Everyone's routine is different here. This is a house of nocturnal animals. Even the big star actress is still asleep.

CHRYSOTHEMIS. It's about time to wake her up.

AEGISTHUS. Oh, leave her alone. She's like a Siamese cat. If you wake her up the wrong way she'll scratch you.

Electra has been standing there, unseen.

AEGISTHUS. You surprised me. You shouldn't be lurking around like that.

ELECTRA. Is it a house rule to make an announcement before entering a room?

AEGISTHUS. Well, you're very good at standing in the background and keeping quiet.

ELECTRA. You say such a thing but . . .

AEGISTHUS. Another noble cat from the Hills of Argos. I'm very impressed. You woke up even later than lazy old me.

ELECTRA. Do you have something against people with low blood pressure?

AEGISTHUS. You're the same as your mother.

ELECTRA. You talk as if you know something. Don't speak about things you know nothing of.

AEGISTHUS. Like mother, like daughter . . .

ELECTRA. Stop it.

AEGISTHUS. Iphigenia might be an actress, but you . . . you are the greatest actress . . .

ELECTRA. I said stop it, old man.

CHRYSOTHEMIS. Elder sister, you're shouting.

AEGISTHUS. Yes, yes, don't shout. (*He is grateful to Chrysothemis for calming things. To Chrysothemis.*) I thank you from the bottom of my heart. Do you have a boyfriend now, Chrysothemis?

CHRYSOTHEMIS. No.

AEGISTHUS. In that case . . . I'd like to introduce you to someone. A nice boy for the nicest girl of her generation. But I only know low-life deadbeats. Like me. Your father's surrounded by such people. You should be careful. Maestro's approval is a gift that requires great caution.

ELECTRA. Once in a while you say something good.

AEGISTHUS. Do you know why, Chrysothemis? Because people like us, we live for the moment. This film is just a short-term job. We all live for now. We don't know what the future holds. So this is no time to think about anyone else. You'd better not get involved with our type.

ELECTRA. So you're talking about yourself again.

CHRYSOTHEMIS. Mother asked me to wake her up. (*Exits.*)

ELECTRA. How long are you going to stay here?

AEGISTHUS. You're being mean, as usual.

ELECTRA. Of course.

AEGISTHUS. Why?

ELECTRA. Ask yourself that question.

AEGISTHUS. Ask myself? You use such stock phrases, such clichés, just like a popular writer.

ELECTRA. You're playing with me.

AEGISTHUS. Not in the least. I just like you.

ELECTRA. So now you're trying to seduce me? First Mother, then daughter. Chicken and egg.

AEGISTHUS. Don't joke.

ELECTRA. What's the joke?

AEGISTHUS. Are you saying that because I visited your mother's bedroom? I was just reading her bedtime stories to help her sleep.

ELECTRA. Bedtime stories?

AEGISTHUS. Yes.

ELECTRA. Who knows what kind of stories? Smooth, soft caresses and heavy panting, I bet.

AEGISTHUS. Electra! Truly shocking thoughts. You may not think so but I am getting old. I don't look it perhaps but I am old. Could you speak a little more politely?

ELECTRA. I'm asking you what of kind story you were reading to my mother. Is it one that you can tell me too?

AEGISTHUS. I was sharing story ideas for a film. From film noir to melodrama, there are many such. Shall I tell you one?

ELECTRA. I'll pass.

AEGISTHUS. You can use it for your novel.

ELECTRA. If it's good enough.

AEGISTHUS. See, that's why you're like . . . (*meaning "your mother."*)

ELECTRA. I said, stop that.

AEGISTHUS. No, you're not. I think you're more like your father. That arrogance . . . I can't hate that completely. I read your novel. It was good, interesting. Especially if you know about this house.

ELECTRA. So you think I just ride on the coat-tails of my parents?

AEGISTHUS. No, you have talent but it is dangerous.

ELECTRA. What do you mean?

AEGISTHUS. Well . . . it's hard to say . . .

ELECTRA. Answer me!

AEGISTHUS. Can you read my script with that dangerous talent of yours? The filming's begun but the Maestro doesn't like the way things are going. He wants more scenes for Andromache. Do you know why, little girl?

ELECTRA. Don't call me "little girl."

AEGISTHUS. I'm just following Chrysothemis.

ELECTRA. This isn't some sleazy cabaret, you know.

AEGISTHUS. I remember how you described such a place in your novel. It was so real. So you did research?

ELECTRA. Stop talking shit. I used to work for them.

AEGISTHUS. I thought you worked for a "heath club," gave massages.

ELECTRA. I did that too.

AEGISTHUS. Sorry, I didn't know you were so experienced. I didn't realize I was speaking to an expert. Do you know what all this Andromache stuff is about?

ELECTRA. Who cares, who gives a shit?

AEGISTHUS. Cassandra's going to play that role.

ELECTRA. . . . Cassandra playing Andromache . . . I think Father is losing his edge.

AEGISTHUS. I suppose you think so, but what if we get Chrysothemis to speak to the director? It's not good for the house, you know.

ELECTRA. I don't care about this house.

AEGISTHUS. Have you met Cassandra?

ELECTRA. Why are you asking such stupid questions?

AEGISTHUS. It's not that important. By the way, how's your brother doing?

ELECTRA. . . . Why?

AEGISTHUS. Because I haven't seen him around. He's called Orestes? I think he should act in the film.

ELECTRA. . . . he's alive.

AEGISTHUS. I know he's alive.

ELECTRA. No, he's dead.

AEGISTHUS. Which one is he?

ELECTRA. None of your business.

AEGISTHUS. Ah, so that's the way it's to be. I know there are family issues to deal with . . . Please read this and give me you honest opinion. (*Takes out the manuscript.*) This film will guarantee trouble. Like *Cleopatra* in the golden age of Hollywood.

ELECTRA. Your example is too old-fashioned.

AEGISTHUS. Maybe a great actress will appear in the last scene—if that works. (*Leaves the manuscript behind and exits.*)

Electra reads.

SCENE 6

Euripedes enters and interrupts Electra.

EURIPIDES. What do you think about the script?

ELECTRA. Who are you?

EURIPIDES. Someone passing by.

ELECTRA. I guess you're part of the film crew.

EURIPIDES. If you say so. I'm the props master. So, is the script interesting?

ELECTRA. The Trojan War, eh? You're a little too late . . .

EURIPIDES. Yes, I know.

SHIMAOKA. Wait up, Euripides. Please don't interfere.

EURIPIDES. What if I do? They were all my characters, after all. This is very different from my version but that's all right. It looks like Agamemnon hasn't been killed yet.

ELECTRA. What are you talking about?

SHIMAOKA. Please! Stop this chatter.

EURIPIDES. At the beginning of my *Electra*, Agamemnon was already murdered by Clytemnestra and Aegisthus. I don't know how you're going be able to kill him off here.

SHIMAOKA. Shush.

ELECTRA. Are you're a fortune-teller or something?

EURIPIDES. If you say so . . . I can read the fortunes of . . . (*those in my play.*)

ELECTRA. So, are you saying my father will be killed by them?

EURIPIDES. Yes. And then you and your younger brother will seek revenge. That's is how the story goes. Can you do that?

ELECTRA. You're mad. Speaking such rubbish . . .

SHIMAOKA. Let's leave it to the characters to decide.

EURIPIDES. You said you were a writer. What did you write?

ELECTRA. None of your business.

EURIPIDES. Have you applied for a new writer's grant?

ELECTRA. . . . well, yes, I have.

EURIPIDES. It must be a self-portrait. The story of an artists' clan and . . . the bad daughter wandering about, looking for love. She rebels against her parents and works in a seedy sex club. She even acts in a pornographic film. Despite all this, somehow or the other, her father understands her. She can't completely reject him, she can't be totally consumed by her hatred of him. Ultimately, she understands his weakness—she shares his fatal flaw.

ELECTRA. You read my story!

EURIPIDES. I already know what happens, even without reading your story.

SHIMAOKA. Excuse me but these are my characters.

EURIPIDES. Oh, don't be so tight-assed . . . I guess you've already begun writing your next play. You should write the naked truth about your family. That's the best thing to do. Show the true story of the famous artist's family. It'll be a best-seller for sure.

ELECTRA. All this talk is annoying me. Cut this fucking crap. (*Exits.*)

EURIPIDES. She's much less friendly than I wrote her.

SHIMAOKA. Shush, someone's coming. Let's hide, quickly.

EURIPIDES. Why do we have to hide?

SHIMAOKA. Someone might report seeing us together and then we might be eliminated.

EURIPIDES. Eliminated? Who would do such a thing?

SHIMAOKA. Not who, what. The history of theater.

SCENE 7

The living room at night. Clytemnestra enters. She picks up the script and turns the pages. Agamemnon enters. Clytemnestra puts the script aside.

CLYTEMNESTRA. So you've come home.

AGAMEMNON. The more I get into this film, the more I realize how many problems there are with the script.

CLYTEMNESTRA. So? You're the director, you can do what you like. It's up to you.

AGAMEMNON. Have you read the script?

CLYTEMNESTRA. Why should I?

AGAMEMNON. I saw you reading it just now.

CLYTEMNESTRA. I thought it was a magazine.

AGAMEMNON. Is Aegisthus working?

CLYTEMNESTRA. I don't know. I guess so. In his own way he is serious.

AGAMEMNON. I thought I saw his light on.

CLYTEMNESTRA. You should go and see what he's up to.

AGAMEMNON. I don't want to disturb him.

CLYTEMNESTRA. That doesn't sound like you at all.

AGAMEMNON. Are you angry?

CLYTEMNESTRA. What about?

AGAMEMNON. About this play. (*Clytemnestra is silent.*) Helen's too young for you to play.

CLYTEMNESTRA (*laughs*). I don't want to be talked to like a little child. Please stop. I'm more worried about Iphigenia. Is she up to it? You cast her, didn't you? You obviously thought she was good . . .

AGAMEMNON. Yes.

CLYTEMNESTRA. Well, that's that, then. There's nothing more to be said.

AGAMEMNON. Are you complaining?

CLYTEMNESTRA. I thought you had someone else in mind.

AGAMEMNON. Who else is there? If you have something to say, speak up.

CLYTEMNESTRA. The question is: Can we be detached and judge our child fairly? After all, you're a father before you're a director?

AGAMEMNON. When I'm on the set I'm a director. I do what it takes to get the best performances. No excuses. I'm very strict.

CLYTEMNESTRA. But you could give her a smaller role to start with. She's easily unnerved.

AGAMEMNON. That's why I want you to play the scene with her. While you're playing Andromache, you can give her advice on how to play Iphigenia.

CLYTEMNESTRA. Do you think that's is a good idea? People will say that she's caught between two parents.

AGAMEMNON. What you really want to say is that you don't want to play Andromache because there aren't enough lines. The role isn't big enough for your talents?

CLYTEMNESTRA (*laughing*). So that's what you think. The great director. Your interpretation's too literal.

AGAMEMNON. There are some who think I'm only a maestro of the ordinary. You think so too . . .

CLYTEMNESTRA. No, that's not what I think.

AGAMEMNON. Yes, it is.

CLYTEMNESTRA. No. You're a great killer of people in your plays. You don't care about a single life as long as it's for your art. Don't worry about me. Just do what ever you think is best. The only one I worry about is Iphigenia. That's all. I can honestly say that Electra's the real actress.

AGAMEMNON. I know.

CLYTEMNESTRA. You should tell her. Make her see it.

AGAMEMNON. She said no. She doesn't want to act.

CLYTEMNESTRA. I thought as much. Because Electra doesn't like me.

AGAMEMNON. That's something different, don't complicate things any more than they are already.

CLYTEMNESTRA. So, at least you acknowledge that she hates me?

AGAMEMNON. You should talk to her and work out your differences.

CLYTEMNESTRA. That might work in most cases, but not for a mother and daughter. The more we talk, the more tangled things become.

AGAMEMNON. Even though you end up arguing, you're still mother and daughter.

CLYTEMNESTRA. It's because we are mother and daughter that things are different. It's not like a quarrel between strangers. We think we should be able to understand each other but we can't. Please, do something for her.

AGAMEMNON. I?

CLYTEMNESTRA. She likes you.

AGAMEMNON. So Electra likes me. But you don't . . .

CLYTEMNESTRA. I'm not saying that . . .

AGAMEMNON. Well, then, at least give me some respect.

CLYTEMNESTRA. I do. You're a great person.

AGAMEMNON. I'm going to bed. (*Exits.*)

CLYTEMNESTRA. Off you go, then. A film director has to wake up very early. (*Picks up the script, tears it into pieces, and throws it in the bin. Iphigenia enters.*) Iphigenia, what's the matter? (*Hiding the bin*) Can't you sleep? (*Iphigenia is silent.*) You can talk to your mother.

IPHIGENIA. You mean you'll listen to me?

CLYTEMNESTRA. Of course I will.

IPHIGENIA. . . . I'm scared.

CLYTEMNESTRA. Scared?

IPHIGENIA. Yes.

CLYTEMNESTRA. What are you scared of, Iphigenia? You can tell me.

IPHIGENIA. . . . I don't think that I can play Helen. That's your role.

CLYTEMNESTRA. What are you saying? Father says you can . . . so you can.

IPHIGENIA. I don't want to sully the family reputation.

CLYTEMNESTRA. You should have more confidence, Iphigenia. I know you can do it.

IPHIGENIA. But I don't have your talent. That I know for sure.

CLYTEMNESTRA. No, that's not true.

IPHIGENIA. It'll look like the lesser talent stealing the role from the greater.

CLYTEMNESTRA. Nonsense. I'm very happy about your debut. Nothing can make me happier. Don't worry, I'll teach you a few tricks of the trade. To calm yourself on the first day, have a chat with the security person.

IPHIGENIA. What if there is no security person?

CLYTEMNESTRA. Then just talk to someone lower down in the pecking order. Someone who doesn't have airs. You'll feel your tension dissolve. And you'll help everyone else as well. Everyone's nervous on the first day.

IPHIGENIA. Thanks for the advice. It's very helpful.

CLYTEMNESTRA. Break a leg. I'll always be there for you . . . Electra (*Electra has been standing unseen by the others. To Electra*). Are you eavesdropping? What did you hear?

ELECTRA. You didn't see me. You were in your own world.

CLYTEMNESTRA. It's your bedtime, Electra.

ELECTRA. Don't speak to me like a child. I'm a grown-up.

CLYTEMNESTRA. For parents, children are children forever.

ELECTRA. It's because of this sort of behavior that your son wanted to leave you.

CLYTEMNESTRA. What?

ELECTRA. Orestes left because he had had enough of being treated like your slave.

IMAGE 6.2 **Electra confronts Clytemenstra.**

Hijiri Kojima as Electra and Yoshiko Sakuma as Clytemnestra. *The White House in the Hills of Argos*, New National Theatre, Tokyo, 2007.

Photograph by Masahiko Yakou.

CLYTEMNESTRA. Slave?

ELECTRA. Yes. We're all slaves obeying your actorly commands.

CLYTEMNESTRA. What? I love all of you. Are you saying I don't love you, Electra?

ELECTRA. Yes. You love me in your own way but what kind of love is that . . . ? You act the nice mother to us. In front of Father, you act the good wife. But I know from your expression that it's all an act. When Father's home you act one way and when he's away you act another. When Aegisthus is at home, you act yet another way. That's why I can't believe you despite your command performances.

CLYTEMNESTRA. You don't know how to be loved. You can't feel it when someone loves you. I know that well because I'm the same.

ELECTRA. Stop saying that. I'm not like you.

CLYTEMNESTRA. You're stubborn. You hold a grudge. Decades after, you still hold on to the slightest smallest transgression that were done to you.

ELECTRA. You don't have to care for me. But you should at least give Father more of your love.

CLYTEMNESTRA. Is that why you hate me?

Electra and Clytemnestra begin to recite their lines from the original text of Electra.

ELECTRA. This next: if, as you say, my father killed your daughter,
What injury have I and my brother done to you?
Why, after you had killed your husband, did you not
Make over to us our father's house? Instead you took
As dowry to your lover what was not your own,
And bought yourself a husband. Aegisthus does not
Suffer exile in payment for Orestes' wrongs,
Nor death for mine, though he inflicts a living death
On me, far crueller than my sister's. And if death
In justice demands death, why, then, I and your son
Orestes must kill you to avenge our father's death;
For if the one revenge is just, so is the other.

CLYTEMNESTRA. My Child, your nature has always been to love your father.
It is natural; some children love their fathers best,
And some their mothers. I'll forgive you. I do not,
In fact exult unduly over what I did.
With what insensate fury I drove myself to take
My grand revenge! How bitterly I regret it now!

ELECTRA. It's too late for regret; you can't undo what's done.
Well, though my father's dead, your son Orestes lives,
Exiled from Argos. Why do you not bring him home?[1]

---

1 This section is taken from Euripides, *Electra*, in *Medea and Other Plays* (Philip Ellicott trans.), (London: Penguin, 1963), p. 142.

CLYTEMNESTRA. Very good. You did really well.

ELECTRA. But I'm not going to be your lovely daughter. Your love will not affect me.

CLYTEMNESTRA. I always gave you the freedom to do what you wanted.

ELECTRA. I am who I am. Father and Orestes are also wounded . . . victims of your . . . love.

CLYTEMNESTRA. Don't speak like that . . . please don't say such things. (*Exits.*)

IPHIGENIA. Electra, you're very good at saying these lines.

ELECTRA. Stop!

IPHIGENIA. Why don't you become an actress?

ELECTRA. Stop talking such rubbish. Who wants to be an actress!

IPHIGENIA. You bully your mother too much.

ELECTRA. Mind your own business.

IPHIGENIA. You should stop talking about Orestes to Mother.

ELECTRA. She asks for it, Iphigenia. Do you know why Orestes left home?

IPHIGENIA. You know everything there is to know.

ELECTRA. I know, even though I don't want to know. I hear, even though I don't want to hear.

IPHIGENIA. It's because you're a writer.

ELECTRA. You're saying I'm a bad person? I guess that's what you want to say. If you don't want to listen then I won't tell you.

IPHIGENIA. No, I want to listen.

ELECTRA. Orestes happened to see Mother and Aegisthus . . .

IPHIGENIA. I guessed as much.

ELECTRA. So you're not surprised.

IPHIGENIA. Why would I be surprised after all these years.

ELECTRA. As I expected. You're the eldest sister and, after all, it doesn't matter to us. But I think it was a big shock for Orestes. I don't know why, though.

IPHIGENIA. I don't understand boys.

ELECTRA. Boys are more sensitive than girls these days.

IPHIGENIA. Is Aegisthus at Mother's tonight as well?

ELECTRA. I heard Father and another man talking in Aegisthus's room.

IPHIGENIA. What about?

ELECTRA. Some script. Father was saying how he'd better change some of the lines. He was complaining about how some of the script didn't work.

IPHIGENIA. I'm not like you. I like Mother. Of course, I like Father too. But I want to leave this house.

ELECTRA. You can leave soon.

IPHIGENIA. Why don't you leave as well?

ELECTRA. Because I can find many stories to inspire me in this White House.

IPHIGENIA. You're scary, Electra.

ELECTRA. So people have been saying since I was little. And because they kept saying it, I kept thinking I had to be scary. The shoot will be fine, Elder Sister. It'll go well. Helen of Troy isn't such a complicated role.

IPHIGENIA (*finds the torn script and takes it out*). Did you do this?

ELECTRA. Why do you think it's me? That bitch did it.

IPHIGENIA. Who?

ELECTRA. Mother.

IPHIGENIA. I don't believe it.

ELECTRA. You just don't understand her. (*Takes a talisman and gives it to Iphigenia.*) Here, take this.

IPHIGENIA. A good-luck charm?

ELECTRA. Take it with you for the shoot.

IPHIGENIA. . . . Thanks.

ELECTRA. First, your debut as Helen of Troy. Next, a contemporary drama. I think you're more suited to that.

IPHIGENIA. Thank you very much, Electra. I'll go to bed now. I think I can sleep.

ELECTRA. Um, yes. (*Iphigenia exits. Electra picks up the torn script.*) I'm sure she did it. That bitch.

Agamemnon enters, holding a whiskey tumbler.

AGAMEMNON (*looking at the script in Electra's hands*). Electra, You don't have to rip it up.

ELECTRA. It wasn't me.

AGAMEMNON. I guess you've read it, then?

ELECTRA. Yes.

AGAMEMNON. Then give me your opinion.

ELECTRA. Fucking rubbish.

AGAMEMNON. As I thought. Why don't you write it?

ELECTRA. It would be a comedy.

AGAMEMNON. That's no good. Filmmaking is men's work, after all.

ELECTRA. Are you serious?

AGAMEMNON. A film location is like a field of battle.

ELECTRA. So women shouldn't be on the battlefield?

AGAMEMNON. Better to leave the fighting to men.

ELECTRA. I feel sorry for such men.

AGAMEMNON. Why?

ELECTRA. He has to live up to his reputation, to being "Maestro," the big brand.

AGAMEMNON. Brand?

ELECTRA. No one makes war films like him.

AGAMEMNON. He can't do anything else. People expect it of him. If he changed now the people would feel betrayed.

ELECTRA. He should betray them.

AGAMEMNON. He can't.

ELECTRA. He won't get divorced for the same reason.

AGAMEMNON. No. That's a different matter.

ELECTRA. Why you are so accepting of Mother and that man? (*Agamemnon is silent.*) Is it so that you can hang around with your mistress too? Or do you want to be seen as open-minded?

AGAMEMNON. That man has something different going for him. My film needs him.

ELECTRA. That man doesn't respect you, Father.

AGAMEMNON. I know that.

ELECTRA. You'd better not drink too much.

AGAMEMNON. I've got to make this film work. Whatever I do, I don't want to become a film director past his prime.

ELECTRA. Don't drink, then.

AGAMEMNON. Yeah, I get what you're saying. But I'm old school. I take my time. Making films—I survived the yakuza and the war: the gangster's short knife and the tank. Women are just there to look after the injured in the heat of the battle. That's enough.

ELECTRA. But those women are battered and raped.

AGAMEMNON. You're criticizing my films?

ELECTRA. I like your films. They have a power beyond words.

AGAMEMNON. Don't lie.

ELECTRA. I'm not. Your films are like a blast of fresh air. But they're also full of sorrow . . .

AGAMEMNON. . . . You know Orestes. How's he getting on?

ELECTRA. I don't know.

AGAMEMNON. Please tell me, it'll be in confidence.

ELECTRA. I said I don't know.

AGAMEMNON. I see.

ELECTRA. Orestes doesn't hate you. He hates your films.

AGAMEMNON. Why?

ELECTRA. Because so many people die in them.

AGAMEMNON. That's stupid. The audience love to watch people die in films.

ELECTRA. Tell that to Orestes. When he was little, he asked me why you weren't arrested though you let so many people die. I tried to explain that it was for the audience, that you were killing them for the audience. You did it to help the audience get what they want.

Agamemnon Exits. Euripedes rushes in.

EURIPIDES. Hi, everyone.

ELECTRA. Here he comes again.

EURIPIDES. Yes. I can't wait around just reading the script. Anyway, it's a totally different story from mine. Well, then. Where's Orestes?

ELECTRA. I said, I don't know. You must know better than me, old man. (*Exits.*)

EURIPIDES. Ahh. I remember now. (*Takes out a script and reads*) "A street at night. Orestes is standing." (*Runs off.*)

Shimaoka enters jumping. His arms, legs, and mouth are bound by tape. He tries to follow Euripides but falls over.

SCENE 8

The street at night, Orestes is standing. Pylades enters.

PYLADES. Are you serious about this, Orestes?

ORESTES. Yes.

PYLADES. How long have you been here?

ORESTES. Five hours

PYLADES. So you've been standing here for five hours?

ORESTES. I had two . . . customers

PYLADES (*in disbelief*). You didn't!

ORESTES. You can check.

PYLADES. Stupid!

ORESTES. It's my life. Let me do what I please.

PYLADES. You'd better get back to the salon.[2]

---

2 A male escort club.

ORESTES. I don't want to do that menial service thing again for those women customers.

PYLADES. You're OK with men, then?

ORESTES. It's the rich women I don't like. I prefer the wrinkled warmth of those old men who secretly try to satisfy their desires by spending what little money they have.

PYLADES. Don't say such stupid things.

ORESTES. I'm trying to find a new way.

PYLADES. Is this your idea of a new way?

ORESTES. Yes.

PYLADES. It's degrading. Don't you remember what you were saying at the beginning? You said you were going to become an actor. And you weren't going to rely on your parents for help.

ORESTES. This is great training for an actor. Now I can see what was not clear before.

PYLADES. What do you think you're going to achieve by torturing yourself?

ORESTES. There is a saying: "There is no success without suffering."

PYLADES. You've had enough suffering already, Orestes. Let's go back to the salon, Number Two (*his salon-escort number*).

ORESTES. I won't, Number Three.

PYLADES. We might be friends but I can't go this route with you.

ORESTES. Go back to the salon, then.

Middle-Aged Man approaches.

MIDDLE-AGED MAN. Shall we go? (*Orestes nods assent.*) Not you. Him.

PYLADES. Me?

MIDDLE-AGED MAN. I'll pay well.

PYLADES. No. Not me . . .

ORESTES. Go for it.

Middle-Aged Man tries to leave, dragging Pylades behind him.

ORESTES. What now? It's a bit quiet.

Euripedes enters.

EURIPIDES. Hi.

ORESTES. . . . Hi there.

EURIPIDES. How're you?

ORESTES. Ha?

EURIPIDES. So, how've you been getting along these days?

ORESTES (*in Osaka dialect*, bochi bochi). So-so . . . OK.

EURIPIDES. You from Osaka?

ORESTES. No.

EURIPIDES. I thought you were someone else. But you're Orestes, aren't you? And that was Pylades who just left, wasn't it?

ORESTES. How do you know?

EURIPIDES. You two are famous around here.

ORESTES. Is that so? Did you hear about us at the salon?

EURIPIDES. The salon?

ORESTES. Host Club "Tragedy."

EURIPIDES. The name doesn't really make me excited about going there.

ORESTES. At "Tragedy," everyone can play the heroine.

EURIPIDES. I'm not interested in being a heroine. How are things though?

ORESTES. About what?

EURIPIDES. About killing your mother. Is it going well?

ORESTES. I don't know what you're talking about.

EURIPIDES. Don't worry. It's been going on since the old days. You're wasting valuable time hanging out here, though. Quick now. Go to your elder sister and get ready.

ORESTES. Ready for what?

EURIPIDES. Ready to kill your mother.

ORESTES. Why do I have to kill my mother?

EURIPIDES. Why? Because your mother and her lover . . . your father . . . Ah . . . (*realizes this part of the play hasn't yet taken place.*)

ORESTES. What's that?

EURIPIDES. I just remembered. Your father hasn't been killed yet. A blind spot. You don't have any reason to kill her yet.

ORESTES. Who did you say I'm supposed to kill?

EURIPIDES. Your mother. As the story goes, your mother kills your father but . . .

ORESTES. Is that so? If it is, it's interesting. So I kill my mother because Mom kills Dad. That means I like my father a lot.

EURIPIDES. Yes, so it does.

ORESTES. But I have a reason to kill my father as well. In fact, I'd like to burn down the whole house.

EURIPIDES. Please don't do that. The story'll get too complicated.

ORESTES. It's my life, I'll do what I want.

EURIPIDES. I wonder what it is you hate so much? Your father's a great man. A rare person. There's only a few like him.

ORESTES. It's like a house of paper.

EURIPIDES. Paper?

ORESTES. It's a house that dwells in writing. A house of writing on paper. Father is like a father, nothing more or less. Mother is like a mother. They are just words that have been written. No one says anything important. I don't want to play the son. If Father's to be killed, then make it soon. Then I'll kill Mother. Finally, I might be able to find love for them. I was always alone in that house.

EURIPIDES. But you've got kind sisters.

ORESTES. Iphigenia doesn't know the truth about our parents. Clytemnestra's just a good girl. Electra . . .

EURIPIDES. Electra?

ORESTES. Is defiant.

EURIPIDES. So you don't get on well with Electra. That's a problem. She's supposed to be your partner in crime.

ORESTES. So Electra and I will kill Mother?

EURIPIDES. It's meant to be.

ORESTES. I see. I feel my destiny is to be like Oedipus.

EURIPIDES. No. You'd better leave that to Sophocles . . .

Pylades, naked, runs on to the stage.

PYLADES. Orestes!

ORESTES. Pylades, why aren't you wearing clothes?

PYLADES. I just can't do it with a man.

Middle-Aged Man enters holding a box-cutter.

MIDDLE-AGED MAN. You tricked me? You little shit! You insulted me. (*Lunges at him with the knife.*)

Euripedes springs to Pylades's defence and disarms Middle-Aged Man.

EURIPIDES. I fear the story is going off the rails a bit. Pylades, haven't you got some important scenes coming up. What're you doing?

PYLADES. I know. Orestes, I just saw on the hotel TV that Iphigenia was in an accident at the shoot. She's unconscious. The TV said it was serious. Apparently Agamemnon let her do her own stunts without a double.

ORESTES. Asshole . . .

EURIPIDES. Go home, Orestes, go back to Argos.

Shimaoka enters running. His legs are untied but his hands and mouth are still bound with gaffer-tape.

ORESTES. Pylades, let's go. Those guys are treating this like a comedy. (*Orestes and Pylades exit.*)

EURIPIDES. Um. My impression is that the cast is very rebellious.

MIDDLE-AGED MAN. What should I do now?

EURIPIDES. Stay here. You won't be sorry. You can trust me.

MIDDLE-AGED MAN. Yes.

EURIPIDES (*to Shimaoka*). Your unfinished play is what's causing all this confusion. (*Peels off the tape from Shimaoka's mouth.*)

SHIMAOKA. No, it's you who's confusing them.

EURIPIDES. You're not giving the cast the right message. You spoil them, that's why they are so selfish. What are you going to do? Do you have an ending in mind?

SHIMAOKA. None.

EURIPIDES. None?

SHIMAOKA. We talked a lot about it, the director and I, but we didn't . . .

SCENE 9

Before anyone realizes Middle-Aged Man changes into Katsuyama.

KATSUYAMA. Let's be original.

SHIMAOKA. That's why I thought about doing it as a musical,

KATSUYAMA. Shimaoka, let's *not* do a musical.

SHIMAOKA. Well, what do you mean by "original?"

KATSUYAMA. A contemporary Japanese Greek tragedy.

SHIMAOKA. That is when I hit the wall . . . Remember the family tree of Atreus? Can you check who was at the top of the tree?

KATSUYAMA (*takes out a piece of paper with the family tree*). Zeus.

SHIMAOKA. Yes. It's Zeus. He's a God, isn't he? That's why people like Agamemnon have so many Gods as relatives. They're human but they're descended from Gods. In Euripides's *Electra* and *Orestes*, the Gods are distant relatives who pass judgment on the main characters. How can we make those Gods come to life in contemporary Japan? How can we have a *deux ex machina* for our time?

KATSUYAMA. *Deux ex machina*? What's that?

SHIMAOKA. It's when the Gods appear in the final scene of the play. *Deux ex machina* is the mechanical God. In the final scene of a Greek Tragedy, a God appears floating above the cast through the use of machinery. The play ends when the God's pass their final judgments on those below. What should I do? Use it or not?

KATSUYAMA. Use it. It's OK.

SHIMAOKA. But I can't. The appearance of the Gods is treated more like a comedy these days.

KATSUYAMA (*thinking*). Ummm. (*Exits pondering this problem.*)

EURIPIDES. You're distressed.

SHIMAOKA. I said that before.

EURIPIDES. Now I really understand.

SHIMAOKA. Understand what?

EURIPIDES. I really understand.

SHIMAOKA. What do you understand?

EURIPIDES. I really understand the problem. Shimaoka my friend, what you need now is a description of war, of the experience of the battlefield.

SHIMAOKA. Umm . . .

EURIPIDES. Your cast needs to truly experience war. War is the mass-production of tragedy. Even now, wars are everywhere.

Mr. Shimaoka, my friend . . . the Japanese people . . . you just avoid the facts of war, you sidestep the true effects of war. So you can't write tragedy. You lost the skill when you shunned war. That's why you need to experience war. Begin by reading about war, Mr. Shimaoka. (*Picks up a manuscript and gives it to Shimaoka*) Read this little piece of a new tragedy. An eruption from the graves of the war dead.

SHIMAOKA. As I thought, you have been writing after all.

EURIPIDES. I haven't. It's the manuscript of the dead. Their thoughts soak the parchment like invisible writing. So, Mr. Shimaoka, read this.

SHIMAOKA (*turning pages and reading*). "The Genocide of Troy." "Or Somewhere Else."

EURIPIDES. To Troy!

SHIMAOKA. Where are we?

EURIPIDES. We're in Troy. Agamemnon's troops are coming for the massacre. They're going to rape and pillage and set fire to everything. They'll do whatever they like. I think the problem of the *deux ex machina* will be solved here as well. Now, here comes a Trojan sword-bearer named Hector.

HECTOR. I am Hector.

EURIPIDES. This is my friend Mr. Shimaoka from the land of peace.

HECTOR. I see. From the look on his face, he looks like he still believes in hope.

SHIMAOKA. I've given up on hope.

HECTOR. That's hard to believe. Your despair is tiny. Like the tears of an ant.

SHIMAOKA. My personal sense of despair and the land of peace are totally separate.

EURIPIDES. Ah. Pray tell me more about your personal sense of despair. I might be able to find out something about the final scene of the tragedy.

SHIMAOKA. I very much doubt that. The tragedy that people expect me to write is a massive drama involving many countries and many Gods. My despair, though, is just a small empty feeling, a blank space in my daily life. I wonder why? I feel like I'm floating on air—without form. When I touch something, I sense it but I don't feel it's real. I suppose the the news of a massacre a day must make everyone feel the same. Like a mass-produced killing machine. People killing people without even realizing. Without feeling.

People may like to think about killing with a passion burning in their heart but that's an illusion. They don't kill to find a passion. They don't find anything. Killing is like a dream—it's almost beyond our understanding.

EURIPIDES. Write that down.

SHIMAOKA. Tragedy is not born from such virtual-reality killing. It's just an endlessly dry landscape. An empty vista.

HECTOR. Let me say a word to the war dead. Such an arid landscape is a luxury for those who don't know about battle.

SHIMAOKA. As a member of this country, I would like to say something. People go on about war all the time. But why don't they talk about the importance of peace? You think that people living in peace aren't qualified to write a play? That peace can't write a play?

HECTOR. It was you who said you couldn't write tragedy.

SHIMAOKA. I did.

HECTOR. So, what are you going to write?

SHIMAOKA. Nothing.

EURIPIDES. You won't write anymore? But there's nowhere for you to go. You should listen to the words of the dead. There's a world that only the dead can see. Just as you can see us now.

SHIMAOKA. What? Wait a minute.

EURIPIDES. You said that the problems of nations and individuals are separate. But that's not right.

HECTOR. Think of the Trojan War. It originated at my foolish younger brother's palace when he had a crush on Helen, Queen of Achaia. He kidnapped her and brought her to Troy. The war that killed thousands of people in Troy and Achaia was begun by one man's love and the anger and jealous rage of another, King Menelaus, who lost his Queen. After long years of war, Troy was ransacked by the terrorist attack of the Trojan Horse. The curtain came down on the Trojan War when the troops of Achaia killed everyone in a single act of ethnic cleansing. The story of this murderous warfare was passed down as one of legendary heroes and became beautified. Achilles, Odysseus, and I. As it happened a long time ago, you may think that nothing can be done. That the will of Greece was determined by one old king's emotions. But the names of the war dead are passed on in writing. Reading them, I thought: People say that modern warfare exists between

IMAGE 6.3 **Euripides, Shimaoka the playwright, and Hector.**

Katsuya Kobayashi as Euripides, Akio Nakamura as Shimaoka, and Yoshiki Arizono as Hector. *The White House in the Hills of Argos*, New National Theatre, Tokyo, 2007.

Photograph by Masahiko Yakou.

countries but where can we see such warlike animus and intent? This thing called the nation-state, this artificial entity, is it so functionally different from one person's humanity and emotions? In fact, conflict between nations is not very different from conflict between one human being and another.

SHIMAOKA. No. The crux of the nation is different from that of the individual.

HECTOR. The system is different. But you can't overestimate the nation-state. It is, after all, a creation that moves by the feelings of those who reside within.

SHIMAOKA. Just the will of the people?

HECTOR. So the feelings of the majority rule, then?

SHIMAOKA. Yes.

HECTOR. If that's the case, the nation is nothing but the integration of people's feelings and emotions. War can happen over anything. Eliminating war from human history is impossible.

SHIMAOKA. What do you hope to achieve by making me seeing this?

EURIPIDES. You've crossed into the place of the Gods. There are many things that I want you to see. It is fated that you must see these things.

SHIMAOKA. The place of the Gods?

EURIPIDES. We're very high up here. Like the top floor of a skyscraper.

SHIMAOKA. What's happening?

EURIPIDES. Look out of the window.

SHIMAOKA. What's that . . . ?

HECTOR. Here they come. The partisans, the survivors of the Trojan Wars, have finally awoken.

SHIMAOKA. Why are they here . . . ? Why now . . . ?

HECTOR (*excited*). Revenge! They come to take a piece of us, to engage in battle. The remnants of the Achaian militia!

EURIPIDES. Now do you understand my friend, Mr. Shimaoka? This is not Troy anymore.

SHIMAOKA. Ah . . . Ummm . . .

The front half of a huge Trojan Horse smashes through the wall onto the stage.

HECTOR (*like a reporter*). This is Argos. Argos and Shinjuku, Shinjuku and Argos. At the beginning of the twenty-first century at 8:45 a.m. the first Trojan Horse crashed into a skyscraper. The first wave of the attack. 9:03 a.m., a second horse crashed through. The second wave of the attack. This city is burning. The death toll is rising. But why are the dead only called dead—surely these are casualties of war?

EURIPIDES. What do you think, Shimaoka? Don't you feel a hatred toward them?

SHIMAOKA. I don't know.

HECTOR. Stop thinking you can be like the dead. Think instead that your family has been killed.

SHIMAOKA. I don't have a family.

HECTOR. What about your parents, brothers, sisters?

SHIMAOKA. I only have a mother.

HECTOR. You should think about her, then.

SHIMAOKA. If you only think about "what if," such thoughts never end.

HECTOR. Stop messing around. You still think you can survive by holding the barren image of the world in front of you. Look around!

SHIMAOKA. Surely we deal with things with a clear head and calm manner.

HECTOR. But don't you have feelings of revenge?

SHIMAOKA. Sorry, but I cannot abide the chain of hatred and revenge.

HECTOR. Can you really say such things in front of the dead? Don't you want to kill me?

SHIMAOKA. But this is not true, it's not reality.

HECTOR. How can you say such a thing?

SHIMAOKA. I want to be rational.

HECTOR. Even if your mother were killed, can you positively say that you would be able to think rationally?

SHIMAOKA. I can't.

EURIPIDES. That's right. Such is the essence of tragedy. The heaps of the dead in tragedy are mass-produced. The *deux ex machina* is our only comfort in the age of tragedy.

SHIMAOKA. So, you're going to use the mechanical God?

EURIPIDES. Read this.

SHIMAOKA (*opens the script and begins to read*). "An American Black Hawk helicopter drops from the sky onto the battlefield of Troy. It is the roadmap to peace." (*Helicopter sound. Hector, Euripedes, and Shimaoka all look up to follow the sound.*) Unbelievable. How the tragedy grows. Amazing. (*Helicopter sound comes closer.*) Don't come here. Let us be. (*Shimaoka picks up some rubble and throws it in the direction of the helicopter. The sound of a machine gun is heard. Shimaoka is shot.*) Mother!!! . . . (*Falls.*)

SCENE 11

A hospital. Shimaoka's mother is standing alone. Katsuyama enters.

SHIMAOKA'S MOTHER. You must be Katsuyama?

KATSUYAMA. Yes.

SHIMAOKA'S MOTHER. Thank you for everything you have done. I am Shimaoka's mother.

KATSUYAMA. Pleased to meet you. How is Shimaoka?

SHIMAOKA'S MOTHER. When he arrived at the hospital his heart had stopped beating and he was no longer breathing.

KATSUYAMA. . . . What can I say? I heard he collapsed in Central Park.

SHIMAOKA'S MOTHER. Yes. I heard that he was drunk and that he fell badly and hit his head.

KATSUYAMA. So it wasn't an accident, then?

SHIMAOKA'S MOTHER. My stupid son. He's been drinking more and more. When he was drunk he kept saying how tragedy would be the end of him.

KATSUYAMA. Killed by tragedy . . .

SHIMAOKA'S MOTHER. Do you know anything about it?

KATSUYAMA. . . . it's about work. He was worried about work.

SHIMAOKA'S MOTHER. Ah. I thought as much.

Old Man, dressed like a homeless man, approaches. He resembles Euripedes.

OLD MAN. Is Katsuyama the director around here?

KATSUYAMA. That's me.

OLD MAN. Ah, so it's you. I was asked to give you this. (*Gives him a manuscript.*) So now I have given it to you. (*Walks away.*)

KATSUYAMA (*looking at the manuscript*). Ah, it's Shimaoka's play. (*Leafing through the manuscript*) It's finished. (*To Old Man*) Wait a minute, Old Man, where did you get this?

OLD MAN. He kept writing even though he was dead. He continued to write under the wreckage of the fallen trees. It was like he was a zombie.

KATSUYAMA. Wreckage? Dead?

OLD MAN. My mistake. My mistake. I meant that he was writing about the dead trees even while he was drunk. I was sleeping in Central Park then, talking to another drunk. He kept talking about the storyline of a play. So I said, "Why don't you write it?" He started writing even though it looked like it was hard for him.

SHIMAOKA'S MOTHER. Were you there when Kiyoshi passed away?

OLD MAN. Umm . . . After writing for a while, he suddenly started running toward the skyscrapers screaming. I don't know what happened after that. He never returned. I found this manuscript near the public toilets. Anyway, who are you to ask?

SHIMAOKA'S MOTHER. I am Shimaoka's mother. Do you know anything about my son?

OLD MAN. So you're Shimaoka's mother. I remember her was talking about his mother. He said he was going to write something about her. That's all. (*Leaving.*)

KATSUYAMA (*to himself*). I think I've met that old man somewhere. Ahh, excuse me, Old Man, who are you?

OLD MAN (*stops walking*). Me? I'm nobody.

Curtain.

ACT II. At the White House

SCENE 1

The Trojan horse is stuck in the wall. The Chorus comprises victims of the Trojan Horse terrorist attack.

CHORUS. Oh how awful history is.
> A terrifying story!
> Here is Argos. Argos and Shinjuku. Shinjuku and Argos.
> We are under attack from terrorists.
> We are dead.
> Because we are dead, we can see everything now.
> Who can speak about the future? Only we can.
> Who can speak of terrifying things? Only we can.

CHORUS MEMBER 1. The war has started.
> Everyone in the government rode the terrorism bandwagon,
> all the citizens too. The Great War has begun.

CHORUS MEMBER 2. Agamemnon's film was propaganda. Aegisthus
> wrote the script and Clytemnestra played the lead after
> Iphigenia was forced to drop out.

CHORUS MEMBER 3. While the military kept on winning, the
> film was popular.
> Deeply moved, many young people joined in the fighting and
> went to the battlefield.

CHORUS MEMBER 4. The whole nation was drunk on war.
> Agamemnon became a hero—the best director, a
> national treasure.

CHORUS. The enemy lost the will to fight.
> But terrorism remained,
> Targeting the occupation forces and the land.
> People became bored with the war.
> The war for justice and the mother country was becoming a
> meaningless war.

CHORUS MEMBER 5. Agamemnon was dragged down from his heroic
> stature.

CHORUS MEMBER 6. I hate war.

CHORUS MEMBER 7. I'm sick of the war!

CHORUS MEMBER 8. Enough of tragedy.

CHORUS. Let's end tragedy.

CLYTEMNESTRA. No. Tragedy must not come to an end in this house. Not yet.

CHORUS. Look, there is Mother. Mother is standing in the wings.

CLYTEMNESTRA. In this house, the tragedy must be accurately portrayed. I am Clytemnestra. Playing Clytemnestra for thousands of years, I know my destiny—I must bring this hatred to an end. That is the destiny of a mother so named Clytemnestra.

CHORUS. Mother? What thing is a mother?
What is a mother of tragedy?
A mother who is killed by her son and daughter . . .

CHORUS MEMBER 9. Do not speak those words now!

CLYTEMNESTRA. Already spoken: I have already been killed thousands of times.

CHORUS. Let us end the chain of hatred.
Let us extinguish the burning fires of revenge.

CLYTEMNESTRA. But you need to see the misfortunes of this house.

CHORUS. We want to see.

CLYTEMNESTRA. Then please look on in silence. Your expectations will be satisfied. Please look on as we reach the pinnacle of tragedy. This I know for sure. There is nothing more interesting than watching someone else's tragedy. We must be seen forever.

The Chorus whisper among themselves and leave.

SCENE 2

Clytemnestra is in the living room of the white house. Agamemnon enters.

AGAMEMNON. Finished.

CLYTEMNESTRA. What's finished?

AGAMEMNON. I am.

CLYTEMNESTRA. What? Don't be foolish. You don't have to worry too much . . . things are always changing.

AGAMEMNON. I don't want to be wrong. What do you think? Please give me your honest opinion.

CLYTEMNESTRA (*ignores what he says*). Darling, I heard Orestes is returning tonight.

AGAMEMNON. Orestes? He made contact?

CLYTEMNESTRA. Electra told me. I'm thinking of getting the whole family together for dinner. Please don't make other plans.

AGAMEMNON. OK. (*Pours himself a whiskey.*)

CLYTEMNESTRA. It's been years since we've had dinner together. Please don't drink too much now. I'm going to cook stew, Orestes's favorite.

AGAMEMNON. Um. He's coming back then? (*Drinks.*)

CLYTEMNESTRA. Stop drinking so early. Please save yourself for dinner.

AGAMEMNON. I'm trying to get in the mood and pretend it's night time.

CLYTEMNESTRA. What will you do then?

AGAMEMNON. Stand in the shadows and get through this time quietly.

CLYTEMNESTRA. That's not possible. You're very visible.

AGAMEMNON. You should become like the night as well.

CLYTEMNESTRA. What would we do? If we both took to drinking?

Chrysothemis enters.

CHRYSOTHEMIS. Mother, can you please taste the stew? I can't tell if it's good.

CLYTEMNESTRA. Yes. (*Takes the whiskey bottle and leaves.*)

AGAMEMNON. Chrysothemis, are you staying home tonight?

CHRYSOTHEMIS. Yes, I heard Orestes is coming.

AGAMEMNON. So I heard. But you can't trust rumors, you know. If you want to go out and play, then go. You can stay out all night . . .

CHRYSOTHEMIS. Why?

AGAMEMNON. Because this story doesn't have you. You can stay at your boyfriend's.

CHRYSOTHEMIS. What do you mean it doesn't have me?

AGAMEMNON. If you don't have money, I can give you some.

CHRYSOTHEMIS. So you want to get rid of me? I knew it. Ever since I was little, I've felt that no one thought me important in this house. Everyone only cares about Electra and Orestes. No one took the time to understand me.

AGAMEMNON. Soon you'll know how things will be better for you.

CHRYSOTHEMIS. Only I in this house know how happiness is boring. All right, I'm leaving and I won't be back. Father, you explain my absence to Mother. She's so excitable: if she notices one person's gone she'll go mad. (*Exits.*)

Aegisthus enters.

AEGISTHUS. Hey, excuse me, Director. What's going on? I want to have a whiskey but I can't find the bottle. It's all right, I'll look for it. Someone's probably hidden it somewhere. (*Exits, then shouts from backstage.*) I've found some Pernod.

AGAMEMNON. Pernod. Well then, I'll have it with champagne. I think there's some in the fridge.

AEGISTHUS (*returning with the bottles*). That's a good idea. (*Trying to remember*) What's the name of that cocktail?

AGAMEMNON. Death in the Afternoon.

AEGISTHUS. That's right.

AGAMEMNON. Hemmingway named it in Paris.

AEGISTHUS. Ah yes, I remember, you're the director who liked Hemmingway. You still do?

AGAMEMNON. I'm not so sure. Reading him made me forget that he took his own life. As I get older, closer to the age when Hemmingway died, I'm beginning to hold a grudge against him.

AEGISTHUS. Is that how it is?

AGAMEMNON. So it's to be Death in the Afternoon.

AEGISTHUS. I remember you planned a movie with that title. Do you remember?

AGAMEMNON. Yes. A war movie.

AEGISTHUS. People won't admit it these days but the fact is that war movies never die out. We come full circle, come back to war. I said "come back" but I don't know where we set out from. Which point do we come back to? When people have nothing better to do with their time, they start a war—that's a fact that never changes.

AGAMEMNON. I heard Orestes is coming back today.

AEGISTHUS (*opening champagne and the sound of the cork popping*). I see. Finally he's coming back to kill me.

Electra runs into the room.

AGAMEMNON. You're just in time. Would you like a drink? (*Taking a glass.*) Why do you look like that?

ELECTRA (*referring to the noise of the cork popping*). . . . that's only champagne.

AEGISTHUS. What did you think it was? A gun? (*Electra doesn't respond.*) I was right! Did you think it's the signal to begin?

ELECTRA. You don't speak!

AEGISTHUS. Cheers

AGAMEMNON. Cheers? To what?

AEGISTHUS. To "Death in the Afternoon." (*Drinks toast.*) So, Orestes is coming home?

ELECTRA. Yes, so?

AEGISTHUS. Have you seen him?

ELECTRA. Yes, so?

AGAMEMNON. How is he?

ELECTRA. He's fine.

AGAMEMNON. He's grown into a fine young specimen, a brave warrior.

ELECTRA. . . . Yes, you could say so . . .

AEGISTHUS. I really hope he's at his best. That he can kill with one clean thrust. I don't like pain.

ELECTRA. Wait until you've done your own job.

AEGISTHUS. I'm sure that I don't know what you mean.

ELECTRA. Father, I'm so sorry. I decided to say my piece, no matter what. It's impossible to hide anything in this house. Everyone knows everything anyway. There're no secrets here. Father, your destiny is a sad thing, but if I don't grab the will of the moment then I am nothing more than a useless irritation to this house.

AEGISTHUS. Wonderful, great. No wonder you're the daughter of a great actress. Why don't you stop with the creative writing and turn your talents to acting?

ELECTRA (*assumes a fighting pose*). Oh, fuck off.

AEGISTHUS. Now, now. It's too early for violence.

AGAMEMNON. Kill me, Aegisthus. I suppose that's what you intend.

AEGISTHUS. The trouble is that I've no such intention. A man without the talent for killing is only half a man. I can say that as the director I have no such murderous feelings toward you. In fact, my affection toward you is deepening. That you get beat up by society and are often ignored is for me even more beautiful.

ELECTRA. Aegisthus is miscast!

Agamemnon stands up.

AEGISTHUS. You haven't touched your drink, Agamemnon.

AGAMEMNON. Not to worry. I'm going to my room.

AEGISTHUS. Why?

AGAMEMNON. There's a manuscript I've been working on . . . (*Exits.*)

AEGISTHUS. An . . . unfinished manuscript . . . (*thinking*) . . . a tragedy . . . a tragedy . . .

ELECTRA. What are you thinking?

AEGISTHUS. I hope he isn't contemplating suicide. (*Electra tries to leave.*) Do you worry about him?

ELECTRA. If Father kills himself, then everything will go wrong.

AEGISTHUS. I'll come with you.

ELECTRA. Why?

AEGISTHUS. Because I'm worried about him too.

ELECTRA. If you're so worried, go and kill him now. (*Aegisthus doesn't respond.*) So you're not going to kill him? (*Aegisthus still doesn't respond.*) After all this, you're not going to kill him? Shit! It's because you're so careless that things have come to this. (*Exits.*)

Chrysothemis and Clytemnestra enter.

CLYTEMNESTRA. Why do you have to go out tonight? What is so important?

CHRYSOTHEMIS. As I said, ask Father. Speaking of whom, where is he?

AEGISTHUS. He's gone back to his room. He didn't say it in so many words but he's going to kill himself.

CLYTEMNESTRA. What? And you said nothing?

AEGISTHUS. Electra's gone after him.

CLYTEMNESTRA. Electra? She can't do anything to help. You should go. Quickly. Go and stop him.

CHRYSOTHEMIS. I'll go and take a look.

CLYTEMNESTRA. Wait, Chrysothemis. It's doesn't make sense for you to go.

CHRYSOTHEMIS. Doesn't make sense?

CLYTEMNESTRA. Aegisthus, kill him before he commits suicide. Quickly now.

Aegisthus exits.

CHRYSOTHEMIS. As I thought. I half expect that our house is . . . (*Tries to leave.*)

CLYTEMNESTRA. Stay here, Chrysothemis. Don't go to his room.

Electra returns.

CLYTEMNESTRA. Has he killed himself?

ELECTRA. He wants a whiskey.

CLYTEMNESTRA. That's good. What's Aegisthus doing?

ELECTRA. Who knows! Is there any whiskey?

CHRYSOTHEMIS. I won't be back home tonight. I don't want to see anything. That's me, such a baby. Such a baby. (*Exits.*)

CLYTEMNESTRA (*to Electra who is leaving*). You'll stay, won't you?

ELECTRA. . . . Yes.

CLYTEMNESTRA. Did you tell her (*meaning Iphigenia*) that Orestes is coming?

ELECTRA. Tell her yourself.

CLYTEMNESTRA. She only speaks to you.

ELECTRA. Have you ever tried to speak to her?

CLYTEMNESTRA. Yes, I did . . .

ELECTRA. I mean, have you really tried?

CLYTEMNESTRA. What do you mean "really?" (*Electra leaves. Clytemnestra sits.*) I'm worried. I'm worried that Orestes's return could be just another of Electra's scheming lies . . . I'm so alone. It this what it means to be a mother? (*Looks down.*)

Aegisthus returns.

AEGISTHUS. It was pretty good.

CLYTEMNESTRA. What?

AEGISTHUS. I'd like to use it in a script.

CLYTEMNESTRA. Stop teasing me. Where have you been?

AEGISTHUS. In the toilet.

CLYTEMNESTRA. You're so hopeless!

AEGISTHUS. Yet again, I'm reminded how beautiful you are.

CLYTEMNESTRA. Stop talking like a servant boy. Orestes is coming back.

AEGISTHUS. So I hear.

CLYTEMNESTRA. You have to kill Agamemnon before he gets here.

AEGISTHUS. I know.

CLYTEMNESTRA. Everything's going wrong. It's supposed to go as straight as a knife edge. I can't seem to cut through, though. It's like swimming in jelly. As though this is not my own body, as though I'm dreaming.

AEGISTHUS. These are the times we're in. War and terror everywhere but no one can see the reality. People live in houses as comfortable as this one . . . it's all bullshit. What about making this into a comedy? I can write it.

CLYTEMNESTRA. You could but you can't laugh. The only way is tragedy. Tragedy is the only thing to do.

AEGISTHUS. I can't help you then. You've chosen your path.

CLYTEMNESTRA. I didn't. I never had the freedom to choose. Never! Nor did you. So stop talking like this has nothing to do with you.

AEGISTHUS. I'm just a supporting actor.

CLYTEMNESTRA. No, you're a partner in crime.

AEGISTHUS. I'm just a houseboy. Not that I mind, I think a servant's life is quite profound. But it doesn't go on forever. I'm leaving this house.

CLYTEMNESTRA. You want to join the main cast?

AEGISTHUS. Don't be so sure about this being a tragedy. You could develop the hero's story instead, you know.

CLYTEMNESTRA. Don't become a hero. You're not like that.

AEGISTHUS. Heroism equals weakness.

CLYTEMNESTRA. You're talking about Agamemnon?

AEGISTHUS. No, generally speaking. The heroes I wrote are all weak people.

CLYTEMNESTRA. He's been drinking more than you.

AEGISTHUS. There's no need for me to be here anymore. Your favorite type is a weak man. So weak that we lost the reason to kill him.

CLYTEMNESTRA. Because you waited too long. The time to kill him has passed.

AEGISTHUS. Your daughter said the same thing.

CLYTEMNESTRA. You're a coward.

AEGISTHUS. I suppose that's why you like me. Because I'm a coward, don't you?

CLYTEMNESTRA. We certainly missed getting on the first-class tragedy ride, that's for sure.

AEGISTHUS. . . . I see.

CLYTEMNESTRA. If you think that only you can become part of the first class here, you're taking too much for granted. After everything that's happened . . . Once again, we need to discover our purpose.

AEGISTHUS. And that is?

CLYTEMNESTRA. Murder.

AEGISTHUS. So that's what's you want? Do you want it so much?

CLYTEMNESTRA. I have to get this house back to being a first-class tragedy house.

AEGISTHUS. I didn't know that there were such differences. First and second-class tragedy.

CLYTEMNESTRA. There are. In the best tragedies, in the final scene, a God always descends from the heavens and shows the survivors the correct path. Then he departs, leaving the humans to their fate.

AEGISTHUS. Do you still believe in such a thing, such an old story?

CLYTEMNESTRA. You'll know it when you experience it. Because this house seems to have been chosen by tragedy itself.

AEGISTHUS. They are the survivors?

CLYTEMNESTRA. As it is written. You know that.

AEGISTHUS. I know, but . . . I can't remember. Because I've abandoned my role, my memory of things has gone blank.

CLYTEMNESTRA. No one understands me.

AEGISTHUS. I do. You may not think so but I'm the only one who understands you in this house. No, not quite so, there is another: Electra understands you too. If we execute this murderous plan, Electra will kill us. At least, I think so.

CLYTEMNESTRA. No. I won't let her. It must be Orestes who stabs me with the cooking knife.

AEGISTHUS. No, no. Only Electra can kill you because only she understands you.

CLYTEMNESTRA. Don't be stupid.

AEGISTHUS. You began this conversation, not me.

CLYTEMNESTRA. I'd rather kill myself than be killed by Electra. (*Exits.*)

AEGISTHUS (*watching her leave*). People in this house are always saying "I'll kill myself," "I'll kill myself," but no one does. Everyone's just waiting, waiting to be killed. It's all talk . . . Useless.

Agamemnon enters with a whiskey bottle.

AGAMEMNON. She's gone.

AEGISTHUS. Yes. Your wife said she was going to kill herself.

AGAMEMNON. She won't. Drink?

They drink.

AEGISTHUS. How's the script going? Well?

AGAMEMNON. Yes. I'm adapting *King Lear*.

AEGISTHUS. *King Lear*! Why do all the desperate old directors do *Lear*?

AGAMEMNON. Well. We just happen to have three sisters in this house.

AEGISTHUS. So you'll take the "sisters" approach. Meaning, you begin to fear your imminent death?

AGAMEMNON. It's not that at all. I've already thought about the next move.

Cassandra enters.

CASSANDRA. Hello.

AGAMEMNON. Here she is . . .

AEGISTHUS. Cassandra.

CASSANDRA. I'm here.

AEGISTHUS. You're here for what?

CASSANDRA. The director called me.

AGAMEMNON. I called her.

CASSANDRA. As I thought. You're drunk!

AGAMEMNON. I'm not drunk. The more I drink, the clearer things become.

CASSANDRA. Why have me enter through the back door? What is it supposed to mean?

AGAMEMNON. I'm thinking about getting together with Cassandra. Today, I think I will finally talk to Clytemnestra. I will be counting on you, Aegisthus.

AEGISTHUS. What's this got to do with me?

AGAMEMNON. Because you won't kill me. I thought this up as a last-ditch measure. It resolves everything nicely.

AEGISTHUS. So who's going to kill who?

AGAMEMNON. As destiny predicts.

CASSANDRA. What's that? You're talking about killing?

AGAMEMNON. Please talk to my wife.

CASSANDRA. Huh? I should talk to her?

AGAMEMNON. Yes.

CASSANDRA. What about?

AGAMEMNON. Oh this and that. You've played the role of the mistress in films often enough, you should be able to talk like one.

CASSANDRA. I wouldn't know what to say. Aegisthus, please write some lines for me. I am no good at ad-libbing.

AGAMEMNON. I knew that. Because I expected as much, I made you enter from the back. Aegisthus, please write something for her to say.

AEGISTHUS. It seems I'm in a delicate position here. Between a rock and a hard place.

CASSANDRA. I'll buy the drinks next time.

AEGISTHUS. Do you love the director?

CASSANDRA. I like him.

AEGISTHUS. Is that all?

CASSANDRA. It's not enough that I like him?

AEGISTHUS. That's not enough to take the place of the wife.

CASSANDRA. You think about it then.

AEGISTHUS. It's difficult.

AGAMEMNON. You should discuss this when I'm not here, secretly, behind my back.

Electra enters.

AGAMEMNON. Ah, Electra! Good timing.

ELECTRA. It's you.

CASSANDRA. Nice to meet you, Electra.

ELECTRA. How dare you come here?

CASSANDRA. I came because I was called.

ELECTRA. I was thinking that I'd like to see you just once. You're not quite as I expected.

AGAMEMNON. You shouldn't say such things, Electra. We're now thinking about how Cassandra will speak to Clytemnestra. Please think about it you two.

ELECTRA. Oh Father, you're losing your edge. You put your efforts into loving such a cheap slut. It's pathetic.

CASSANDRA. Hey, little girl! Don't speak to your father like that. You go too far. I am who I am, a self-made woman. Deal with it . . . I can smell something foul here (*meaning Electra*).

ELECTRA. You got that right.

CASSANDRA. You live in a good house and have an easy life. You're so easy to read, transparent in fact. We're both in the same place, as bad as each other.

ELECTRA. I like you, film actress.

CASSANDRA. Thanks, little girl.

ELECTRA. But that woman—Clytemnestra—can do better than you, I think. Whether you take the baton from her or not, its strength of character. But I think that's impossible. You don't know how frightening that woman is.

CASSANDRA. I'll give it my best shot. By these little girl's words I am resolved to try. Things have come to this and I will face "the great actress" and get the old man.

AGAMEMNON. That's the way. I'm counting on you!

ELECTRA. Can you do it?

CASSANDRA. I don't need anyone's help anymore, I'll just ad-lib that's all.

AGAMEMNON. You can't just ad-lib.

CASSANDRA. Let me. Is the camera ready?

AGAMEMNON. No. You're too excited. Let's forget it for today and go home.

Clytemnestra has been standing unnoticed.

CLYTEMNESTRA. Am I supposed to go on now? No one gave me my call.

AGAMEMNON. Ahh . . .

CLYTEMNESTRA. It looks like the camera's ready, Cassandra. (*Cassandra is silent.*) Cassandra, please take your place. (*Cassandra walks in front of Clytemnestra and stands.*) We were both in the last movie but we didn't have a scene together. Too bad.

CASSANDRA. Yes, it was. I was really looking forward to working with such a great actress.

CLYTEMNESTRA. Umm. People thought we shouldn't have a scene together. Such meddling folk. (*To Agamemnon*) Please say "action!"

AGAMEMNON. Eh?

CLYTEMNESTRA. It's your call.

AGAMEMNON. . . . "Action."

CASSANDRA. Nice to meet you, I'm the director's mistress. Cassandra is my name.

CLYTEMNESTRA. I know all about you. What brings you here today?

CASSANDRA. I came here to ask you to leave the director.

CLYTEMNESTRA. Thank you for coming today. When should I leave him?

CASSANDRA. When? Why are you taking about "when?"

CLYTEMNESTRA. My husband has to finish one more film. One last film of one last first-class tragedy. After he's finished, I'll give him to you, gift-wrapped.

CASSANDRA. Please ask him to finish as soon as possible, then.

CLYTEMNESTRA. All right. I will. I'll get him ready at once.

CASSANDRA. Can I stay here until then?

CLYTEMNESTRA. Of course.

CASSANDRA. I'm sorry for disturbing you.

CLYTEMNESTRA. Not at all. This is a big house, one or two more people makes no difference.

CASSANDRA. Ready, then?

CLYTEMNESTRA. Yes, of course.

They look at each other.

AGAMEMNON. . . . and cut!

CASSANDRA. No. It hasn't finished yet. Keep rolling.

AGAMEMNON. That's enough. I said, "Cut!"

CASSANDRA. But I'm not satisfied. This house is at the center of the story but the story isn't working. All of the connections are completely outrageous. People of the White House of Argos, do you really remember the story of Cassandra?

CLYTEMNESTRA. Um . . . I wonder. I don't really know what you're talking about.

CASSANDRA. I was born in Troy. After the war, my hometown was reduced to rubble. Since the director brought me here, I got used to this country. I thought I could adapt and become like everyone else living here. But now I know that I am different. These thoughts have continued to grow and so I expected that a day like today would eventually come to pass. Your people attacked Troy and Troy was destroyed. All the buildings were torn down and we remember Troy no more. Many people died and we remember the feelings of pain no more. You have eliminated memory. Without memories, we are dead already. We are dead people. I have been living without knowing it. I was killed a long time ago. I cannot become a part of your country's story. I cannot support this telltale narrative covered with a membrane of gentle warmth. I cannot forgive the arrogance and irreverence of those who cry out to start the war even as they deny the war's existence. I'm an actress born in Troy. I'm a women from the land of women who were raped by the troops of Achaia. I'm a women from a country that has been destroyed. A country that is no more. I'm a women from a rogue state. I'm a women who is already dead. Now I end this story. I cut it like a knife. (*Rips off her clothes to reveal a suicide-bomber corset that she tries to activate by pushing a button on her chest. Sounds of gunfire. Cassandra is hit in the arm by a bullet.*)

Pylades enters in a wheelchair pushed by a woman, her face covered by a veil. Pylades holds a gun.

PYLADES. Remove that outfit. Now!

Electra leans over to Cassandra and removes the corset.

ELECTRA. This is the terrorist who destroys the story!

CLYTEMNESTRA. Let her go.

ELECTRA. She may try it again, though . . .

CLYTEMNESTRA. We'll have to complete our tragedy before she does. Why get her involved in the first place?

AGAMEMNON (*to Clytemnestra*). I wanted to make you so jealous that you'd kill me.

CLYTEMNESTRA. The motive for your murder would then be reduced to my single act of rage. And I would be reduced to a shallow woman. What a stupid idea. It's just too much for you: you can't write, after all! This woman brought such a political story into this house. This should not happen. She's just a distraction for the high-class tragedy of our house. Let her go.

Electra stops holding Cassandra.

CASSANDRA. High-class tragedy? Don't flatter yourself. (*Exits.*)

AGAMEMNON. What a surprise, that she had such a thing in mind. Why didn't she just kill me instead of taking all that extra effort?

CLYTEMNESTRA. I wouldn't let her.

AEGISTHUS. Anyway, she couldn't satisfy her desire by killing only the director. She's a full-fledged terrorist, she must have wanted to kill all the people in this house.

PYLADES. Be careful. It's wartime now.

CLYTEMNESTRA. You've become careless. Be strong, darling. I don't want to say this, Agamemnon, but you are useless.

AGAMEMNON. Finally, you tell me the honest truth.

ELECTRA. Orestes has come home.

AGAMEMNON. Eh? What?

CLYTEMNESTRA. Orestes. (*Everyone turns to the wheelchair.*) No, that's not Orestes. He's not Orestes.

Woman pushing the wheelchair removes her veil: it is Orestes dressed as a woman.

ORESTES. It's me. Mother, Father, I'm home.

ELECTRA. Look, he's so valiant. Orestes.

AEGISTHUS. . . . what can I say . . .

CLYTEMNESTRA. Orestes . . . .

AGAMEMNON. That . . . that . . . Um . . .

ELECTRA. I have another younger sister. She is a pretty one, don't you think?

AGAMEMNON. I need a whiskey. Quick.

CLYTEMNESTRA. Here you are. (*Pours whiskey for Agamemnon but, distracted, she overfills his glass.*)

AGAMEMNON. Hey, that's enough.

CLYTEMNESTRA. I'm sorry. Please excuse my clumsiness.

ELECTRA. It must be a quite a shock for you all. I was deeply shocked when I first found out. But as long as he does what he has to, I don't care. Man or woman, it's no different.

AEGISTHUS. Calm down everyone and think rationally about this. Orestes, are you a woman?

ORESTES. Yes, I am.

AEGISTHUS. How far have you gone?

ORESTES. I am a perfect woman.

AGAMEMNON. What a fuck-up!

AEGISTHUS. Who's this young man, then?

ORESTES. My best friend, Pylades.

AEGISTHUS. He's not your lover, then?

ORESTES. Half.

PYLADES. I lost my legs in the war. These are artificial ones. We were ambushed by terrorists. I saw my legs flying through the air. I thought I was dead. But when I woke up I was in hospital back home.

AEGISTHUS. Did you volunteer for this?

PYLADES. Yes.

AGAMEMNON. I won't accept this, Orestes!

ELECTRA. Won't accept what?

AGAMEMNON. A son who's become a daughter.

ORESTES (*pushing the wheelchair toward Agamemnon*). Father!

AGAMEMNON. Don't come any closer.

ORESTES. Father, look at him carefully. This is one of your injured soldiers.

AGAMEMNON. My what?

ORESTES. This is a young man who went to war after watching one of your movies. He lost both his legs and now he's come back. *Agamemnon empties the glass of whiskey.*

CLYTEMNESTRA. That's all right. I forgive you. Man or woman, I'm just glad he's back in one piece. Orestes, welcome home. I'm cooking your favorite dish tonight. Stew, your favorite.

AGAMEMNON. I hope his tastes haven't changed now that he has.

ORESTES. Father, you're still alive! My sister said that by the time I came home you'd be dead.

CLYTEMNESTRA. We had a problem along the way . . . things changed.

ORESTES. Father, don't you understand? It was you who made me into a woman. "Live like a man" you said to me over and over. I am what I am. Those words made me who I am.

ELECTRA. Don't misplace the target of your rage. Don't you want to say something to this woman, your mother.

CLYTEMNESTRA. I don't care. Whatever he says to me, I'm his mother.

ELECTRA. Grotesque!

CLYTEMNESTRA. Shut your mouth. You don't understanding a mother's feelings. Orestes is my son.

ELECTRA. A son is not your private possession.

CLYTEMNESTRA. Yes, he is because I gave him life. Once you become a mother, you'll understand.

ELECTRA. Looking at you there's no way I want to be a mother.

ORESTES. Mother, Sister, I'm now a daughter.

CLYTEMNESTRA. Son or daughter, I don't care. Orestes is my daughter.

ELECTRA. Orestes, why did you leave home? Because you disliked Father? Or was there some other reason? What did you see this woman doing (*meaning Clytemnestra*)? Tell us now.

ORESTES. Mother and Aegisthus . . .

ELECTRA. What happened? What did they do?

ORESTES. Holding each other in embrace.

AGAMEMNON. Shush. These are secrets, only to be shared quietly in corners.

ELECTRA. No more secrets! If you keep hiding things, the story won't go anywhere.

AEGISTHUS. Did you actually see anything?

ELECTRA. What are you saying?

AEGISTHUS. What you're saying is that your mother and I were holding each other. Is that right?

ORESTES. Yes. That's what I saw.

ELECTRA. That's right. Orestes saw you.

AEGISTHUS. What exactly did you see?

ORESTES. In Mother's room. I saw this man lying with my naked mother.

AEGISTHUS. I see. Then your mother was lying with her face up? (*Orestes is silent.*) Your mother was lying face up? Or was she lying face down?

ORESTES. Face down.

AEGISTHUS. And was I naked too?

ORESTES. . . . No. You had your clothes on.

AEGISTHUS. Listen, Orestes. That is what we do, your mother and I. I was relaxing your mother's tired body. It's called a massage.

ORESTES. A massage?

AEGISTHUS. Massage uses the hands to knead the muscles and heal the body from stress.

ORESTES. Massage . . .

ELECTRA. Hang on. You don't know how far the massage goes.

AEGISTHUS. As you said, no more secrets. You say I'm a pitiful lover? That's what I feel too. Madam's lover. That's what you've called me for long years behind my back. But it was an honor undeserved. I am impotent. So, everyone, thank you for nothing.

AGAMEMNON. . . . What did you just say?

AEGISTHUS. Mr. Director, I'm impotent.

CLYTEMNESTRA. That's enough, Aegisthus.

AEGISTHUS. No. I have to testify to your innocence too. Everyone, listen please. I'm a man who doesn't have such a skill. That is why she kept me close to her side. Madam needs a person like me. Anyway, Orestes, you didn't have to leave home.

ELECTRA. Say something, Orestes. Don't be taken in by this glib talk.

AEGISTHUS. It's true, I'm impotent. If you doubt me, you need but try . . .

ELECTRA. Don't be stupid! Nothing's been decided. My efforts to bring Orestes home have come to nothing.

CLYTEMNESTRA. Yes. I harbored my hatred and now it is full fledged. I want you to disappear from this world, Agamemnon. Your control over me was strong. What you took away from me will never come back.

AEGISTHUS. What about forgiveness? Can you forgive him?

CLYTEMNESTRA. I cannot forgive this film director. Everything goes his way. He'll even cry like a baby to get what he wants. You took everything from me: my womankind, my culture. You patronize me, treat me like a child. You order me to act while you rob me of my talent, my creativity, my art. You took my son away: Orestes hated you so much that he left home. You wouldn't let me stop being an actress, you took my home, my family. Now you took my daughter. You took Iphigenia's future away.

ELECTRA. You're making yourself out as the only victim.

CLYTEMNESTRA. How can you say such a thing?

ELECTRA. You're always like that. Can't you see how you are a victimizer too? What happened to Iphigenia was no accident.

CLYTEMNESTRA. What are you talking about?

ELECTRA. It was no accident.

CLYTEMNESTRA. Just what are you implying, Electra?

ELECTRA. Father, do you remember that scene from the film?

AGAMEMNON. The one with the aircraft carrier on the way to battle. It was attacked by enemy bombers. A woman soldier was meant to jump into the burning ocean. Iphigenia mistimed her cue. She jumped before the ocean was ready.

ELECTRA. Iphigenia said she was pushed. Someone pushed her overboard.

AGAMEMNON. What? Iphigenia said so?

ELECTRA. Yes. I must be the only one she said it to. That day was the day when that great actress was on the sets, to encourage her daughter. Father, please try to remember: Who was standing behind Iphigenia?

AGAMEMNON. I can't remember.

ELECTRA. I do.

CLYTEMNESTRA. Don't you lie to me! You weren't there.

ELECTRA. I'm not talking about that. What I want to say is about you. When you came home. I saw what happened. When they decided that Iphigenia couldn't continue in the role, I saw your cunning smile. You went to your room and started to learn the lines. You were in your element. You spared no thought to your dying daughter.

CLYTEMNESTRA. What an awful child you are!

ELECTRA. I'm your daughter.

CLYTEMNESTRA. Oh God!!

ORESTES. Mother! So it's true that you were there on that day?

CLYTEMNESTRA. You too, talking rubbish.

ORESTES. I'm not saying you pushed her. I just want to confirm the truth.

CLYTEMNESTRA. Stop this idle chatter. I'm always alone in this house.

ELECTRA. Mothers are always the best actors.

AGAMEMNON. That's enough from you two. I take full responsibility for everything.

ORESTES. Precisely. And how do you intend to do so?

AGAMEMNON. . . . By being a good parent. Parenting the right way.

CLYTEMNESTRA. So why did you cast Iphigenia in the first place?

AGAMEMNON. Why are you asking that now?

CLYTEMNESTRA. You didn't cast me because you wanted to give Cassandra's career a boost? You wanted her to become a great actress?

AGAMEMNON. What's done is done. Let's not talk about the past. You acted in the film and the film was a great success for which I am grateful. If Iphigenia had done the role, it might not have been so good.

CLYTEMNESTRA. After everything . . . so you admit your responsibility?

AGAMEMNON. . . . Yes.

AEGISTHUS. So Iphigenia was sacrificed and the blockbuster juggernaut was successfully launched. At the end, only she rode the waves of destiny.

CLYTEMNESTRA. The tragedy plumbs the lower depths in that case.

ORESTES. So . . . How is Iphigenia doing now?

ELECTRA. She's *hikikomori*. She rarely leaves her room.

No one speaks for a while. Iphigenia, her face wrapped in bandages, enters quietly.

IPHIGENIA. I suppose you're all talking about me . . . Welcome home, Orestes.

ORESTES. Iphigenia.

IPHIGENIA. I'm glad you returned.

ORESTES. Sister! Your face . . . (*Cries.*)

IPHIGENIA. So you heard about the botch-up during the shoot?

ELECTRA. Didn't someone push you?

IPHIGENIA. . . . Yes.

ELECTRA. Who?

IPHIGENIA. . . . It's no one's fault. No one is to blame. It's just that the God's of Film didn't like me. That's why it happened. Shall we eat dinner?

ELECTRA. Are you sure about that?

IPHIGENIA. That's enough, Electra. Dinner isn't ready? It smells like we're having stew.

CLYTEMNESTRA. Yes. I forgot about the stew. (*About to leave.*)

IPHIGENIA. You were my mother until you took over from me, you took over my role.

CLYTEMNESTRA. Yes . . .

IPHIGENIA. I'm happy to hear you say so.

CLYTEMNESTRA. . . . Yes.

IPHIGENIA. Being a woman is a hard cross to bear. Why do you want to be a woman, Orestes?

ORESTES. Father talking about how to live life as a man gave me some ideas. But Mother always scolded me for not behaving like a man. She told me I should always take control no matter what the situation and become a film director, just like Father. When I came home after playing with my friends, Mother always told me off, "Why aren't you the leader?" Secretly she'd watch me play and see how I wasn't in charge.

ELECTRA. See, it's her fault too.

CLYTEMNESTRA. Only I had your best interests at heart, Orestes.

ORESTES. Leadership, leadership. Be a man, be a leader . . . all the while I was becoming a woman.

IPHIGENIA. I see. That's how it was. You've suffered too, Orestes. You've endured great suffering—like an operation—you stuck a scalpel into your flesh. Compared to you, my pain is nothing. I'm so stupid, thinking I'm the only one who's hurt. All the while my brother was suffering so deeply. I take off these bandages. (*Removes her bandages.*)

CLYTEMNESTRA. Iphigenia, you don't have to.

IPHIGENIA. I want to.

As the bandages are removed, her face becomes visible. It is unmarked: there is no sign of any injury.

CLYTEMNESTRA. Iphigenia, you . . .

AGAMEMNON. You're still as beautiful . . . as before!

ELECTRA. There are no marks, sister.

IPHIGENIA. Really? Everyone's just saying that to make me feel better.

CLYTEMNESTRA. Iphigenia, you're completely fine.

AGAMEMNON. It was an illusion. Your anxiety made you think you had a scar. It was probably also an illusion that someone pushed you. You couldn't face the fact that it was your own fault and so you had to create this delusion. Blaming your mother and me was the easy way. It's all right, you've been ill. People accused me after the shoot but it was not as dangerous as they claimed. (*To Clytemnestra*) Don't you think so? A new actress should try and do such a scene, otherwise we can't say she is up-and-coming. Don't you agree, Iphigenia? Your mother went through this and became a great star. You might just possibly lack such talent, eh?

CLYTEMNESTRA. Be quiet. . .

ORESTES (*to Agamemnon*). So you're saying you bear no responsibility? You're always like that, denying responsibility for everything. What kind of a man are you?

ELECTRA. Stop it, Orestes.

ORESTES. Do you know how many men died as a result of your film, how many died admiring the men in your film. The cast had to take the blame instead of you.

ELECTRA. Your hatred points the wrong way.

ORESTES. Say something, Pylades.

PYLADES. I volunteered for the war after watching your film. But what I experienced on the field of battle was totally different from the film. There were no heroes, no bravery . . . everyone just wanted to survive and go home. We were living in a muddy swamp, thinking about survival every minute of every day. Give me back my legs. And take responsibly for those who died, one by one, on the field of battle.

AGAMEMNON. . . . . I want to die. . . . . I want to die now. Kill me, quickly. I have lived too long in this world. If no one kills me I'll kill myself.

AEGISTHUS. Madam, it would seem to be your turn.

CLYTEMNESTRA. You won't do it?

AEGISTHUS. I have no reason to. The world has already done that.

CLYTEMNESTRA. No, it hasn't. That just makes him stronger. Such ebbs and flows of the world. We must bear the fortunes of fate while others look on in amusement. (*Clytemnestra holds a kitchen knife.*) I should have done this a long time ago. Before Orestes came back. Nothing is harder than reliving a story that's already been written. (*Holds the knife in front of Agamemnon.*)

AGAMEMNON. Finally, the day has come. I am ready to accept what fate holds. You all take me to be a fool of a man. But now that it has come to this, I will show you what it means to be a man until the very end. You forget that true manhood made this country what it is, developed the economy and made for a prosperous land. True manhood is a simple honest thing. A thing that transforms dreams into reality and proceeds without thought to consequences. You know nothing! In my film I transferred the dreams of men as easily as if I was burning a DVD. In one of those dreams, Clytemnestra, you are radiant and beautiful. Those dreams are the simple dreams of men, without complication. And your image is of a beautiful woman. Through the screen I swear my eternal love for you. It is from love that I made the massacre: *Eros plus Massacre*. Because of you I could make the war film. You say you were just a slave to the male imagination but there's nothing I can do about that. A simple man like me can't read your thoughts. I ask you all, what kind of dreams will you have in the place of these simple dreams of men? What kind of dreams will cinema reproduce? I have lived in my own film for all these months, a life of my own creating, a life of cinematic imagination. I lived with you Clytemnestra. I don't care how reality treats me anymore. Do it, Clytemnestra! Do it! (*Asking Clytemnestra to stab him.*)

CLYTEMNESTRA. Once again, please show us your arrogant self.

AGAMEMNON. Not a chance.

Clytemnestra is on the verge of stabbing Agamemnon but cannot.

CLYTEMNESTRA. I can't. Now that he is so weak, I can't kill him.

ELECTRA. Then nothing will happen. Nothing will move forward.

CLYTEMNESTRA. I know, Electra. I must do something. For the Gods to come to us, we must begin to kill each other. The present situation is no good for anyone. The audience, the society, no one will accept this situation. If we don't do something, we'll become nobodies. They'll forget about us completely. The memory of our family line will vanish.

AGAMEMNON. That might be the destiny of this house. Finally, it is time for us to abandon our name.

ELECTRA. Who will I be if I am no longer Electra?

AEGISTHUS. We will fade beyond the horizon of the story. Like so many other forgotten characters.

ELECTRA. No! That's not what I want.

CLYTEMNESTRA. . . . Let's pretend . . .

ELECTRA. Pretend?

CLYTEMNESTRA. Yes. Pretend.

ELECTRA. Pretend what?

CLYTEMNESTRA. Pretend to kill. (*Throws the knife away.*) All right, my darling, I'm going to stab you now so please pretend that I have you and that you are dead. Aegisthus, if we are pretending, maybe you can do it too?

AEGISTHUS. No. I'll leave all that to you. I'm the writer, I'm no good at acting.

CLYTEMNESTRA. As you wish. (*To Agamemnon*) Darling, you're not a director now. Show us your best acting.

AGAMEMNON. Acting . . .

CLYTEMNESTRA. You were such a strict acting coach, I'm sure you can do it. (*Stabs Agamemnon with an imaginary kitchen knife. Agamemnon cries out in pain then abruptly dies.*) Excellent, you did well. Electra, Orestes, it's your turn now.

Everyone is petrified and frozen in their places.

IPHIGENIA. Mother, don't you think that's enough?

CLYTEMNESTRA. No, it's not.

ELECTRA. Pretend-killing. How silly . . . (*Tries to leave.*)

CLYTEMNESTRA. Where do you think you're going, Electra? You can't leave. Don't you hate me as your mother? Haven't you wanted to kill me so many times?

ELECTRA. Yes, many times. Why was that? Your shifting back and forth between being a mother and actress was so annoying. Your selfish prevarications got on our nerves. It's easy to talk about what you did but I don't anymore. There is no reason behind my desire to kill you. We just can't live in the same world. Giving birth to me was a mistake! We should not breathe the same air.

CLYTEMNESTRA. Do it if you think like that. Kill me, go on.

ELECTRA. Just pretending? Is that enough?

CLYTEMNESTRA. This is the only way for us. We have to act, Electra. We have to pretend. So now, act!

ELECTRA. You can't give me orders anymore. Orestes, I am going to kill this woman. So will you, Aegisthus. (*Passes an imaginary kitchen knife to Orestes.*)

AEGISTHUS. Please, one stab to the heart.

ORESTES. I can't do this. This is too much.

ELECTRA. Then you're not going to kill Mother?

ORESTES. No. You're so selfish, my sister.

ELECTRA. I'm taking control. I'll do your work for you. This is our destiny, the fate of the House of Atreus. We are fated from birth to finish the tragedy.

CLYTEMNESTRA. Bravo, Electra. You're great.

ELECTRA. Let's do this together, then!

CLYTEMNESTRA. In praise of high-class tragedy!

Electra stabs Clytemnestra and Orestes stabs Aegisthus. Orestes stabs with one clean blow while Electra stabs repeatedly. Clytemnestra is graceful in death. Truly a splendid anagnorisis— the magnificent finale of a great tragedian. Aegisthus and Clytemnestra freeze, now dead. Electra and Orestes stand, petrified by their actions.

ORESTES. So what happens now?

ELECTRA. The Gods will come down.

ORESTES. What?

ELECTRA. The Gods descend from the heavens to tell us what we should do.

ORESTES. So we're going to wait for that?

ELECTRA. Yes, we're going to wait.

They wait, silently. The sound of a helicopter comes closer and then fades away.

ORESTES. . . . No one's coming.

PYLADES. Are you sure? What did you think? What is it about this house? Everyone pretending to be dead? Maybe this is how you keep your sense of comfort. But it seems I overestimated you. I thought that if I came here then someone would take responsibility for my pain.

CLYTEMNESTRA (*still lying as if dead*). You can't understand our pain.

PYLADES. I can just leave it here. Orestes, I'm leaving. Goodbye.

ORESTES. You're leaving me?

PYLADES. Yes. You're all right now. Your mother and sister are strong.

Everyone is silent while Pylades exits, pushing his own wheelchair. Eventually Aegisthus speaks.

AEGISTHUS (*still lying as if dead*). I've been thinking something over these past few days. Now that I'm finally dead I can share it with you. I'm thinking about leaving this house and going to war. To an authentic battlefield like the one I wrote for the film. I'm not taking responsibility, that's not what I mean. But I'm thinking of rewriting the war story after I've experienced a war. I've volunteered.

Everyone listens quietly. Chrysothemis runs in.

CHRYSOTHEMIS. Everyone, I'm home. No one thought about me so I came back. (*Looks around her.*) Why are they all sleeping?

ELECTRA. They're being dead.

CHRYSOTHEMIS. What?

IPHIGENIA. I feel refreshed somehow. We can all kill each other many times.

Chrysothemis is silent.

CLYTEMNESTRA (*standing, relaxed*). I remember now. I was cooking some stew. Let's all have some. It must be very tasty. (*Moves to leave.*)

ELECTRA. Mother, the Gods didn't come.

CLYTEMNESTRA. So we will live. (*Exits.*)

Everyone gradually recovers from playing dead.

CHRYSOTHEMIS. You must be Orestes?

ORESTES. Yes.

CHRYSOTHEMIS. The whole family's here. It's been a long time.

AGAMEMNON. . . . Survived . . . we have survived.

The sound of a large number of jet bombers in the distance. This is the sound of war. The sounds come closer. Everyone anxiously looks up in their direction.

SCENE 3

An image of the city under siege. Clytemnestra is stirring the stew pot. Chorus enters.

CHORUS. Here is a mother. A mother standing amid the city of terror.

CHORUS MEMBER 1. Mother, strong mother.

CHORUS MEMBER 2. Mother, clever mother.

CHORUS MEMBER 3. Mother, cheating mother.

CHORUS MEMBER 4. Mother, arrogant mother.

CHORUS MEMBER 5. Mother, kind mother.

CHORUS MEMBER 6. Mother, cruel mother.

CHORUS MEMBER 7. Mother, cool mother.

CHORUS MEMBER 8. Mother, impetuous mother.

CHORUS MEMBER 9. Mother, mother to all.

CHORUS MEMBER 10. Mother, solitary mother.

CHORUS MEMBER 11. Here is a mother. A mother standing amid the city of terror. Here is Mother. Mother standing in the ashes of destroyed buildings.

CLYTEMNESTRA (*stirring the stew*). Tragedy is a story. The story of fate. But I could not carry my blood-soaked destiny. That is the tragedy of this house. Now I know that the Gods will not come. This is the only way for us to live: Keeping close to our hearts the tragedy that will remain forever incomplete . . . Mother? Well, it's true that you are not born a mother but that you *become* one. In such a world as the one in which we live, someone must play the mother's role. Is there no one from our generation who will do so? I have played the role a thousand times. Playing a mother, I become a mother. A mother who kills and who is killed, I have refused to play it again. My survival for some might be a nuisance but survive I have. This is the only thing I could do. I lived through everything only by using my mother's instinct. But when I saw that my ego was like a flower, I could no longer continue this story, a story like a prison. Becoming a mother is to experience the blooming of flowers inside one's body. I think I finally understand that. Different flowers for different people. I could not cut the flower out from inside me, even as I knew of people's dislike and hatred of me. This is Argos. Shinjuku *and* Argos. Argos *and* Shinjuku. The war has started. A mother cannot stop war. A mother is like a beautiful flower that the sons and daughters of war call to mind as they die. Who knows, flowers might burst into bloom across the battlefield . . .

SCENE 4

Ashes. This could be the stage setting for the play within a play that has just taken place. Or it could be the setting for the city in ruins. Shimaoka is squatting in a dark corner. Euripedes enters.

EURIPIDES. Hey. The play is over. Come out from there.

SHIMAOKA (*emerging from his corner*). Finally, it is becoming clear where I am. That night I was dead drunk and passed out in Shinjuku Central Park. I might have fallen over and knocked my head. Or maybe someone attacked me. I met you in the world between life and death. You took me to the battlefield and I died in the terrorist attack. Am I right?

EURIPIDES. Yes, something like that.

SHIMAOKA. I kept writing under the wreckage of the collapsed buildings. But after my death it was the writing of a dead man.

EURIPIDES. He (*indicating Shimaoka*) was pretty good after all.

SHIMAOKA. . . . Finally, I understand that I was dead.

EURIPIDES. So, should I say congratulations . . . ?

SHIMAOKA. Did you see the play?

EURIPIDES. Yes. The curtain went up. Good for them . . .

SHIMAOKA. I doubt it.

EURIPIDES. What's your problem?

SHIMAOKA. After all that I could not write about killing. Killing each other.

EURIPIDES. That's all right.

SHIMAOKA. I couldn't write like you . . . to let people die.

EURIPIDES. Can I ask you something?

SHIMAOKA. What?

EURIPIDES. What will happen to this family now? If you haven't thought about it, that's all right.

SHIMAOKA. I wrote a scene after this one but I cut it. (*Takes out the manuscript.*)

EURIPIDES. Can you tell me what happens?

SHIMAOKA. Everyone is going to live ordinary lives. There is nothing dramatic about the world. Even if something out of the ordinary happens, it is momentary. Just a moment of normality. No more do I long for dramatic characters. Everyday characters are good enough. I wonder: Do I think like this because I'm dead?

EURIPIDES. I'd like to know what happens to Orestes.

SHIMAOKA. He gets a job as a manager at a talent agency.

EURIPIDES. And Electra?

SHIMAOKA. She becomes a novelist. She leaves the house and writes novels. As the daughter of a famous actress, her private life becomes a stream of steamy scandals. Adultery, attempted suicide, abortion, traffic accidents, violence, court cases, gaol. All the time, the city lives in the fear of terrorism. In a corner of the city, in an out of the way place, a sister and brother meet once again.

Electra and Orestes appear.

ELECTRA. What are you doing now Orestes?

ORESTES. Management.

ELECTRA. What for?

ORESTES. Uh? I am managing my mother.

ELECTRA. I see.

ORESTES. Mother said she'd like to see you. (*Electra is silent.*) Just so you know, yeah. (*Exits.*)

SHIMAOKA. This is the dialogue for the last scene.

Shimaoka gives some of the script to Electra. She reads it and then tries out the lines.

ELECTRA. I've been watching my brother's back. Is this Mother's final victory, I wonder? I haven't seen her for a long time. All of a sudden I feel the need to see her. I want to go back to that house. The house filled with angry words, thoughts, and deeds. The house of broken hopes and dreams. The incomplete house that lets down the story. In a time of endless war, I have decided to write about Mother once again, I have decided to walk up the hill of Argos again. Seven years have gone by. The path is narrower and steeper than I remember. Soon the white house in the hills of Argos comes into view. The front door opens as if welcoming me.

Clytemnestra is standing in the open doorway.

CLYTEMNESTRA. Welcome, Electra.

ELECTRA. . . . I'm home.

CLYTEMNESTRA. Please come in. Let's talk. Girl-talk.

Curtain

The End